THE JUDAISM BEHIND THE TEXTS

SOUTH FLORIDA STUDIES IN THE HISTORY OF JUDAISM

Edited by
Jacob Neusner
William Scott Green, James Strange
Darrell J. Fasching, Sara Mandell

Number 99
THE JUDAISM BEHIND THE TEXTS
The Generative Premises of Rabbinic Literature
III.
The Later Midrash Compilations:
Genesis Rabbah, Leviticus Rabbah,
and Pesiqta deRab Kahana
by
Jacob Neusner

THE JUDAISM BEHIND THE TEXTS

The Generative Premises of
Rabbinic Literature

III.

The Later Midrash Compilations:
Genesis Rabbah, Leviticus Rabbah,
and Pesiqta deRab Kahana

by

Jacob Neusner

Scholars Press
Atlanta, Georgia

THE JUDAISM BEHIND THE TEXTS
The Generative Premises of Rabbinic Literature
III.
The Later Midrash Compilations:
Genesis Rabbah, Leviticus Rabbah,
and Pesiqta deRab Kahana

©1994
University of South Florida

Publication of this book was made possible by a grant from the Tisch Family Foundation, New York City. The University of South Florida acknowledges with thanks this important support for its scholarly projects.

Library of Congress Cataloging in Publication Data
Neusner, Jacob, 1932-
  The Judaism behind the texts : the generative premises of rabbinic literature. III, The later midrash compilations: Genesis Rabbah, Leviticus Rabbah, and Pesiqta deRab Kahana / by Jacob Neusner.
      p. cm. — (South Florida studies in the history of Judaism ; no. 99)
  Includes index.
  ISBN 1-55540-947-4
  1. Midrash rabbah. Genesis—Sources. 2. Midrash rabbah. Leviticus—Sources. 3. Pesikta de-Rav Kahana—Sources. 4. Bible. O.T. Genesis—Criticism, interpretation, etc. 5. Bible. O.T. Leviticus—Criticism, interpretation, etc. 6. Judaism—Essence, genius, nature. I. Title. II. Series.
BM517.M65N49 1994
296.1'4—dc20   93-48298
                                                CIP

Printed in the United States of America
on acid-free paper

Table of Contents

Preface

...One must press behind the contents of the Mishnah and attempt to discover what the contents of the Mishnah presuppose....
E.P. Sanders[1]

Carrying forward Volumes I and II, we move into two volumes of examination of Midrash compilations. The results shift in character, but their implications remain uniform, as I shall explain in the Introduction. Sanders's correct insistence that we "press behind" the contents of the documents – had he an authentic interest in Judaism on its own terms, he of course would not limit matters to the Mishnah! – yields a result no one could have anticipated, one that is only now emerging. In time I shall spell out the results of answering what is now proving to be not a wrong question, but a wrong-headed one.

It suffices here to explain that this protracted exercise asks a deceptively simple question of theory, applied systematically to the principal documents of Rabbinic Judaism in its formative age. It is, if I know this, what else do I know? If an author or compiler of a Judaic text tells me something, what else does he thereby tell me about what he is thinking or how? Can I press behind the contents of a Rabbinic document and attempt to discover what the contents presuppose? Can I ask about the author's premises: what he knows and how he thinks he knows it? Can I move back from the text to the intellectual context the text presupposes? The only way to find the answers to these questions is to reread documents, line by line, and see what lies behind what is there. This I do in a multi-volume exercise on selected, critical documents of Rabbinic Judaism. I now proceed to the second set of Midrash compilations, organized around books of Scripture, the ones produced

---

[1]E.P. Sanders, "Puzzling Out Rabbinism," in William Scott Green, ed., *Approaches to Ancient Judaism*. II (Chicago, 1980: Scholars Press for Brown Judaic Studies), p. 73.

(according to conventional opinion) in association with the Talmud of the Land of Israel, in the fifth century C.E.

All these writings, like the two Talmuds, are exegetical composites, and, it goes without saying, identifying premises and presuppositions in documents that are built as amplifications and clarifications of prior writings is not so simple. We have to eliminate from consideration what these documents have learned from the ones on which they depend, since what is secondary and derivative tells us not premises of later authors but lessons imparted by earlier ones. Hence our interest lies in what is fresh to the compilations under study: What do these writers bring to their work? That question forms the complement to the one we addressed to the Mishnah and the earliest Midrash compilations in sequence: What do these writers know before they start their work? In the case of the writings at hand, of course, what they know at the outset is Scripture; then what they think they know about Scripture forms the center of interest.

The goal of this project has now clarified itself. What I want ultimately to find out is whether I can identify premises that circulate among all or at least most of the Rabbinic compilations of Mishnah and Scripture exegesis. In the case of this Judaism, with its sizable canon of authoritative and holy books – Scripture, the Mishnah, Tosefta, two Talmuds, score of Midrash compilations – we want to know how the various writings hold together. Can we identify a set of premises that animate all writers, presuppositions that guide every compilation's compositions' authors and compositors' framers? If we can, then we shall have found what makes that Judaism into a single coherent religious system. If we cannot, then we shall have to ask a fresh set of descriptive questions concerning the theology of that religious system – a different set from those that guide the present work. When at the end of this exercise I reach the conclusion, in *Judaism from before 70 to 600: The Judaism That Is Taken for Granted,* I shall exploit the facts that will turn up in the present book and its companions: Is there a Judaism behind the texts at all? And if not, what explains the coherence of the Judaism of the Dual Torah – for, by all reckoning, it is a remarkably cogent and stable religious system, with a body of ideas that for centuries have formed a single statement and today, with numerous variations and nuances, continues to say some one thing in many ways. Let me state with heavy emphasis what I want to find out:

At stake is not only the Mishnah and its premises (presumably bringing us back into circles of first-century thinkers) but the presuppositions of numerous representative documents of Rabbinic Judaism throughout its formative period. .

The second question vastly outweighs the one that animates interest in premises and presuppositions: Is there a Judaism that infuses all texts and forms of each part of a coherent whole? At issue in the quest for presuppositions is not the Judaism that lies beyond the texts (which the texts by definition cannot tell us and indeed do not pretend to tell us), but the Judaism that holds together all of the texts and forms the substrate of conviction and conscience in each one.

That body of writings is continuous, formed as it is as commentaries on the Written Torah or the Mishnah, and the period in which they took shape for formal and substantive reasons also is continuous and of course not to be truncated at its very starting point, with the Mishnah, as Sanders's formulation proposes. For the Mishnah presents only the first among a long sequence of problems for analysis, and cutting that writing off from its continuators and successors, in both Midrash compilations and Talmuds, represents a gross error, one commonplace, to be sure, among Christian scholars of Judaism, for whom, as in Sanders's case, Judaism ends in the first century or early second and ceases beyond that point to require study at all. But the Judaism of the Dual Torah, viewed in its formative canon, is single and whole, and the premises and presuppositions of any of its writings, treated in isolation from those of all the others, contain nothing of interest for the analysis of that massive and complex Judaic system, only for the Judaism of a given piece of writing.

Let place into the context of contemporary debates the results presented here and in the companion volumes. An important premise of the sectarian study of the Jews and Judaism, besides the dogmas of a single, unitary, linear, and incremental Judaism and of the historicity of its sources, insists on the uniformity of all writings classified as canonical, that is, treated as the oral part of the Torah. The concept of a single, normative Judaism, on the one side, and of the facticity and historicity of all sources, on the other, explains why scholarship under parochial auspices ignored the lines of structure and order that marked the beginning of one document and the end of another. A theological premise, serving the religious institutions, drew attention to the status, as Torah, of all writings; if each document finds its undifferentiated place within the (oral part of the) Torah, then little effort will go toward differentiating one document from another. A historical premise concerning the contents of documents serves equally well to account for the problems not ordinarily addressed in the same setting. If, as we have seen, we take as fact all statements (except those concerning miracles) in all writings of the canon, then our inquiry concerns the facts documents supply; we shall take a position of indifference to the venue, origin, auspices, and authority, as to historical fact, of a given document and to relationships of documents to one another. All are held to draw indifferently upon a corpus of "tradition," deemed to have circulated orally hither and yon before coming to rest in a particular compilation.

Therefore, it was taken for granted, we open a document and come up with a fact, and which document yields what fact bears little meaning.

Not only so, but the paramount trait of all documents – their constant attribution of sayings to named authorities – afforded a distinct point of differentiation, namely, the names of authorities. Whatever is given to a specific name, whether in a document that reached closure ("only") two hundred years after he flourished or as long as five hundred or a thousand years later, serves equally well to tell us what said authority really thought and stated. Lives of Talmudic masters, along with histories of Talmudic times, therefore brought together, collected, and arranged in intelligible order, attributed sayings without a shred of interest in the time or place or circumstance of the documents that preserved them. The upshot, once more, was simple: considerations of time and circumstance do not register; every writing is equally useful; all may be assumed to wish to make the same, factual contribution to "the Torah," and, for the secular, history consists in opening a document, pointing to a sentence, paraphrasing the sense of that sentence, and speculating on its meaning: a labor of paraphrase and pure fabrication.

These theological and secular historical premises of course represented welcome labor-saving devices, since people took for granted it is not necessary to examine documents one by one, whole, complete, and in their own context. Not only so, but literary studies could take up a given trait or form, for example, the parable, and examine all evidences of the same without the slightest concern for comparing and contrasting the form of the phenomenon as diverse compilations portray it. And, still more common, scholars working on something we might call "the history of ideas" routinely set forth "the Talmudic view of...," collecting, arranging, and paraphrasing everything from everywhere, with little or no attention to questions of social context (not imagined, to begin with, to matter) or literary origin. Entire careers devoted to expounding the Rabbinic, the Talmudic, or the Talmudic-Midrashic view of one thing after another yielded an entire library of monographs resting on the simple presuppositions now generally dismissed: [1] a single Judaism [2] revealed in a unitary tradition of completely reliable historical veracity [3] comes down to us in a variety of undifferentiated writings – a single book, with many chapters, not a library, made up of many free-standing, but cogently selected, volumes. That set of coherent premises explains why, moreover, people translated the documents in long columns of undifferentiated words, rendering impossible any sort of analytical work on the character, composition, and construction of documents, each viewed on its own, such as can be done if we identify chapter and verse, on the one side, or compose a still more serviceable reference system, on the other. The upshot was, the governing premises of the sectarian institutions dictated the character of the presentation of the sources in critical texts and translations and also predetermined the modes of characterization of their contents.

Today, by contrast, people understand that the documents viewed as free-standing and autonomous require description, analysis, and interpretation. Each exhibits its own differentiating traits. Not only do people grasp that the Mishnah is different from Leviticus Rabbah which is different from the Talmud of Babylonia. They also understand that each of those documents sets forth its own program in its own way. Systematic analyses of distinguishing traits of rhetoric, the logic of coherent discourse, and the topical programs of the various documents leave no ambiguity. Each writing exhibits its own formal traits, and each sets forth its own message. No document is readily confused with any other. Many, though not all, exhibit a cogency of program, working on the same few questions time and again. What that means for the received, sectarian episteme is simple. The point of origin of a given saying or story governs our reading and use of the item. True, some sayings and stories occur in more than a single document. The changes and developments of these items as they make their journey from here to there have to be traced, accounted for, if possible, in terms of the interests of the framers of the documents that make use of them. Among the parochial scholars, occurrence of the same sayings in the name of a single authority in two or more documents yielded "he often said." A different conception now prevails.

Scholars who take for granted that the Gospels yield not a single, harmonious life of Jesus but several distinct statements will hardly find surprising these simple rules of analysis. Each of the Rabbinic documents – the Mishnah, Tosefta, Midrash compilations, the two Talmuds – represents its own compilers, their taste and judgment in selecting from available compositions what they used and neglecting what they did not, their program in organizing and arranging and formulating matters in one way, rather than in some other. The collective statement and consensus of authorships (none is credibly assigned to a single author and all are preserved because they are deemed canonical and authoritative) show us how those authorships proposed to make a statement to their situation.

In fact, the question of a single, unitary, harmonious tradition, set forth in diverse compilations that themselves are not to be differentiated, is now settled. While most in the sectarian setting, and some in the academic one, may have yet to catch up to matters, the study of the Rabbinic writings has drawn abreast of the study of the Gospels and other early Christian ones, and work on the characterization of documents, comparable to that on the Gospels, as well as on the differentiation of writings by appeal to their salient formal traits, is well advanced. As noted just now, documents are now perceived in three relationships: first, as autonomous writings; second, as writings connected with others of the same class; and, finally, as parts of a complete corpus deemed unitary and coherent: autonomy, connection, continuity beyond the key words to portray perspective. The labor is one of description, analysis, and interpretation, and it involves study of the text, its literary context, and its intellectual matrix.

DESCRIPTION OF THE TEXT AS AUTONOMOUS: a document is set on display in its own terms, examining the text in particular and in its full particularity and immediacy. The text will be described in accord with three distinct, differentiating traits: its rhetoric, logic, and topic: the formal traits of the writing, the principles of cogency that dictate how one sentence will link up with another, and the topical, and even propositional, program that the entire document addresses.

ANALYSIS OF THE TEXT IN ITS CONTEXT THROUGH COMPARISON AND CONTRAST WITH INTERSECTING AFFINES IN CONNECTION: a document connects with others in two ways, first and less important, through shared sayings or stories, but, second and far more important, through recurrent points of emphasis found in a number of documents. A set of documents may address a single prior writing, Scripture or the Mishnah; they may pursue a single exegetical program or take up a common question, deemed urgent in two or more compilations. They may intersect in other ways. Groups of documents may take shape out of an inductive examination of points of differentiation and aggregation.

INTERPRETATION OF THE MATRIX THAT BRINGS ALL CANONICAL TEXTS INTO A SINGLE CONTINUITY: the examination of the entire corpus of Rabbinic writings (or the writings found in the library at Qumran, or other groups of writings deemed by common consensus to form a textual community), finally, leads outward toward the matrix in which a variety of texts find their place. Here description moves from the world of intellectuals to the world they proposed to shape and create. That inquiry defines as its generative question how the social world formed by the texts as a whole proposes to define and respond to a powerful and urgent question, that is, I read the canonical writings as response to critical and urgent questions. A set of questions concerning the formation of the social order – its ethics, ethos, and ethnos – for example will turn out to produce a single set of answers from a variety of writings. If that is the case, then we may describe not only documentary cogency and the coherence of two or more writings but the matrix in an intellectual system that the continuity among many documents permits us to outline. That is the work that proceeds in the present part of the project.

The plan of the work as a whole is to examine important and representative writings – not every canonical document but only those that strike me as systemically generative, on the one side, or exemplary, on the other. My sense is that, if there really are premises of systemic consequence, they should turn up nearly everywhere, so that a sample of the documents must suffice. If that should not be the case, then the very notion of a single Judaism behind the Rabbinic texts will prove parlous, beyond all examination, testing, and demonstration, and probably untenable. But for now, I retain as my given the notion that the canonical writings of Rabbinic Judaism do come together and cohere, on which account a sample will suffice; others may pursue the same questions in the analysis of omitted documents. The following indicates how I plan to proceed with this project in particular:

In Print

The Judaism behind the Texts. The Generative Premises of Rabbinic Literature. I. *The Mishnah.* A. *The Division of Agriculture* (Atlanta, 1993: Scholars Press for South Florida Studies in the History of Judaism).

The Judaism behind the Texts. The Generative Premises of Rabbinic Literature. I. *The Mishnah.* B. *The Divisions of Appointed Times, Women, and Damages (through Sanhedrin)* (Atlanta, 1993: Scholars Press for South Florida Studies in the History of Judaism).

The Judaism behind the Texts. The Generative Premises of Rabbinic Literature. I. *The Mishnah.* C. *The Divisions of Damages (from Makkot), Holy Things and Purities* (Atlanta, 1993: Scholars Press for South Florida Studies in the History of Judaism).

The Judaism behind the Texts. The Generative Premises of Rabbinic Literature. II. *The Tosefta, Tractate Abot, and the Earlier Midrash Compilations: Sifra, Sifré to Numbers, and Sifré to Deuteronomy* (Atlanta, 1993: Scholars Press for South Florida Studies in the History of Judaism).

Next

The Judaism behind the Texts. The Generative Premises of Rabbinic Literature. IV. *The Latest Midrash Compilations: Song of Songs Rabbah, Ruth Rabbah, Esther Rabbah I, and Lamentations Rabbati. And The Fathers According to Rabbi Nathan* (Atlanta, 1994: Scholars Press for South Florida Studies in the History of Judaism).

The Judaism behind the Texts. The Generative Premises of Rabbinic Literature. V. *The Talmuds of the Land of Israel and Babylonia.* A. *Tractate Qiddushin*

Chapters One and Two (Atlanta, 1994: Scholars Press for South Florida Studies in the History of Judaism).

The Judaism behind the Texts. The Generative Premises of Rabbinic Literature. VI. The Talmuds of the Land of Israel and Babylonia. B. Tractate Erubin Chapter One, Moed Qatan Chapter Three, and Hagigah Chapter Three (Atlanta, 1994: Scholars Press for South Florida Studies in the History of Judaism).

The Judaism behind the Texts. The Generative Premises of Rabbinic Literature. VII. The Talmuds of the Land of Israel and Babylonia. C. Tractate Gittin Chapters One and Five and Nedarim Chapter One (Atlanta, 1994: Scholars Press for South Florida Studies in the History of Judaism).

The Judaism behind the Texts. The Generative Premises of Rabbinic Literature. VIII. The Talmuds of the Land of Israel and Babylonia. D. Tractate Niddah Chapter One, Baba Mesia Chapter One, and Makkot Chapters One and Two (Atlanta, 1994: Scholars Press for South Florida Studies in the History of Judaism).

Judaism from before 70 to 600: The Judaism That Is Taken for Granted.

How the documents will break up beyond Volume IV I cannot now predict, but the groupings seem to me justified. If there are results that will sustain the final title on this list, the *Vorstudien* contemplated here will yield them, if not, not. The final listed work should yield a sustained book, not just a research report, and that will survey the main premises that are identified in the documentary analysis and will ask how the various premises and presuppositions hold together: the intellectual foundations of Judaism. That will present my first effort at defining the unity of the Oral Torah, identifying the main principles that transcend various documents but animate them all.

No work of mine can omit reference to the exceptionally favorable circumstances in which I conduct my research as Distinguished Research Professor in the Florida State University System at the University of South Florida. I wrote this book as part of my labor of research scholarship, expressed through both publication and teaching at the University of South Florida, which has afforded me an ideal situation in which to conduct a scholarly life. I express my thanks for not only the advantage of a Distinguished Research Professorship in the Florida State University System, which for a scholar must be the best job in the world, but also of a substantial research expense fund, ample research time, and some stimulating and cordial colleagues. In the prior chapters of my career, I never knew a university that prized professors' scholarship and publication and treated with respect those professors who actively and methodically pursue research.

The University of South Florida, among all ten universities that comprise the Florida State University System as a whole, exemplifies the high standards of professionalism that prevail in publicly sponsored higher education in the United States and provides the model that privately sponsored universities would do well to emulate. Here there are rules, achievement counts, and presidents, provosts, and deans honor and respect the University's principal mission: scholarship, scholarship alone – both in the classroom and in publication. Here at last I find integrity, governing in the lives of people true to their vocation and their mission.

I defined the work at hand in conversation with Professor William Scott Green, who gave me substantial help in clearly formulating my problem in its own terms. As ever, I acknowledge my real debt to him for his scholarly acumen and perspicacity.

JACOB NEUSNER

Distinguished Research Professor of Religious Studies
UNIVERSITY OF SOUTH FLORIDA
Tampa, FL 33620-5550 USA

Introduction

How are we to read all of the writings of the Judaism of the Dual Torah as these reached closure with the Talmud of Babylonia? Since, I have argued, we cannot assume everything is the same thing as everything else, we have first to read each writing in its own terms, describing its distinctive traits of rhetoric, logic of coherent discourse, and topical and even propositional program. This I have now completed for the bulk of the documents. But then, what joins document to document, and makes of the whole a single, coherent statement? That question defines the goal of this project. Once I have demonstrated that each document bears its own integrity, the natural next question is, then how do the documents fit together? And it is only by uncovering the results put forth here and in related projects that that question is to be answered.

This project takes a considerable step forward in a large-scale account of the systemic statement of the documents of the Judaism of the Dual Torah, read as a whole. Before turning to a recapitulation of what is at stake here and how I proceed to do the work, let me place this, presently rather tedious, research report into its larger context. That will help those who consult this work (it is hard to imagine anyone reading it from one page to the next) to know the direction in which I am heading. We begin with the now-settled question: documents have to be read one by one, not as a mass of undifferentiated "traditions," all of equal valence. But when we dismiss as wrong-headed the reading of documents all together and all at once, it is because that reading contradicts the material traits of the documents themselves. It is not because we exempt ourselves from the task of saying how things fit together, what they said when read whole as a coherent statement. It is the simple fact that all of the writings of a given Judaism cohere in the community of those who valued those writings and regarded them as authoritative. It follows that a question neglected until now is simple: What holds together the various writings deemed canonical by a given

Judaism? Is there a Judaism behind these texts, to the task of the expression of some aspect of which each text is assigned? Or, viewing the authoritative writings as a whole, are we able to identify premises that govern throughout, presuppositions that characterize all these writings but no others?

That question cannot trouble the scholars who under sectarian auspices study Judaism, since they know in advance that everything forms a single statement. But given the issues that have now been settled, we have to raise in our own terms a question that is opened by our own results. It is this: What explains the coherence of the Judaism of the Dual Torah? For, by all reckoning, it is a remarkably cogent and stable religious system, with a body of ideas that for centuries have formed a single statement and today, with numerous variations and nuances, continues to say some one thing in many ways. At stake is not only the Mishnah and its premises (presumably bringing us back into circles of first-century thinkers) but the presuppositions of numerous representative documents of Rabbinic Judaism throughout its formative period. Is there a Judaism that infuses all texts and forms of each part of a coherent whole? At issue in the quest for presuppositions is not the Judaism that lies beyond the texts (which the texts by definition cannot tell us and indeed do not pretend to tell us), but the Judaism that holds together all of the texts and forms the substrate of conviction and conscience in each one.

These questions, while theological in character, demand the attention of the academy. For at stake in any study of a religion is the definition of that religion and of religion. Hence, in this context, we have to find the correct way to define Judaism in its formative age, which is to say, describe, analyze, and interpret the earliest stage in the formation of the Judaism of the Dual Torah. To that project the question of premise and presupposition is critical. No one can imagine that the explicit statements of a generative text, such as the Mishnah or the Talmud of Babylonia, for example, exhaust all that that text conveys – or means to convey. But it is not enough to posit such premises; we have in detail to identify just what they were. So it is the task of learning to explore the premises, presuppositions, and processes of imagination and of critical thought, that yield in the end the statements that we find on the surface of the writings. But the work has to be done systematically and not episodically, in a thorough way and not through episode, anecdote, and example. We address an entire canon with the question: Precisely what are the premises demonstrably present throughout, the generative presuppositions not in general but in all their rich specificity? Here I take up this analytical problem, having completed my descriptive work.

The project thus presents an exercise in the further definition of the Judaism of the Dual Torah that encompasses not only what its principal documents make articulate but also what they mean to imply, on the one end, and how what they presuppose coheres (if it does), on the other. Since many of the answers to those questions are either obvious or trivial or beg the question, we have to refine matters with a further critical consideration. It is this: Among the presuppositions, the critical one is, which ones matter? And how can we account for the emergence of the system as a whole out of the presuppositions demonstrably present at the foundations of systemic documents?

These statements left unsaid but ubiquitously assumed may be of three kinds, from [1] the obvious, conventional, unsurprising, unexceptional, uninteresting, [2] the routine and systemically inert to [3] the highly suggestive, provocative and systemically generative.

First, a statement in a text may presuppose a religious norm of belief or behavior (*halakhah* or *aggadah*, in the native categories). For one example, if a rule concerns itself with when the Shema is to be recited, the rule presupposes a prayer, the Shema – and so throughout. Such a presupposition clearly is to be acknowledged, but ordinarily, the fact that is taken for granted will not stand behind an exegetical initiative or intellectual problem to which a document pays substantial attention.

Second, a statement in a text may presuppose knowledge of a prior, authoritative text. For instance, rules in the Mishnah take for granted uncited texts of Scripture, nearly the whole of Tractate Yoma providing a particularly fine instance, since the very order and structure of that tractate prove incomprehensible without a verse-by-verse review of Leviticus Chapter Sixteen. Knowing that the framers of a document had access to a prior holy book by itself does not help us to understand what the framers of that document learned from the earlier one; they will have selected what they found relevant or important, ignoring what they found routine; we cannot simply assign to the later authorship complete acquiescence in all that a prior set of writers handed on, merely because the later authorship took cognizance of what the earlier one had to say. It is one thing to acknowledge, it is another to make use of, to respond to, a received truth.

Third, a concrete statement in a text may rest upon a prior conception of a more abstract character, much as applied mathematics rests upon theoretical mathematics, or technology upon principles of engineering and physics. And this set of premises and presuppositions does lead us deep into the foundations of thought of a given, important and systematic writing. In the main, what I want to know here concerns the active and generative premises of Rabbinic documents: the things the writers had to know in order to define the problems they wished to solve. I seek the key to the exegesis of the law that the framers of the Mishnah put forth, the exegesis of Scripture that they systematically provided. When we can say not only what they said but also what they took for granted, if we can explain their principles of organization and the bases for their identification of the problems they wished to solve, then, but only then, do we enter into that vast Judaic system and structure that their various writings put forth in bits and pieces and only adumbrated in its entirety.

We all know that the sages of the Rabbinic writings deemed the Scriptures of ancient Israel, which they knew as the written part of the Torah, to be authoritative; they took for granted the facticity and authority of every line of that writing, to be sure picking and choosing, among available truths, those that required emphasis and even development. That simple fact permits us to take for granted, without laboring to prove the obvious, that the Judaism not articulated in the Rabbinic literature encompassed the way of life and worldview and conception of Israel that, in broad outlines, Scripture set forth. But that fact standing on its own is trivial. It allows for everything but the main thing: what characterized the specific, distinctive character of the Judaic system set forth in Rabbinic writings, and, it goes without saying, how the particular point of view of those writings dictated the ways in which Scripture's teachings and rules gained entry into, and a place for themselves in, the structure and system of the Judaism of the Dual Torah.

Prior to a vast number of rulings, generating the problems that require those rulings, a few fundamental conceptions or principles, never articulated, await identification. And, once identified, these several conceptions or principles demand a labor of composition: How does the generative problematic that precipitates the issues of one tractate, or forms the datum of that tractate's inquiry, fit together with the generative problematic of some other tractate and its sustained exegesis of the law? Once we know what stands behind the law, we have to ask, what holds together the several fundamental principles, all of them of enormous weight and vast capacity for specification in numerous detailed cases? Before we know how to define this Judaism, we have to show that a coherent metaphysics underpins the detailed physics, a cogent principle the concrete cases, a proportioned, balanced, harmonious statement the many, derivative and distinct cases of which the law and theology of Judaism are comprised.

Here we revert to the distinction between what is necessary and what is sufficient. Some premises are necessary to any Judaism, but insufficient to account for the shape and structure of any particular Judaism. What makes a Judaic system important is what marks that system as entire and imparts to that system its integrity: what makes it different from other systems, what holds that system together. Defining that single, encompassing "Judaism" into which genus all species, all Judaisms, fit helps us understand nothing at all about the various Judaisms. But all we really have in hand are the artifacts of Judaisms. Efforts to find that one Judaism that holds together all Judaisms yields suffocating banalities and useless platitudes: we do not understand anything in particular any better than we did before we had thought up such generalities. So by "generative premises," I mean, the premises that counted: those that provoked the framers of a document's ideas to do their work, that made urgent the questions they address, that imparted self-evidence to the answers they set forth.

Now to come to the project at hand. At stake in any study of a religion is the definition of that religion and of religion, and what I am trying to do here is to find the correct way to define Judaism in its formative age, which is to say, describe, analyze, and interpret the earliest stage in the formation of the Judaism of the Dual Torah. To that project, which has occupied me for thirty years, the question of premise and presupposition is critical. No one can imagine that the explicit statements of a generative text, such as the Mishnah or the Talmud of Babylonia, for example, exhaust all that that text conveys – or means to convey – about God's truth. With what Sanders correctly emphasizes no one can argue, and with that obvious premise, none has argued. To the contrary, even in the founding generation of the field that used to be called "Talmudic history," the true founder and greatest mind in the field, Y. I. Halevi, *Dorot harishonim* (Vienna-Berlin, 1923 et seq.), insisted that a statement rested on a prior history of thought, which can and should be investigated, and that premises of available facts yield a pre-history that we can describe. Everybody understands that the definitive documents of a religion expose something, but contain everything. Sanders is in good company.

What Rabbinic documents tell us that bears consequence for the definition of their Judaism in particular – not merely what was likely to be common to all Judaism, for example, a sacred calendar, a record of generations' encounter with God and the like – then requires specification, and the third of the three types of presuppositions or premises points toward the definition of what is at stake and under study here. That is, specifically, the deeper, implicit affirmations of documents: what they know that stands behind what they say, the metaphysics behind the physics (to resort to the metaphor just now introduced). For a close reading of both law and lore, *halakhah* and *aggadah*, yields a glimpse at a vast structure of implicit conceptions, those to which Sanders makes reference in his correct prescription of what is to be done: "...one must press behind the contents of the Mishnah and attempt to discover what the contents of the Mishnah presuppose."

Some of these implicit conceptions pertain to law, some to questions of philosophy and metaphysics, some to theology. Once we have examined important constitutive documents, we shall see that all of them circulate hither and yon through the law and the theology of the various documents; and only when we identify the various notions that are presupposed and implicit and show how they coalesce shall we understand the details of the Judaic system – law and theology alike – that comes to concrete expression in the Rabbinic writings. I have already set forth a systematic account, treating the Mishnah as a whole, of the document's premises in regard to philosophy, politics, and economics. These are large-scale exercises in answering the question, "if I know this, what else do I know?" My answer is, if I know the specific rulings of the Mishnah on topics relevant to economics and politics, I know that the Mishnah sets forth a philosophical politics and a philosophical economics. If I know how the Mishnah formulates and solves a problem, I know that the framers of the Mishnah thought philosophically – but mostly, though not entirely, about questions of a very different order from those that philosophers pursued.

This detailed work follows a simple and consistent program. Let me undertake to spell out the procedures of this and its companion volumes. What is needed is a patient sifting of details. Therefore I review the entire document under study here, and in each of its divisions and subdivisions examine data by the following criteria:

1. UNARTICULATED PREMISES. THE GIVENS OF CORRECT PUBLIC CONDUCT: I want to know what generative practices the halakhah at hand takes for granted, which customs or rites or social rules and laws are refined and improved, applied and analyzed, being simply givens. Very frequently, the law will provide detailed exegeses, in terms of a number of distinct cases and problems, of a single principle. The law therefore shows how in concrete and practical ways a principle operates. That is what is critical in this category.

2. UNARTICULATED PREMISES. THE GIVENS OF RELIGIOUS CONVICTION: At issue here are the givens of generative conviction: this category is identical to the foregoing, now with attention to matters within the native category of aggadah and the academic category of theology and exegesis. Where many texts presuppose the same premise

but none articulates it, or the premise is never made explicit in such a way as to extend to a variety of cases, I classify the matter as an unarticulated premise. But, I readily concede, the difference between this category and the next is not always obvious to me.

3. MATTERS OF PHILOSOPHY, NATURAL SCIENCE AND METAPHYSICS: This category covers general principles that concern not theological but philosophical questions. "Natural science" and "philosophy" for our documents coincide, being two ways of referring to the same corpus of knowledge. The questions that fall into the present category are not theological but concern issues of natural philosophy, science, and metaphysics, for example, sorting out matters of doubt, discovering the rules of classification, working out problems of applied logic and practical reason, and the like. Now as a matter of fact, many rulings presuppose answers to philosophical questions of a broad and abstract character. Here we identify the premises of the documents that operate widely but do not concern questions particular to the situation of Israel.[1]

In *Judaism behind the Texts.* Volume I. Part A, readers will recall, I asked also about two other matters: points of stress and traits of self-differentiation. But these produced nothing of sustained interest, only some casual and episodic entries at which I thought a tractate or a major component of a tractate struck me as laying heavy emphasis on a given proposition, on the one side, or point of difference between the document's "Israel" and the rest of the Jews, on the other. I found the categories too subjective for further use, since I could not always identify the objective and indicative traits that would lead me to categorize an item's premise as either a point of stress or a point of differentiation. Accordingly, I omit these categories from further use.

---

[1]In some measure, also, I recapitulate the findings of *The Philosophical Mishnah.* Volume I. *The Initial Probe* (Atlanta, 1989: Scholars Press for Brown Judaic Studies); *The Philosophical Mishnah.* Volume II. *The Tractates' Agenda. From Abodah Zarah to Moed Qatan* (Atlanta, 1989: Scholars Press for Brown Judaic Studies); *The Philosophical Mishnah.* Volume III. *The Tractates' Agenda. From Nazir to Zebahim* (Atlanta, 1989: Scholars Press for Brown Judaic Studies); *The Philosophical Mishnah.* Volume IV. *The Repertoire* (Atlanta, 1989: Scholars Press for Brown Judaic Studies). But the work done here is not focused so narrowly as the survey accomplished in those volumes; I am more interested in finding as broad a range of premises and presuppositions as I can. In *The Philosophical Mishnah,* my program was carefully framed to identify clearly-philosophical matters.

What I want to undertake in due course is a cogent account of all of the premises that appear to me to play a role in the specific rulings of the law, on the one side, and in the concrete propositions of theology and exegesis, on the other. But that ultimate goal concerning the unity and coherence of the Judaism of these writings – the unity of the oral part of the Torah – is not going to be easily attained. Once we have assembled the data of all sixty-two tractates of the Mishnah (excluding Tractate Abot), we shall see how they relate to one another and even coalesce into a metaphysical structure and system.

It remains to explain that, when I refer to "generative premises," I mean to exclude a variety of other givens that strike me as demonstrably present but systemically inert. There are many facts our documents know and acknowledge but leave in the background; there are others, that is, premises and presuppositions, that generate numerous specific problems, indeed that turn out, upon close examination of the details of documents, to stand behind numerous concrete inquiries. The former are systemically inert, the latter, systemically provocative and formative. Such premises as the sanctity of Israel and the Land of Israel, the election of Israel, the authority of the Torah (however defined), and the like in these writings prove systemic givens, assumed but rarely made the focus of exegetical thought.

Not only so: a very long list of platitudes and banalities can readily be constructed and every item on the list shown to be present throughout the documents under study here; but those platitudes and banalities make no contribution to the shaping of our documents and the formulation of their system. Therefore, having proven that the sun rises in the east, from those systemically inert givens, we should know no more about matters than we did beforehand. True, to those in search of "Judaism," as distinct from the diverse Judaic systems to which our evidence attests, that finding – God is one, God gave the Torah, Israel is God's chosen people, and the like – bears enormous consequence. But that God is one in no way accounts for the system's specific qualities and concerns, any more than does the fact that the laws of gravity operate.

There is another class of items that I do not catalogue: matters of narrow exegetical or philological interest. Where a Midrash compilation amplifies the sense of a passage, or where it sets forth a localized virtue, for example, arrogance and pride offend, humility pleases, God, I do not include that item on my lists, for example, of theological premises. I search for large-scale and global presuppositions; I have no interest in paraphrasing, in general terms, concrete allegations about one virtue or another, or one type of action or attitude or another. A single example suffices:

I

V.1   A.   R. Huna in the name of Bar Qappara commenced [discourse by citing the following verse]: "'Let the lying lips be made dumb [which arrogantly speak matters kept secret against the righteous]' (Ps. 31:19).

      B.   "[Translating the Hebrew word for dumb into Aramaic one may use words meaning] 'bound,' 'made dumb,' or 'silenced.'

      C.   "'Let [the lying lips] be bound,' as in the following verse: 'For behold, we were binding sheaves' (Gen. 37:7).

      D.   "'Let the lying lips be made dumb,' as in the usage in this verse: 'Or who made a man dumb ' (Ex. 4:11).

      E.   "'Let them be silenced' bears the obvious meaning of the word."

      F.   "Which arrogantly speak matters kept secret against the righteous" (Ps. 31:19):

      G.   "...which speak against the Righteous," the Life of the Ages, matters that he kept secret from his creatures [Freedman: the mysteries of creation].

      H.   "With pride" (Ps. 31:19):

      I.   That is so as to take pride, saying, "I shall expound the work of creation."

      J.   "And contempt" (Ps. 31:19): Such a one treats with contempt the honor owing to me.

      K.   For R. Yosé b. R. Hanina said, "Whoever gains honor through the humiliation of his fellow gains no share in the world to come.

      L.   "For one does so through the honor owing to the Holy One , blessed be He, how much the more so!"

      M.   And what is written after the cited verse [Ps. 31:19]?

      N.   "How abundant is your goodness, which you have stored away for those who revere you" (Ps. 31:20).

      O.   Rab said, "Let one [who reveals the mysteries of creation] not have any share in your abundant goodness.

      P.   "Under ordinary circumstances, if a mortal king builds a palace in a place where there had been sewers, garbage, and junk, will not whoever may come and say, 'This palace is built on a place where there were sewers, garbage and junk,' give offense? So, too, will not whoever comes and says, 'This world was created out of chaos, emptiness, and darkness' give offense?"

      Q.   R. Huna in the name of Bar Qappara: "Were the matter not explicitly written in Scripture, it would not be possible to state it at all: 'God created heaven and earth' (Gen. 1:1) – from what? From the following: 'And the earth was chaos' (Gen. 1:2). [Freedman: God first created chaos and emptiness, and out of these he created the world, but this is not to be taught publicly.]"

The point here is that there are things about which one must not speak openly. I could easily have added such a point to my catalogue of theological premises. But restating as a generalization what is set forth in mythic and concrete language does not advance the purpose of this study, but makes the work ungainly. Hence a measure of subjectivity operates in what I exclude as premise. Exclusions of the sort just now given rest on the judgment that the point, while fundamental, is systemically inert, being too local to bear much influence beyond the passage at hand. Clearly, others will find solid reason to differ from that judgment, which underscores the fact that this first study of the premises of the documents invites others to review the results and propose their own.

What makes a Judaic system important is what marks that system as entire and imparts to that system its integrity: what makes it different from other systems, what holds that system together. Defining that single, encompassing "Judaism" into which genus all species, all Judaisms, fit helps us understand nothing at all about the various Judaisms. But all we really have in hand are the artifacts of Judaisms. As the Prologue to Volume I.A has already argued, efforts to find that one Judaism that holds together all Judaisms yields suffocating banalities and useless platitudes: we do not understand anything in particular any better than we did before we had thought up such generalities. So by "generative premises," I mean, the premises that counted: those that provoked the framers of a document's ideas to do their work, that made urgent the questions they address, that imparted self-evidence to the answers they set forth. This brings us to the documents under study in this part of the work.

In the earliest Midrash compilations, not to mention the Tosefta, premises and presuppositions – "the Judaism behind the texts" – prove rare and episodic. The reason is that the character of the documents under study imposes limitations upon the free exercise of speculation. They undertake the systematic exposition of a prior document. Consequently, most of the task finds its definition in the statements that have been received and now require paraphrase, clarification, extension, and augmentation. The way in which this work is done – the hermeneutics that govern the exegesis of Scripture – yields no premises or presuppositions susceptible of generalization. And the result of the exegesis itself proves from our perspective sparse and anecdotal. Let me commence with a single example of how a sublime text is treated in a manner that, while not trivial, still in no way yields the kind of theological or moral or legal principles that at various points in the Mishnah show the document to rest upon deep foundations of thought. Our example is the exposition of the priestly benediction, and it shows us what to expect in Midrash compilations, therefore explaining, also, why the results of the survey prove frustrating – yielding what is necessary but not sufficient to the task of description, analysis, and interpretation of the system that forms the intellectual subtext of the documents overall:

XXXIX

I.1   A.   "The Lord said to Moses, Say to Aaron and his sons: Thus shall you bless the people of Israel. [You shall say to them: 'The Lord bless you and keep you, the Lord make his face to shine upon you and be gracious to you, the Lord lift up his countenance upon you and give you peace.' So shall they put my name upon the people of Israel, and I will bless them]" (Num. 6:22-27):

       B.   Since the deed required in the present passage is to be carried out by Aaron and his sons, the statement that is made is not only to Moses but also to Aaron and his sons.

       C.   For this is the encompassing rule:

       D.   Whenever the statement is made to the priests, then the deed is required only of the priests.

       E.   When the statement is made to Israel, then the entirety of what is required is incumbent on Israel.

       F.   When the statement is made to Israel but the deed is to be done by everyone, then one has to encompass proselytes as well.

II.1   A.   "The Lord said to Moses, Say to Aaron and his sons: Thus shall you bless the people of Israel":

       B.   The blessing is to be said in the Holy Language [Hebrew].

       C.   For any passage in which reference is made to "responding" or "saying" or "thus," the statement is to be made in Hebrew.

III.1   A.   "The Lord said to Moses, Say to Aaron and his sons: Thus shall you bless the people of Israel":

       B.   [This must be done when the priests are] standing.

       C.   You maintain that this must be done when the priests are standing.

       D.   But perhaps it may be done either standing or not standing?

       E.   Scripture states, "And these shall *stand* to bless the people" (Deut. 27:42).

       F.   The word "blessing" occurs here and the word "blessing" occurs there. Just as the word "blessing" when it occurs at the later passage involves the priests' standing, so here, too, the word blessing indicates that the priests must be standing.

       G.   R. Nathan says, "It is not necessary to invoke that analogy. For it is said, 'And the Levitical priests shall draw near, for the Lord has chosen them to serve him and to bestow a blessing in the name of the Lord' (Deut. 21:5). The act of bestowing a blessing is compared to the act of service. Just as service is performed only when standing, so bestowing a blessing is bestowed when standing."

IV.1   A.   "The Lord said to Moses, Say to Aaron and his sons: Thus shall you bless the people of Israel":

       B.   It must be done by raising the hands.

       C.   You say it must be done by raising the hands.

       D.   But perhaps it may be done either by raising the hands or not by raising the hands?

       E.   Scripture says, "And Aaron raised his hands toward the people and blessed them" (Lev. 9:22).

       F.   Just as Aaron bestowed the blessing by raising his hands, so his sons will bestow the blessing by raising their hands.

       G.   R. Jonathan says, "But may one then say that just as that passage occurs in the setting of a blessing bestowed at the new moon, on the occasion of a public offering, and through the medium only of the high priest, so here, too, the blessing may be bestowed only at the new moon, on the occasion of a public offering, and through the medium only of the high priest!

H.   "Scripture states, 'For the Lord your God has chosen him above all your tribes' (Deut. 18:5). The Scripture compares his sons to him: just as he bestowed the blessing by raising his hands, so his sons will bestow the blessing by raising their hands."

V.1   A.   "The Lord said to Moses, Say to Aaron and his sons: Thus shall you bless the people of Israel":

B.   It is to be done by expressing the fully spelled out Name of God.

C.   You maintain that it is to be done by expressing the fully spelled out Name of God. But perhaps it may be done with a euphemism for the Name of God?

D.   Scripture says, "So shall they put my name upon the people of Israel" (Num. 6:27).

V.2   A.   "In the sanctuary it is to be done by expressing the fully spelled out Name of God. And in the provinces it is to be done by a euphemism," the words of R. Josiah.

B.   R. Jonathan says, "Lo, Scripture states, 'In every place in which I shall cause my name to be remembered' (Ex. 20:20). This verse of Scripture is out of order, and how should it be read? 'In every place in which I appear before you, there should my Name be mentioned.' And where is it that I appear before you? It is in the chosen house [the Temple]. So you should mention my name [as fully spelled out] only in the chosen house.

C.   "On this basis sages have ruled: 'As to the fully spelled out Name of God, it is forbidden to express it in the provinces [but only in the sanctuary].'"

VI.1   A.   "The Lord said to Moses, Say to Aaron and his sons: Thus shall you bless the people of Israel":

B.   On this basis I know only that the blessing is directed to Israel.

C.   How do I know that it is directed to women, proselytes, and bondsmen?

D.   Scripture states, "...and I will bless *them*" (Num. 6:27), [encompassing not only Israel, but also women, proselytes, and bondsmen].

VI.2   A.   How do we know that a blessing is bestowed on the priests?

B.   Scripture states, "...and I will bless them" (Num. 6:27).

VII.1   A.   "The Lord said to Moses, Say to Aaron and his sons: Thus shall you bless the people of Israel":

B.   It must be done face to face [with the priests facing the people and the people facing the priests].

C.   You say that it must be done face to face [with the priests facing the people and the people facing the priests]. But may it be back to face?

D.   Scripture says, "You shall say *to* them" (Num. 6:23), [which can only be face to face].

VIII.1 A.   "The Lord said to Moses, Say to Aaron and his sons: Thus shall you bless the people of Israel":

B.   The sense is that the entire congregation should hear what is said.

    C.   Or may it be that the priests say the blessing to themselves [and not in audible tones]?

    D.   Scripture says, "*Say* to them...," (Num. 6:23), meaning that the entire congregation should hear the blessing.

    E.   And how do we know that the leader of the prayers has to say to the priests, "Say..."?

    F.   Scripture says, "*You* shall say to them" (Num. 6:23).

Whatever the hermeneutics that is taken for granted, the unarticulated layer of law and theology is scarcely to be discerned; the givens are Scripture and its facts and formulations, on the one side, and a set of principles of exegesis deriving from a transparent hermeneutics, on the other. For our survey, I find nothing in the treatment of a passage of surpassing interest to enrich our grasp of the law or theology behind the text. What we see is what there is – that alone. When I observe that most of the documents surveyed here generate little of interest to an inquiry into the Judaism behind the texts, this passage speaks for me. What we derive is refinement and clarification, but the passage scarcely suggests that taken for granted is a deep layer of theological or moral speculation. What we see is what we get, which is, a text with some minor points of refinement.

Even though these results prove paltry, the issues remain vital, and a negative result itself bears formidable implications. Let me spell out what I conceive to be at stake in this protracted study. In fact, the issue of premises, the question, if I know this, what else do I know? – these form the entry point. But my goal is other. For the task of history of religions always is that of definition of religions: what we can possibly mean by those encompassing categories, "Judaism" or "Buddhism" or "Islam" or "Christianity" that descriptively conform to data. In the case of "Judaism," I want to know whether the construct refers to documents that cohere, or whether the fabricated category is imposed thereon. So I aim at finding out whether, and how, the various documents valued by the Judaism of the Dual Torah relate, not in imputed but in substantive ways. Do I find that the various writings that the Judaism of the Dual Torah produced in late antiquity rest upon shared and common fundamental convictions, that is, this "Judaism behind the texts," or does each piece of writing stand essentially on its own? It is clear that as a matter of theory documents that are held by those who deem them authoritative to cohere relate in three ways. First, they stand each on its own, that is, each is autonomous. Second, in some ways they may intersect, for example, citations or long quotations of one writing appear in some other. They are therefore connected in some specific ways. But, third, do these writings also form a continuous whole? That is what I want to find out in this exercise. Let me spell out these three dimensions of relationship: autonomy, connection, and continuity.

Documents – cogent compositions made up of a number of complete units of thought – by definition exist on their own. That is to say, by invoking as part of our definition the trait of cogency of individual units as well as of the entire composite, we complete a definition of what a document is and is not. A document is a cogent composite of cogent statements. But, also by definition, none of these statements is read all by itself. A document forms an artifact of a social culture, and that in diverse dimensions. Cogency depends on shared rhetoric, logic of intelligible discourse, topic and program – all of these traits of mind, of culture. Someone writes a document, someone buys it, an entire society sustains the labor of literature. But people value more than a single document, so we want to know how several documents may stand in connection with one another.

Each document therefore exists in both a textual and literary context, and also a social dimension of culture and even of politics. As to the former, documents may form a community whose limits are delineated by shared conventions of thought and expression. Those exhibiting distinctive, even definitive traits, fall within the community, those that do not, remain without. These direct the author to one mode of topic, logic, and rhetoric, and not to some other. So much for intrinsic traits. As to the extrinsic ones, readers bring to documents diverse instruments of intelligibility, knowledge of the grammar of not only language but also thought. That is why they can read one document and not some other. So one relationship derives from a literary culture, which forms the authorship of a document, and the other from a social culture. The literary bond links document to document, and the essentially social bond links reader to document – and also document (through the authorship, individual or collective) to reader. The one relationship is exhibited through intrinsic traits of language and style, logic, rhetoric, and topic, and the other through extrinsic traits of curiosity, acceptance and authority. While documents find their place in their own literary world and also in a larger social one, the two aspects have to remain distinct, the one textual, the other contextual.

It follows that relationships between and among documents also matter for two distinct reasons. The intrinsic relationships, which are formal, guide us to traits of intelligibility, teaching us through our encounter with one document how to read some other of its type or class. If we know how to read a document of one type, we may venture to read another of the same type, but not – without instruction – one of some other type altogether. The extrinsic relationships, which derive from context and are relative to community, direct us to how to understand a document as an artifact of culture and society. Traits not of documents but of doctrines affecting a broad range of documents come into play. The document, whatever its contents, therefore becomes an instrument of social culture, for example, theology and politics, a community's public policy. A community then expresses itself through its choice of documents, the community's canon forming a principal mode of such self-definition. So, as I said, through intrinsic traits a document places itself within a larger community of texts. Extrinsic traits, imputed to a document by not its authorship but its audience, select the document as canonical and make of the document a mode of social definition. The community through its mode of defining itself by its canonical choices forms a textual community – a community expressed through the books it reads and values.

So to summarize: the relationships among the documents produced by the sages of Judaism may take three forms: complete dependence, complete autonomy, intersection in diverse manner and measure. That second dimension provokes considerable debate and presents a remarkably unclear perspective. For while the dimensions of autonomy and continuity take the measure of acknowledged traits – books on their own, books standing in imputed, therefore socially verified, relationships – the matter of connection hardly enjoys the same clear definition. On the one side, intrinsic traits permit us to assess theories of connection. On the other, confusing theological and social judgments of continuities and literary and heuristic ones of connection, people present quite remarkable claims as to the relationships between and among documents, alleging, in fact, that the documents all have to be read as a single continuous document: the Torah. As we shall now see, some maintain that the connections between and among documents are such that each has to be read in the light of all others. So the documents assuredly do form a canon, and that is a position adopted not in some distant past or alien society but among contemporary participants to the cultural debate.

While I take up a community of texts and explore those intrinsic traits that link book to book, my inquiry rests on the premise that the books at issue derive from a textual community, one which, without reference to the intrinsic traits of the writings, deems the set of books as a group to constitute a canon. My question is simple but critical:

If in advance I did not know that the community of Judaism treats the writings before us (among others) as a canon, would the traits of the documents have told me that the writings at hand are related?

In this study, these "traits of documents" are the most profound and pervasive: premises and presuppositions. I cannot think of a more penetrating test of the proposition that the documents form a unity and are continuous with one another. The inquiry is inductive, concerns intrinsic traits of rot form or proposition but premise, and therefore pursues at the deepest layers of intellect, conviction, attitude, and even emotion the matte. of connection between document and document.

What makes the work plausible and nec˕ssary? It is a simple fact. All of the writings of Judaism in late antiquity copiously cite Scripture. Some of them serve (or are presented and organized) as commentaries on the former, others as amplifications of the latter. Since Judaism treats all of these writings as a single, seamless Torah, the one whole Torah revealed by God to Moses, our rabbi, at Mount Sinai, the received hermeneutic naturally does the same. All of the writings are read in light of all others, and words and phrases are treated as autonomous units of tradition, rather than as components of particular writings, for example, paragraphs – units of discourse – and books – composite units of sustained and cogent thought. The issue of connection therefore is legitimate to the data. But the issue of continuity is a still more profound and urgent one, and it is that issue that the present project is formulated to address.

With reference to the determinate canon of the Judaism of the Dual Torah, therefore, I ask about what is unstated and presupposed. I want to know the large-scale premises that form the foundations for the detailed statements of those writings. I turn to what is beneath the surface because I have completed my account of what lies right on the surface: the canon's articulated, explicit statements. It is time to look beneath the surface. In my tripartite program for the study of the Judaism of the Dual Torah in its formative age, an enterprise of systematic description, analysis, and interpretation, I have now completed the first stage and proceed to the second. Now that I know what the canonical writings say and have described the whole in the correct, historical manner and setting, I proceed to ask about what they do not say but take for granted. That defines the question here.

These questions bear a more profound implication than has been suggested. What I really want to find out here is not the answer to the question, if I know this, what else do I know? It is, rather, what are the things that all of the documents that make up the writings accorded the status of the Oral Torah know and share? When I ask about the Judaism behind the texts, I mean to find out what convictions unite diverse writings and form of them all a single statement, a cogent religious system. As I have explained, every document stands on its own; each is autonomous. Many documents furthermore establish points of contact or intersection; they are connected. But, as a matter of fact, the Judaism of the Dual Torah maintains that every writing is continuous with all other writings, forming a whole, a statement of comprehensive integrity.

If that is so, then at the premises or presuppositions of writings I ought to be able to identify what is continuous, from one writing to another, and what unites them all at their deepest layers of conviction, attitude, or sentiment. That is what is at stake in this study.

Accordingly, the experimental work of an analytical character that is undertaken here and in the companion volumes form a natural next step, on the path from description through analysis to interpretation. From my beginning work on the Mishnah, in 1972, I have undertaken a sustained and systematic description of that Judaism. In 1992, twenty years later, that sustained and uninterrupted work reached its conclusion in the two volumes that state the final results of the two programs that I pursued simultaneously: description of the literature, description of the history of the religious ideas set forth in that literature. The results are now fully in print in a variety of books and have now been systematically summarized, for a broad academic audience, in my *Introduction to Rabbinic Literature* and *Rabbinic Judaism: A Historical Introduction* (New York, 1994 and 1995, respectively: Doubleday Anchor Reference Library). These two books state my final results for the description of the literature and the history of Rabbinic Judaism; at this time, I have nothing to add to the descriptive process, and not much to change in the results set forth over this long span of time.

In finding the way into the deeper layers of conviction and consciousness of the Rabbinic documents, I propose to move inward from my description of Rabbinic Judaism, its writings and its historical development, document by document, to the analysis of the inner structure of that Judaism; and this search, in due course, should open the way to an interpretation of the system of that same Judaism. Here I offer more results of the analytical work, consequent upon completed description, that I have considered for some time.

A word particular to this and the next part of the larger project serves to complete this introduction. The documents of Midrash compilation that are examined in this part of the study, as well as in the part that follows, yield only modest results. We find little of legal interest, nothing at all of philosophical concern. The theological premises that occur throughout prove familiar and unremarkable. Any notion that behind the texts we may identify deep layers of coherent conviction, everywhere forming the foundation of sensibility and thought, proves not wrong but trivial. That is so – but so what? All we can show out of the sizable study at hand is that our sages of blessed memory read (those parts of) Scripture (that they deemed determinative). But that we knew before we began the work. As the project unfolds, it leads us into a different set of problems from that which at the outset appeared definitive, and the formulation of matters by Sanders, which struck me as productive, proves shallow and ignorant. But I did not know that when I started the work, nor could I have predicted the shape and structure of the results that are beginning to emerge. However, I leave until the end a complete and encompassing account of what we learn from a systematic study of the Judaism behind the texts. We end not where we thought we were going, and we began in a direction that led nowhere. But that is the way of learning, and that is why learning feeds curiosity, the energy of all intellectual quest.

Part One

GENESIS RABBAH

1

Genesis Rabbah to
Parashat Bereshit (I-XXIX)

I. The Character of Genesis Rabbah

In Genesis Rabbah, generally supposed to have reached closure in the mid-fifth century, sometime after the Talmud of the Land of Israel, the entire narrative of Genesis is so formed as to point toward the sacred history of Israel, the Jewish people: its slavery and redemption; its coming Temple in Jerusalem; its exile and salvation at the end of time – the whole a paradigm of exile and return, resentment and remission. In the rereading of the authorship of Genesis Rabbah, Genesis proclaims the prophetic message that the world's creation commenced a single, straight line of significant events, that is to say, history, leading in the end to the salvation of Israel and through Israel all humanity. The single most important proposition of Genesis Rabbah is that, in the story of the beginnings of creation, humanity, and Israel, we find the message of the meaning and end of the life of the Jewish people in the here and now of the fifth century. The deeds of the founders supply signals for the children about what is going to come in the future. So the biography of Abraham, Isaac, and Jacob also constitutes a protracted account of the history of Israel later on.

Genesis Rabbah is a composite document. As with the Talmud that it accompanies, so in Genesis Rabbah, some of the material in the compilation can be shown to have been put together before that material was used for the purposes of the compilers. Many times a comment entirely apposite to a verse of Genesis has been joined to a set of comments in no way pertinent to the verse at hand. Proof for a given syllogism, furthermore, will derive from a verse of Genesis as well as from numerous verses of other books of the Bible. Such a syllogistic argument therefore has not been written for exegetical purposes particular to the verse at hand. To the contrary, the particular verse subject to attention serves that other, propositional plan; it is not the focus of discourse; it has not generated the comment but merely provided a proof for a syllogism. That is what it means to say that a proposition yields an exegesis. That fundamental proposition, displayed throughout Genesis Rabbah, which yields the specific exegeses of many of the verses of the book of Genesis and even whole stories, is that the beginnings point toward the endings, and the meaning of Israel's past points toward the message that lies in Israel's future. The things that happened to the fathers and mothers of the family, Israel, provide a sign for the things that will happen to the children later on.

What is at stake is the discovery, among the facts provided by the Written Torah, of the social rules that govern Israel's history. At stake is the search for the order yielded by the chaos of uninterpreted data. It follows that, as with the Mishnah, the governing mode of thought is that of natural philosophy. It involves the classification of data by shared traits, yielding descriptive rules, the testing of propositions against the facts of data, the whole aimed at the discovery of underlying rules out of a multiplicity of details, in all, the proposing and testing, against the facts provided by Scripture, of the theses of Israel's salvation that demanded attention just then. But the issues were not so much philosophical as religious, in the sense that while philosophy addressed questions of nature and rules of enduring existence, religion asked about issues of history and God's intervention in time. Within that rough-and-ready distinction between nature, supernature, and sanctification, typified by the Mishnah and the Tosefta and the legal enterprise in general, on the one side, and society, history, and salvation, typified by Genesis Rabbah, Leviticus Rabbah, Pesiqta deRab Kahana, and the theological inquiry into teleology, on the other, we may distinguish our documents.

Specifically, we may classify the document before us and its successors and companions as works of profound theological inquiry into God's rules for history and society in the here and now and for salvation at the end of historical time. That fundamental proposition concerning the search, in the account of the beginnings, of the ending and meaning of Israel's society and history – hence the rules that govern and permit knowledge of what is to come – constitutes the generative proposition that yielded the specific exegesis of the book of Genesis in Genesis Rabbah.

Genesis Rabbah in its final form emerges from that momentous century in which the Roman Empire passed from pagan to Christian rule, and, in which, in the aftermath of Julian's abortive reversion to paganism, Christianity adopted that politics of repression of paganism that rapidly engulfed Judaism as well. The issue confronting Israel in the

Land of Israel therefore proved immediate: the meaning of the new and ominous turn of history, the implications of Christ's worldly triumph for the other-worldly and supernatural people, Israel, whom God chooses and loves. The message of the exegete compositors addressed the circumstance of historical crisis and generated remarkable renewal, a rebirth of intellect in the encounter with Scripture, now in quest of the rules not of sanctification – these had already been found – but of salvation. So the book of Genesis, which portrays how all things had begun, would testify to the message and the method of the end: the coming salvation of patient, hopeful, enduring Israel.

That is why in the categories of philosophy, including science and society, and religion, including a prophetic interpretation of history and teleology, Genesis Rabbah presents a deeply *religious* view of Israel's historical and salvific life, in much the same way that the Mishnah provides a profoundly *philosophical* view of Israel's everyday and sanctified existence. Just as the main themes of the Mishnah evoke the consideration of issues of being and becoming, the potential and the actual, mixtures and blends and other problems of physics, all in the interest of philosophical analysis, so Genesis Rabbah presents its cogent and coherent agendum as well. That program of inquiry concerns the way in which, in the book of Genesis, God set forth to Moses the entire scope and meaning of Israel's history among the nations and salvation at the end of days. The mode of thought by which the framers of Genesis Rabbah work out their propositions dictates the character of their exegesis, as to rhetoric, logical principle of cogent and intelligible discourse, and, as is clear, even as to topic.

In view of the framers of the compilation, the entire narrative of Genesis is so formed as to point toward the sacred history of Israel, the Jewish people: its slavery and redemption; its coming Temple in Jerusalem; its exile and salvation at the end of time. In the reading of the authors at hand, therefore, the powerful message of Genesis proclaims that the world's creation commenced a single, straight line of events, leading in the end to the salvation of Israel and through Israel all humanity. That message – that history heads toward Israel's salvation – sages derived from the book of Genesis and contributed to in their own day. Therefore in their reading of Scripture a given story will bear a deeper truth about what it means to be Israel, on the one side, and what in the end of days will happen to Israel, on the other. True, their reading makes no explicit reference to what, if anything, had changed in the age of Constantine. But we do find repeated references to the four kingdoms, Babylonia, Media, Greece, Rome – and beyond the fourth will come Israel, fifth and last. So sages' message, in their theology of history, was that the present anguish prefigured the coming vindication of God's people.

It follows that sages read Genesis as the history of the world with emphasis on Israel. So the lives portrayed, the domestic quarrels and petty conflicts with the neighbors, all serve to yield insight into what was to be. Why so? Because the deeds of the patriarchs taught lessons on how the children were to act, and, it further followed, the lives of the patriarchs signaled the history of Israel. Israel constituted one extended family, and the metaphor of the family, serving the nation as it did, imparted to the stories of Genesis the character of a family record. History become genealogy conveyed the message of salvation. These propositions really laid down the same judgment, one for the individual and the family, the other for the community and the nation, since there was no differentiating. Every detail of the narrative therefore served to prefigure what was to be, and Israel found itself, time and again, in the revealed facts of the history of the creation of the world, the decline of humanity down to the time of Noah, and, finally, its ascent to Abraham, Isaac, and Israel.

Rhetoric

The document undertakes two tasks. First comes the exegesis of clauses of verses, read in sequence, just as we noted in Sifra and Sifré to Numbers. Second, a not quite fresh, but vigorous and now fully exploited, exegetical technique involves the introduction, at the beginning of a sustained composition, of a verse other than the one under analysis. That other verse intersects with the verse under discussion, and – as before, with Sifré to Numbers – the one is called the intersecting verse and the other the base verse. This formal arrangement of verses predominates from Genesis Rabbah forward. The power of this form – the juxtaposition of two verses, one derived from the document at hand, the other from some other document altogether – which will dominate from the present document (ca. 400-450) onward, is simple. On the surface, the intersecting verse expands the frame of reference of the base verse, introducing data otherwise not present. But just beneath the surface lies the implicit premise: both the intersecting verse and the base verse make the same point, and, in their meeting, each rises out of its narrow framework as a detail or an instance of a rule and testifies to the larger picture, the encompassing rule itself. The intersecting verse/base verse construction therefore yields a proposition that transcends both verses and finds proof in the cases of each, and that powerful way of composing something new forms the centerpiece of the present document and the two that follow.

The reason that this rhetorical program – intersecting verse/base verse – serves so well derives from the program of the document. It is to demonstrate that there are reliable rules that govern Israel's history, specifically to discover and validate those fixed and governing rules within the details of stories of the origins of the family of Abraham, Isaac, and Jacob, which Israel now constitutes. A process of search for the governing laws of history and society requires not specific cases but general rules, and an inductive process will demand that sages generate rules out of cases. The meeting of rhetoric, logic, and topic takes place here. Putting together the cases represented by two verses, one deep within the narrative of Genesis, the other far distant from that narrative, the exegetes found it possible to state a case and along with the case to point toward an implicit generalization yielded by the two or more cases at hand. The rhetoric involves the recurrent arrangement of verses, the logic, the inquiry into the general rule that holds together two cases and makes of them a single statement of an overriding law, and the topic, the direction of the history of Israel, specifically, its ultimate salvation at the end of time.

The first of the three forms of the document is the recurrent mode of organization: the base verse/intersecting verse construction. In the sort of passage under discussion, (1) a verse of the book of Genesis will be followed by (2) a verse from some other book of the Hebrew Scriptures. The latter (2) will then be subjected to extensive discussion. But in the end the exposition of the intersecting verse will shed some light, in some way, upon (1) the base verse, cited at the outset. The second paramount form, which always follows in sequence as well, is the exegesis of a verse, which is familiar: a verse of the book of Genesis will be subjected to sustained analysis and amplification, but not with reference to some other intersecting verse but now, commonly with regard to numerous prooftexts, or to no prooftexts at all. Finally, the syllogism form will cite a variety of verses, drawn from a broad range of books of the Hebrew Scriptures, ordinarily composed in a list of like grammatical and syntactical entries.

In the aggregate Genesis Rabbah conforms to two important literary patterns. First we are able to classify the bulk of its completed units of thought among three forms or patterns, as specified. Second, the formal types of units of discourse are arranged in accord with a single set of preferences, with the intersecting verse/base verse always standing at the head of a composite, followed by the exegetical form. Within the formal structures may be discerned miscellaneous material as well. Form 1, for example, with its reference to an intersecting verse followed by its treatment of the base verse, not uncommonly carried in its wake materials of a formally quite miscellaneous character. Form 2 still more commonly permits characterization only in the simplest way: first comes the citation of a verse of the book of Genesis, then comes some sort of comment on that verse. Within the requirements of so simple a pattern, a variety of arrangements and formulations found ample place. Form 3, to be sure, presents more striking formal traits, with its emphasis upon the construction of a list of facts to prove a given proposition. In the cases of form 2 and form 3, the patterns find a place not in the center but at the edges of the compositions in which they occur. These forms make only a superficial, external impact on the compositions in which they occur.

Logic of Coherent Discourse

Genesis Rabbah is made up of one hundred *parashiyyot*, and each *parashah* is comprised of from as few as five to as many as fifteen subdivisions. These subdivisions in the main formed cogent statements, that is to say, words joined together to form autonomous statements, sentences. Sentences then coalesced into cogent propositions, paragraphs. Paragraphs then served a larger purpose, forming a cogent proposition of some sort. All together, therefore, discrete words turned into sentences, and sentences into whole thoughts, that we can discern and understand. The smallest whole units of thought of Genesis Rabbah contain cogent thought. We can discern the ideas presented in the composition at hand. The use of the word "composition" is justified: there is thought, in logical sequence, in proportion, in order, with a beginning, a middle, and an end. Genesis Rabbah then is composed of a long sequence of these smallest whole units of thought, strung together for some purpose or another.

What differentiates this document from its predecessors, as noted at the outset, is that these smallest whole units of discourse or thought join together for a larger purpose. The document intellectually is more than an anthology of discrete passages. How so? Among all the diverse smaller units of discourse, sayings, stories, exegeses of verses of Scripture, protracted proofs of a single proposition, and the like, ordinarily served a purpose cogent to the whole subdivision of a *parashah*. That is to say, whatever finished materials are present have been made by the compositors – the authorities who selected the smallest completed units of thought and arranged them as we now have them – to serve their goals, that is, purposes of the compositors of the larger unit of thought of which the several smallest units of thought now form a part. That is why form-analysis worked its way from the largest components of the document, the *parashiyyot*, to the next largest, and so on down.

The analysis of the logic of coherent discourse shows a kind of writing not apparent in Rabbinic literature in prior documents. The coherence of the document derives from the program of the document as a whole, rather than from the joining of the smaller into the larger units of discourse and thought. True, we find compositions of that present syllogistic argument; we find passages joined by the teleological logic of narrative; and the compilation has its share of passages that hold together only through the logic of fixed association. But, overall, the document holds together through what we may call the governing purpose of the entire compilation, not only the sewing together of its components. What accomplishes the ultimate unification of the writing is that the framers of Genesis Rabbah wished to do two things. First, they proposed to read the book of Genesis in light of other books of the Hebrew Scriptures, so underlining the unity of the Scriptures. Second, they planned to read the book of Genesis phrase by phrase, so emphasizing the historical progression of the tale at hand, from verse to verse, from event to event.

So the book of Genesis now presents more than a single dimension. It tells the story of things that happened. The exegetes explain the meaning of these events, adding details and making explicit the implicit, unfolding message. Read from beginning to end, time in the beginning moved in an orderly progression. The book of Genesis also tells the laws that govern Israel's history. These laws apply at all times and under all circumstances. Facts of history, emerging at diverse times and under various circumstances, attest to uniform and simple laws of society and of history. That is why verses of Scripture originating here, there, everywhere, all serve equally well to demonstrate the underlying rules that govern. Read out of all historical sequence but rather as a set of exemplifications of recurrent laws, the stories of Genesis do not follow a given order, a single sequence of timely events. Time now moves in deep, not shallow, courses; time is cyclical, or, more really, time matters not at all. The long stretches of timeless rules take over. Sequential exegeses, citing and commenting on verses, classified as form 2, express the former of the two dimensions, and exercises in the clarification of a verse of Genesis through the message of a verse in another book of the Scriptures altogether, on the one side, and propositional or syllogistic compositions, on the other, forms 1 and 3, express the latter. The book of Genesis is made greater than its first reading would suggest. Hence, Genesis Rabbah, meaning (from a later angle of vision only) a greater conception of the book of Genesis, vastly expands the dimensions of the story of the creation of the world, humanity, and Israel. The document finds its coherence in the vast conception that it wishes to put forth.

Topical Program

In Genesis Rabbah the entire narrative of Genesis is so formed as to point toward the sacred history of Israel, the Jewish people: its slavery and redemption; its coming Temple in Jerusalem; its exile and salvation at the end of time. The powerful message of Genesis in Genesis Rabbah proclaims that the world's creation commenced a single, straight line of events, leading in the end to the salvation of Israel and through Israel all humanity. Israel's history constitutes the counterpart of creation, and the laws of Israel's salvation form the foundation of creation. Therefore a given story out of Genesis, about creation, events from Adam to Noah and Noah to Abraham, the domestic affairs of the patriarchs, or Joseph, will bear a deeper message about what it means to be Israel, on the one side, and what in the end of days will happen to Israel, on the other. So the persistent theological program requires sages to search in Scripture for meaning for their own circumstance and for the condition of their people. The single most important proposition of Genesis Rabbah is that, in the story of the beginnings of creation, humanity, and Israel, we find the message of the meaning and end of the life of the Jewish people. The deeds of the founders supply signals for the children about what is going to come in the future. So the biography of Abraham, Isaac, and Jacob also constitutes a protracted account of the history of Israel later on. If the sages could announce a single syllogism and argue it systematically, that is the proposition upon which they would insist.

As a corollary to the view that the biography of the fathers prefigures the history of the descendants, sages maintained that the deeds of the children – the holy way of life of Israel – follow the model established by the founders long ago. So they looked in Genesis for the basis for the things they held to be God's will for Israel. And they found ample proof. Sages invariably searched the stories of Genesis for evidence of the origins not only of creation and of Israel, but also of Israel's cosmic way of life, its understanding of how, in the passage of nature and the seasons, humanity worked out its relationship with God. The holy way of life that Israel lived through the seasons of nature therefore would make its mark upon the stories of the creation of the world and the beginning of Israel

Part of the reason sages pursued the interest at hand derived from polemic. From the first Christian century theologians of Christianity maintained that salvation did not depend upon keeping the laws of the Torah. Abraham, after all, had been justified and he did not keep the Torah, which, in his day, had not yet been given. So sages time and again would maintain that Abraham indeed kept the entire Torah even before it had been revealed. They further attributed to Abraham, Isaac, and Jacob rules of the Torah enunciated only later on, for example, the institution of prayer three times a day. But the passage before us bears a different charge. It is to Israel to see how deeply embedded in the rules of reality were the patterns governing God's relationship to Israel. That relationship, one of human sin and atonement, divine punishment and forgiveness, expresses the most fundamental laws of human existence.

The world was created for Israel, and not for the nations of the world. At the end of days everyone will see what only Israel now knows. Since sages read Genesis as the history of the world with emphasis on Israel, the lives portrayed, the domestic quarrels and petty conflicts with the neighbors, as much as the story of creation itself, all serve to yield insight into what was to be. We now turn to a detailed examination of how sages spelled out the historical law at hand. The lives of the patriarchs signaled the history of Israel. Every detail of the narrative therefore served to prefigure what was to be, and Israel found itself, time and again, in the revealed facts of the history of the creation of the world, the decline of humanity down to the time of Noah, and, finally, its ascent to Abraham, Isaac, and Israel. In order to illustrate the single approach to diverse stories, whether concerning Creation, Adam, and Noah, or concerning Abraham, Isaac, and Jacob, we focus on two matters, Abraham, on the one side, and Rome, on the other. In the former we see that Abraham serves as well as Adam to prove the point of it all. In the latter we observe how, in reading Genesis, the sages who compiled Genesis Rabbah discovered the meaning of the events of their own day.

One rule of Israel's history is yielded by the facts at hand. Israel is never left without an appropriate hero or heroine. The relevance of the long discourse becomes clear at the end. Each story in Genesis may forecast the stages in Israel's history later on, beginning to end. A matter of deep concern focused sages' attention on the sequence of world empires to which, among other nations, Israel was subjugated, Babylonia, Media, Greece, and Rome – Rome above all. What will follow? Sages maintained that beyond the rule of Rome lay the salvation of Israel:

XLII

IV.1   A.   "And it came to pass in the days of Amraphel" (Gen. 14:1):

IV.4   A.   Another matter: "And it came to pass in the days of Amraphel, king of Shinar" (Gen. 14:1) refers to Babylonia.

       B.   "Arioch, king of Ellasar" (Gen. 14:1) refers to Greece.

       C.   "Chedorlaomer, king of Elam" (Gen. 14:1) refers to Media.

       D.   "And Tidal, king of Goiim [nations]" (Gen. 14:1) refers to the wicked government [Rome], which conscripts troops from all the nations of the world.

E.   Said R. Eleazar bar Abina, "If you see that the nations contend with
one another, look for the footsteps of the king messiah. You may
know that that is the case, for lo, in the time of Abraham, because
the kings struggled with one another, a position of greatness came
to Abraham."

Obviously, No. 4 presents the most important reading of Genesis 14:1,
since it links the events of the life of Abraham to the history of Israel and
even ties the whole to the messianic expectation. I suppose that any list
of four kings will provoke inquiry into the relationship of the entries of
that list to the four kingdoms among which history, in Israel's
experience, is divided. The process of history flows in both directions.
Just as what Abraham did prefigured the future history of Israel, so what
the Israelites later on were to do imposed limitations on Abraham. Time
and again events in the lives of the patriarchs prefigure the four
monarchies, among which, of course, the fourth, last, and most
intolerable was Rome.

   Genesis is read as if it portrayed the history of Israel and Rome. For
that is the single obsession binding sages of the document at hand to
common discourse with the text before them. Why Rome in the form it
takes in Genesis Rabbah? And how come the obsessive character of
sages' disposition of the theme of Rome? Were their picture merely of
Rome as tyrant and destroyer of the Temple, we should have no reason
to link the text to the problems of the age of redaction and closure. But
now it is Rome as Israel's brother, counterpart, and nemesis, Rome as the
one thing standing in the way of Israel's, and the world's, ultimate
salvation. So the stakes are different, and much higher. It is not a
political Rome but a Christian and messianic Rome that is at issue: Rome
as surrogate for Israel, Rome as obstacle to Israel. Why? It is because
Rome now confronts Israel with a crisis, and, I argue, the program of
Genesis Rabbah constitutes a response to that crisis. Rome in the fourth
century became Christian. Sages responded by facing that fact quite
squarely and saying, "Indeed, it is as you say, a kind of Israel, an heir of
Abraham as your texts explicitly claim. But we remain the sole
legitimate Israel, the bearer of the birthright – we and not you. So you
are our brother: Esau, Ishmael, Edom." And the rest follows.

   By rereading the story of the beginnings, sages discovered the
answer and the secret of the end. Rome claimed to be Israel, and, indeed,
sages conceded, Rome shared the patrimony of Israel. That claim took
the form of the Christians' appropriation of the Torah as "the Old
Testament," so sages acknowledged a simple fact in acceding to the
notion that, in some way, Rome, too, formed part of Israel. But it was the
rejected part, the Ishmael, the Esau, not the Isaac, not the Jacob. The
advent of Christian Rome precipitated the sustained, polemical, and, I

think, rigorous and well-argued rereading of beginnings in light of the end. Rome then marked the conclusion of human history as Israel had known it. Beyond? The coming of the true Messiah, the redemption of Israel, the salvation of the world, the end of time. So the issues were not inconsiderable, and when the sages spoke of Esau/Rome, as they did so often, they confronted the life-or-death decision of the day.

In Genesis Rabbah the sages show in detail the profound depths of the story of the creation of the world and Israel's founding family. Bringing their generative proposition about the character of the Scripture to the stories at hand, they systematically found in the details of the tales the history of the people Israel portrayed in the lives and deeds of the founders, the fathers and the mothers of this book of the Torah. It is no accident that the exegetes of the book of Genesis invoke large-scale constructions of history to make fundamental judgments about society – Israel's society. Nor is it merely happenstance that the exegetes bring into juxtaposition distinct facts – passages – of scriptural history or appeal to a typological reading of the humble details of the scriptural tale, the simple statement that the shepherds had brought their flocks to the well, for example. A large proposition has governed the details of exegesis, and the individual verses commonly, though not always, address their facts in the proof of an encompassing hypothesis, a theorem concerning Israel's fate and faith.

II. Unarticulated Premises: The Givens of Religious Conduct

1.   The rites imitate God's actions on comparable occasions:

III

VI.2   A.   "And God saw the light" (Gen. 1:3):

         B.   R. Zeira son of R. Abbahu gave an exposition in Caesarea: "How do we know that **people may not say a blessing [for the rite of Habdalah, separating the Sabbath from the ordinary week] making use of a light, unless they have actually made use of its light** [M. Ber. 8:5]?

         C.   "From the following statement: 'And God saw...then God divided...' [as in saying a blessing to divide the Sabbath from the ordinary weekday. So God first made use of the light by looking at it and only then divided it.]"

III. Unarticulated Premises: The Givens of Religious Conviction

1.   God consulted the Torah in creating the world; the Torah is the divine design of the world:

I

I.2   A.   Another matter:

      B.   The word means "workman."

C. [In the cited verse] the Torah speaks, "I was the work plan of the Holy One, blessed be He."

D. In the accepted practice of the world, when a mortal king builds a palace, he does not build it out of his own head, but he follows a work plan.

E. And [the one who supplies] the work plan does not build out of his own head, but he has designs and diagrams, so as to know how to situate the rooms and the doorways.

F. Thus the Holy One, blessed be He, consulted the Torah when he created the world.

G. So the Torah stated, "By means of 'the beginning' [that is to say, the Torah] did God create..." (Gen. 1:1).

H. And the word for "beginning" refers only to the Torah, as Scripture says, "The Lord made me as the beginning of his way" (Prov. 8:22).

2. If one wishes to know the secrets of creation, that person will study the Torah:

I

VI.4   A. Said R. Judah bar Simon, "To begin with, when the world was being created, 'He reveals deep and secret things,' for it is written, 'In the beginning God created the heaven (Gen. 1:1).' But the matter was not spelled out.

B. "Where then was it spelled out?

C. "Elsewhere: 'Who stretches out the heaven as a curtain' (Isa. 40:22).

D. "'....and the earth' (Gen. 1:1). But this matter, too, was not then spelled out.

E. "Where then was it spelled out?

F. "Elsewhere: 'For he says to the snow, "Fall on the earth"' (Job 37:6).

G. "And God said, 'Let there be light' (Gen. 1:3).

H. "And this, too, was not spelled out.

I. "Where then was it spelled out?

J. "Elsewhere: 'Who covers yourself with light as with a garment' (Ps. 104:2)."

3. There is only one God, there are not two gods:

I

VII.1   A. R. Isaac commenced [discourse by citing the following verse]: "'The beginning of your word is truth [and all your righteous ordinance endures forever]' (Ps. 119:16)."

B. Said R. Isaac [about the cited verse], "From the beginning of the creation of the world, 'The beginning of your word was truth.'

C. "'In the beginning God created' (Gen. 1:1).

D. "'And the Lord God is truth' (Jer. 10:9).

E. "Therefore: 'And all your righteous ordinance endures forever' (Ps. 119:16).

F. "For as to every single decree which you lay down for your creatures, they accept that decree as righteous and receive it in good faith, so that no creature may differ, saying 'Two powers gave the Torah, two powers created the world.'

G. "[Why not?] Because here it is not written, 'And gods spoke,' but rather, 'And God spoke' (Ex. 20:1).

H. "'In the beginning [gods] created' is not written, but rather, 'in the beginning [God] created' [in the singular]."

3. God had the right to assign the Land of Israel to Israel, because God made the entire world and is owner by right of all creation, so God can do what he wants with everything:

I

II.1   A. R. Joshua of Sikhnin in the name of R. Levi commenced [discourse by citing the following verse]: "'He has declared to his people the power of his works, in giving them the heritage of the nations' (Ps. 111:6).

B. "What is the reason that the Holy One, blessed be He, revealed to Israel what was created on the first day and what on the second?

C. "It was on account of the nations of the world. It was so that they should not ridicule the Israelites, saying to them, 'Are you not a nation of robbers [having stolen the land from the Canaanites]?'

D. "It allows the Israelites to answer them, 'And as to you, is there no spoil in your hands? For surely: "The Caphtorim, who came forth out of Caphtor, destroyed them and dwelled in their place" (Deut. 2:23)!

E. "'The world and everything in it belongs to the Holy One, blessed be He. When he wanted, he gave it to you, and when he wanted, he took it from you and gave it to us.'

F. "That is in line with what is written, '....in giving them the heritage of the nations, he has declared to his people the power of his works' (Ps. 111:6). [So as to give them the land, he established his right to do so by informing them that he had created it.]

G. "He told them about the beginning: 'In the beginning God created...' (Gen. 1:1)."

4. The world was created because of Israel, or Israel and the Torah, or Israel's service of God in the Land:

I

IV.1   A. ["In the beginning God created" (Gen. 1:1):] Six things came before the creation of the world, some created, some at least considered as candidates for creation.

B. The Torah and the throne of glory were created [before the creation of the world].

C. The Torah, as it is written, "The Lord made me as the beginning of his way, prior to his works of old" (Prov. 8:22).

D. The throne of glory, as it is written, "Your throne is established of old" (Ps. 93:2).

E. The patriarchs were considered as candidates for creation, as it is written, "I saw your fathers as the first ripe in the fig tree at her first season" (Hos. 9:10).

F. Israel was considered [as a candidate for creation], as it is written, "Remember your congregation, which you got aforetime" (Ps. 74:2).

G. The Temple was considered as a candidate for creation], as it is written, "You, throne of glory, on high from the beginning, the place of our sanctuary" (Jer. 17:12).

H. The name of the Messiah was kept in mind, as it is written, "His name exists before the sun" (Ps. 72:17).

I. R. Ahbah bar Zeira said, "Also [the power of] repentance.

J. "That is in line with the following verse of Scripture: 'Before the mountains were brought forth' (Ps. 90:2). From that hour: 'You turn man to contrition and say, Repent, you children of men' (Ps. 90:3)."

K. Nonetheless, I do not know which of these came first, that is, whether the Torah was prior to the throne of glory, or the throne of glory to the Torah.

L. Said R. Abba bar Kahana, "The Torah came first, prior to the throne of glory.

M. "For it is said, 'The Lord made me as the beginning of his way, before his works of old' (Prov. 8:22).

N. "It came prior to that concerning which it is written, 'For your throne is established of old' (Ps. 93:2)."

IV.2 A. R. Huna, R. Jeremiah in the name of R. Samuel b. R. Isaac: "Intention concerning the creation of Israel came before all else.

B. "The matter may be compared to the case of a king who married a noble lady but had no son with her. One time the king turned up in the marketplace, saying, 'Buy this ink, inkwell, and pen on account of my son.'

C. "People said, 'He has no son. Why does he need ink, inkwell, and pen?'

D. "But then people went and said, 'The king is an astrologer, so he sees into the future and he therefore is expecting to produce a son!'

E. "Along these same lines, if the Holy One, blessed be He, had not foreseen that, after twenty-six generations, the Israelites would be destined to accept the Torah, he would never have written in it, 'Command the children of Israel.' [This proves that God foresaw Israel and created the world on that account.]"

IV.3 A. Said. R. Benaiah, "The world and everything in it were created only on account of the merit of the Torah.

B. "'The Lord for the sake of wisdom [Torah] founded the earth' (Prov. 3:19)."

C. R. Berekiah said, "It was for the merit of Moses.

D. "'And he saw the beginning for himself, for there a portion of a ruler [Moses] was reserved' (Deut. 33:21)."

IV.4 A. R. Huna in the name of Rab repeated [the following]: "For the merit of three things was the world created, for the merit of dough-offerings, tithes, and first fruits.

B. "For it is said, 'On account of [the merit of] what is first, God created...' (Gen. 1:1).

    C. "And the word 'first' refers only to dough-offering, for it is written, 'Of the first of your dough' (Num. 15:20).

    D. "The same word refers to tithes, as it is written, 'The first fruits of your grain' (Deut. 18:4).

    E. "And the word 'first' refers to first fruits, for it is written, 'The choicest of your land's first fruit' (Ex. 23:19)."

5. The condition of the natural world corresponds to the condition of the world of humanity, and the supernatural condition of Israel is attested in nature as well; this point recurs, but is registered here alone:

I.1

    A. ["And the earth was unformed..." (Gen. 1:2):]

    B. R. Judah b. R. Simon interpreted the verse as referring to coming generations, [as follows]:

    C. "'The earth was unformed' refers to Adam, who was [Freedman:] reduced to complete nothingness [on account of his sin].

    D. "'And void' refers to Cain, who sought to return the world to unformedness and void.

    E. "'And darkness was upon the face of the deep' (Gen. 1:2) refers to the generation of Enosh: 'And their works are in the dark' (Isa. 29:15).

    F. "'Upon the face of the deep' (Gen. 1:2) refers to the generation of the flood: 'On the same day were all the fountains of the great deep broken up' (Gen. 7:11).

    G. "'And the spirit of God hovered over the face of the water' (Gen. 1:2): 'And God made a wind pass over the earth' (Gen. 8:1).

    H. "Said the Holy One, blessed be He, 'For how long will the world make its way in darkness. Let light come.'

    I. "'And God said, "Let there be light"' (Gen. 1:3). This refers to Abraham. That is in line with the following verse of Scripture: 'Who has raised up one from the earth, whom he calls in righteousness to his foot' (Isa. 41:23).

    J. "'And God called the light day' (Gen. 1:3) refers to Jacob.

    K. "'And the darkness he called night' (Gen. 1:30) refers to Esau.

    L. "'And there was evening' refers to Esau.

    M. '"'And there was morning' refers to Jacob.

    N. "'One day'– for the Holy One, blessed be He, gave him one day, and what is that day? It is the Day of Atonement. [Freedman, p. 17, n. 1: It is the one day over which Satan, symbolizing the wickedness of Esau, has no power.]"

II.1

    A. R. Simeon b. Laqish interpreted the verses at hand to speak of the empires [of the historical age to come].

    B. "'The earth was unformed' refers to Babylonia, 'I beheld the earth and lo, it was unformed' (Jer. 4:23).

    C. "'And void' refers to Media: 'They hasted [using the letters of the same root as the word for void] to bring Haman' (Est. 6:14).

    D. "'Darkness' refers to Greece, which clouded the vision of the Israelites through its decrees, for it said to Israel, 'Write on the horn of an ox [as a public proclamation for all to see] that you have no portion in the God of Israel.'

E.   "'...upon the face of the deep' refers to the wicked kingdom [of Rome].

F.   "Just as the deep surpasses investigation, so the wicked kingdom surpasses investigation.

G.   "'And the spirit of God hovers' refers to the spirit of the Messiah, in line with the following verse of Scripture: 'And the spirit of the Lord shall rest upon him' (Isa. 11:2)."

The same point is made in a different way, when the creation of the world is shown as a paradigm for the actions and condition of humanity:

III

VIII.1 A.   Said R. Yannai, "At the beginning of the creation of the world the Holy One, blessed be He, foresaw the deeds of the righteous and the deeds of the wicked.

B.   "'And the earth was unformed and void' refers to the deeds of the wicked.

C.   "'And God said, "Let there be light"' refers to the deeds of the righteous.

D.   "'And God saw the light, that it was good,' refers to the deeds of the righteous.

E.   "'And God divided between the light and the darkness' means, [he divided] between the deeds of the righteous and the deeds of the wicked.

F.   "'And God called the light day' refers to the deeds of the righteous.

G.   "'And the darkness he called night' refers to the deeds of the wicked.

H.   "'And there was evening' refers to the deeds of the wicked.

I.   "'And there was morning' refers to the deeds of the righteous.

J.   "'One day,' for the Holy One, blessed be He, gave them one day, [and what day is that]? It is the day of judgment."

The same point registers when nature is portrayed as obeying God's commandments in relationship to Israel:

V

V.1   A.   Said R. Jonathan, "The Holy One, blessed be He, made a stipulation with the sea to split open before the Israelites.

B.   "That is in line with this verse of Scripture: 'And the sea returned to its former strength', which word may be read, 'in accord with the stipulation that it had given' (Ex. 14:27)."

C.   Said R. Jeremiah b. Eleazar, "It was not with the sea alone that the Holy One, blessed be He, made such a stipulation, but he made the same stipulation with everything that was created in the six days of creation.

D.   "That is in line with this verse of Scripture: 'I, even my hands, have stretched out the heavens and all their host have I commanded' (Isa. 45:12).

E.   "'I commanded' the sea to divide.

F. "'I commanded' the heaven to be silent before Moses: 'Give ear, heaven' (Deut. 32:1).

G. "'I commanded' the sun and the moon to stand still before Joshua.

H. "'I commanded' the ravens to bring food to Elijah.

I. "'I commanded' the fire not to harm Hananiah, Mishael, and Azariah.

J. "'I commanded' the lions not to harm Daniel, the heaven to open before Ezekiel, the fish to vomit up Jonah."

6. God is both merciful and just:

VIII

IV.1 A. Said R. Berekhiah, "When God came to create the first man, he saw that both righteous and wicked descendants would come forth from him. He said, 'If I create him, wicked descendants will come forth from him. If I do not create him, how will the righteous descendants come forth from him?'

B. "What did the Holy One, blessed be He, do? He disregarded the way of the wicked and joined to himself his quality of mercy and so created him.

C. "That is in line with this verse of Scripture: 'For the Lord knows the way of the righteous, but the way of the wicked shall perish' (Ps. 1:6).

D. "What is the sense of 'shall perish'? He destroyed it from before his presence and joined to himself the quality of mercy, and so created man."

7. Israel's devotion to the Temple contrasts with ordinary peoples' devotion to the affairs of the natural world:

XIII

II.2 A. All conversation of ordinary mortals concerns only what has to do with the earth: "Has the earth produced a good harvest?" or "has the earth not produced a good harvest?"

B. And all prayers of ordinary mortals concern only the earth: "May my Lord make the earth produce a crop," or "may my Lord make the earth succeed."

C. But the prayers of Israel concern only the house of the sanctuary: "My Lord, rebuild the Temple," and "When will you build the Temple?"

8. Adam was created because of the merit of Abraham:

XV

IV.2 A. "[There he put] the man..." (Gen. 2:9):

B. It was on account of the merit owing to Abraham [who is, we recall, the model and the perfect man].

C. So it is written, "You know my sitting down and my standing up. You understand my thought from afar" (Ps. 139:2).

D. "My sitting down" refers to my settling in the Garden of Eden.

E.   "My standing up" refers to my being driven forth from it.

F.   "You understand my thought from afar" (Ps. 139:2): on account of the merit of whom did you determine to create me? It was on account of the merit of him who came from a far place: "Calling a bird of prey from the east, the man of my counsel from a far country" (Isa. 46:11). [This is taken to refer to Abraham, who answered God's call from a far place.]

9.   The four kingdoms who have ruled the world up to now correspond to nature, and all four will give way to Israel's ultimate dominion:

XVI

IV.1   A.   R. Tanhuma in the name of R. Joshua b. Levi said to him, "In the future the Holy One, blessed be He, is destined to give a cup of bitterness to the nations to drink from the place from which this [river] goes forth. And what is the verse that so indicates? 'A river flowed out of Eden to water the garden' (Gen. 2:10).

B.   "This refers to the four kingdoms, forming the counterpart to the four heads [into which the river is divided].

C.   "'The name of the first is Pishon' (Gen. 2:11) refers to Babylonia, in line with this verse: 'And their horsemen spread (*pashu*) themselves' (Hab. 1:8). And it also responds to [Freedman:] the midget dwarf, who was smaller than a handbreadth [that is, Nebuchadnezzar].

D.   "'It is the one which flows around the whole land of Havilah' [again, referring to Babylonia,] for [Nebuchadnezzar] came up and encompassed the entire Land of Israel, concerning which it is written, 'Hope you in God, for I shall yet praise him' (Ps. 42:6). [There is a play on the words for Havilah and hope.]

E.   "'...where there is gold' (Gen. 2:11) speaks of words of Torah, which are 'more to be desired than gold and than much fine gold' (Ps. 19:1). [Compare above, XVI:II.3.B. "Actual gold, not something that symbolizes something else of great value."]

F.   "'And the gold of that land is good' (Gen. 2:11) teaches that there is no Torah like the Torah of the Land of Israel, and there is no wisdom like the wisdom of the Land of Israel.

G.   "'Bdellium and onyx stone are there' (Gen. 2:12) refers to Scripture, Mishnah, Talmud, supplementary teachings, and lore.

H.   "'And the name of the second river is Gihon' refers to Media, for Haman [who was a Median] had [because of his deranged hatred of Israel] inflamed eyes like those of a serpent, on the count: 'On your belly (GHWNK) you will go, and dust you will eat all the days of your life' (Gen. 3:14).

I.   "It is the one which flows around the whole land of Cush' (Gen. 2:13). This allusion is to [Ahasueros, the Median, as in this verse]: 'Who reigned from India even to Cush' (Est. 1:1).

J.   "'And the name of the third river is Tigris' (Gen. 2:14) refers to Greece, which was sharp and speedy in making evil decrees, saying to Israel, 'Write on the horn of an ox [as a public proclamation] that you have no share in the God of Israel.'"

IV.2   A.   "...which flows east of Assyria" (Gen. 2:14):

> B. Said R. Huna, "In three matters did the kingdom of Greece take precedence [a play on the word for 'east' and 'precedence'] over the wicked kingdom [Rome]: in navigation, in setting up camp, and in language."

IV.3 A. R. Huna in the name of R. Aha, "All kingdoms bear the name of Assyria because they get rich on account of exacting their taxes from Israel [a play on the word for 'rich' and 'Assyria']."

> B. Said R. Yosé bar Judah, "All kingdoms are called Nineveh because they ornament themselves at the expense of Israel."
> C. Said R. Yosé bar Halapta, "All kingdoms are called 'Egypt,' because they oppress Israel [a play on the words 'oppress' and 'Egypt']."

IV.4 A. "And the fourth river is the Euphrates" (Gen. 2:14):
> B. This refers to Rome.
> C. It is called the Euphrates (PRT) because it unsettled and harassed his world.
> D. It is called the Euphrates because it became abundant on account of the blessing of the old man [Jacob, who blessed Esau, standing for Rome].
> E. It is called the Euphrates because: "In the future I am going to destroy it, at the end."
> F. It is called the Euphrates because of what will happen at the end of it: "I have trodden the winepress alone" (Isa. 63:3).

10. Israel's history in the Land is comparable to Adam's history in Eden:

XIX

IX.2 A. R. Abbahu in the name of R. Yosé bar Haninah: "It is written, 'But they are like a man [Adam], they have transgressed the covenant' (Hos. 6:7).

> B. "'They are like a man,' specifically, like the first man. [We shall now compare the story of the first man in Eden with the story of Israel in its land.]
> C. "'In the case of the first man, I brought him into the garden of Eden, I commanded him, he violated my commandment, I judged him to be sent away and driven out, but I mourned for him, saying "How..."'[which begins the book of Lamentations, hence stands for a lament, but which, as we just saw, also is written with the consonants that also yield, 'Where are you'].
> D. "'I brought him into the garden of Eden,' as it is written, 'And the Lord God took the man and put him into the garden of Eden' (Gen. 2:15).
> E. "'I commanded him,' as it is written, 'And the Lord God commanded...' (Gen. 2:16).
> F. "'And he violated my commandment,' as it is written, 'Did you eat from the tree concerning which I commanded you' (Gen. 3:11).
> G. "'I judged him to be sent away,' as it is written, 'And the Lord God sent him from the garden of Eden' (Gen. 3:23).
> H. "'And I judged him to be driven out.' 'And he drove out the man' (Gen. 3:24).

I.   "'But I mourned for him, saying, "How...."' 'And he said to him,
      "Where are you"' (Gen. 3:9), and the word for 'where are you' is
      written, 'How....'

J.   "'So, too, in the case of his descendants, [God continues to speak,] I
      brought them into the Land of Israel, I commanded them, they
      violated my commandment, I judged them to be sent out and
      driven away but I mourned for them, saying, "How...."'

K.   "'I brought them into the Land of Israel.' 'And I brought you into
      the land of Carmel' (Jer. 2:7).

L.   "'I commanded them.' 'And you, command the children of Israel'
      (Ex. 27:20). 'Command the children of Israel' (Lev. 24:2).

M.   "'They violated my commandment.' 'And all Israel have violated
      your Torah' (Dan. 9:11).

N.   "'I judged them to be sent out.' 'Send them away, out of my sight
      and let them go forth' (Jer 15:1).

O.   "'....and driven away.' 'From my house I shall drive them' (Hos.
      9:15).

P.   "'But I mourned for them, saying, "How...."' 'How has the city sat
      solitary, that was full of people' (Lam. 1:1)."

11. Israel and Adam are counterparts, but opposites; what Adam did not
    succeed in accomplishing, Israel realized in abundance: obedience to
    the Torah.

XXIV

V.2   A.   Said R. Yudah, "The first man [Adam] was worthy to have the
            Torah given through him. What is the verse of Scripture that so
            indicates? 'This is the book of the generations of man' (Gen. 5:1).
            ["This book can be given over to man."]

      B.   "Said the Holy One, blessed be He, 'He is the creation of my hands,
            and should I not give it to him?' Then he reversed himself and said,
            'I gave him no more than six commandments to follow, and he did
            not stand by them, so how can I now give him six hundred thirteen
            commandments, two hundred forty-eight commandments of things
            to do and three hundred sixty-five commandments of things not to
            do?'

      C.   "'And he said to man,' meaning, 'not-to-man' [reading the L before
            the consonants for 'man,' read as 'to man,' as though it bore the
            negative]. To man I shall not give it. And to whom shall I give it?
            To his children.' 'This is the book that belongs to the children of
            man' (Gen. 5:1)."

V.3   A.   Said R. Jacob of Kefar Hanan, "The first man was worthy to
            produce the twelve tribes. What is the verse of Scripture that so
            indicates? 'This is the book of man.'

      B.   "The word 'this' in Hebrew has consonants with the numerical
            value of twelve (ZH).

      C.   "Said the Holy One, blessed be He, 'He is the creation of my hands,
            and should I not give it to him?' Then he reversed himself and said,
            "Two sons I gave him, and one of them went and killed his fellow.
            How shall I then give him twelve?'

D. "'And he said to man,' (Job 28:27) meaning, 'not-to-man' [reading the L before the consonants for man as though it bore the negative]. To man I shall not give it. And to whom shall I give it? To his children: 'This is the book that belongs to the children of man' (Gen. 5:1)."

IV. Matters of Philosophy, Natural Science and Metaphysics

1. There are numerous discussions about the mysteries of the creation of the natural world, for example, creatio e nihilo in the following:

I

IX.1
A. A philosopher asked Rabban Gamaliel, saying to him, "Your God was indeed a great artist, but he had good materials to help him."
B. He said to him, "What are they?"
C. He said to him, "Unformed [space], void, darkness, water, wind, and the deep."
D. He said to him, "May the spirit of that man [you] burst! All of them are explicitly described as having been created by him [and not as pre-existent].
E. "Unformed space and void: 'I make peace and create evil' (Isa. 45:7).
F. "Darkness: 'I form light and create darkness' (Isa. 45:7).
G. "Water: 'Praise him, you heavens of heavens, and you waters that are above the heavens' (Ps. 148:4). Why? 'For he commanded and they were created' (Ps. 148:5).
H. "Wind: 'for lo, he who forms the mountains creates the wind' (Amos 4:13).
I. "The depths: 'When there were no depths, I was brought forth' (Prov. 8:24)."

The basic view that operates throughout is that investigation of the origins of things must begin with creation, not with what is prior to creation:

I

X.1
A. ["In the beginning God created" (Gen. 1:1):] R. Jonah in the name of R. Levi: "Why was the world created with [a word beginning with the letter] B?
B. "Just as [in Hebrew] the letter B is closed [at the back and sides but] open in front, so you have no right to expound concerning what is above or below, before or afterward."
C. Bar Qappara said, "'For ask now of the days past which were before you, since the day that God created man upon the earth' (Deut. 4:32).
D. "Concerning the day *after* which days were created, you may expound, but you may not make an exposition concerning what lies before then."
E. "'And from one end of the heaven to the other' (Deut. 4:32).

F.   "[Concerning that space] you may conduct an investigation, but you may not conduct an investigation concerning what lies beyond those points."

G.   R. Judah b. Pazzi gave his exposition concerning the story of creation in accord with this rule of Bar Qappara.

In this context, the premise must be classified as anti-philosophical.

2

Genesis Rabbah to Parashat Noah (XXX-XXXVIII)

I. Unarticulated Premises: The Givens of Religious Conduct

Nothing qualifies for this list.

II. Unarticulated Premises: The Givens of Religious Conviction

1. God is merciful to Israel, when Israelites show mercy to one another:

XXXIII

III.2

A. In the time of R. Tanhuma Israel had need of a fast [on account of the lack of rain]. People came to him. They said to him, "Our master, decree a fast." He decreed a fast for one day, then for a second day, then for a third day, but it did not rain.

B. He went up and preached to them, saying to them, "My children, show mercy for one another, and the Holy One, blessed be He, will show mercy to you."

C. While they were passing out charity, they saw a man giving money to a woman whom he had divorced. They came to [Tanhuma] and said to him, "How can we sit here while someone is doing such a thing!"

D. He said to them, "What did you see?"

E. They said to him, "We saw Mr. So-and-so paying off the woman he had divorced [so we assumed he was buying her sexual services]."

F. He sent the people to the man, and they brought him to the sage. He said to him, "Why did you give money to the woman you divorced?"

G. He said to him, "I saw her in great need and I felt pity for her."

H. R. Tanhuma raised his face upward and said, "Lord of all ages, now, if this man, who was under absolutely no obligation to provide food for the woman, could see her in need and be filled with mercy for her, you, concerning whom it is written, 'The Lord is full of compassion and gracious' (Ps. 103:8), and whose children we

43

are, that is, the children of those who are precious to you, children of Abraham, Isaac, and Jacob, how much the more so should you be filled with mercy for us!"

I.   Forthwith the rain came and the world returned to prosperity.

2.   God responds to the devotion of Israel and remembers in behalf of a later generation the achievements of an earlier one; God responds especially to the devotion of those who are persecuted in his name:

XXXIV

IX.4   A.   "And when the Lord smelled the pleasing odor, [the Lord said in his heart, 'I will never again curse the ground because of man, for the imagination of man's heart is evil from his youth']" (Gen. 8:21):

B.   He smelled the fragrance of the flesh of Abraham, our father, coming up from the heated furnace.

C.   He smelled the fragrance of the flesh of Hananiah, Mishael, and Azariah, coming up from the heated furnace.

D.   The matter may be compared to the case of a king, whose courtier brought him a valuable present. It was a fine piece of meat on a lovely plate [following Freedman].

E.   His son came along and brought him nothing. His grandson came along and brought him a present. He said to him, "The value of the gift you brought is equivalent to the value of the gift your grandfather brought."

F.   So God smelled the fragrance of the sacrifice of the generation of persecution.

III. Matters of Philosophy, Natural Science and Metaphysics

The question presented by this category of items does not pertain to the document analyzed here.

3

Genesis Rabbah to Parashat Lekh Lekha (XXXIX-XLVII)

I. Unarticulated Premises: The Givens of Religious Conduct

1. The law derives from the acts of the patriarchs and matriarchs:

XLV

III.2   A. "So after Abram had dwelt ten years in the land of Canaan" (Gen. 16:3):

      B. R. Ammi in the name of R. Simeon b. Laqish: "How on the basis of Scripture do we know that rule that we have learned in the Mishnah: **If one has married a woman and lived with her for ten years and not produced a child, he is not allowed to remain sterile [but must marry someone else]** [M. Yeb. 15:6]? Proof derives from this verse: 'So after Abram had dwelt ten years.' The statement, '...in the land of Canaan...' further proves that the years of marriage spent outside of the Land of Israel do not count."

II. Unarticulated Premises: The Givens of Religious Conviction

1. What happens to the patriarchs happens also to their descendants, Israel:

XL

VI.1   A. "And for her sake he dealt well with Abram" (Gen. 12:16):

      B. "And Pharaoh gave men orders concerning him, [and they set him on the way, with his wife and all that he had]" (Gen. 12:20).

      C. R. Phineas in the name of R. Hoshaiah said, "The Holy One, blessed be He, said to our father, Abraham, 'Go and pave a way before your children.' [Set an example for them, so that whatever you do now, they will do later on.] [We shall now see how each statement about Abram at Gen. 12:10-20 finds a counterpart in the later history of Israel, whether Jacob or the children of Jacob.]

      D. "You find that whatever is written in regard to our father, Abraham, is written also with regard to his children.

45

E.   "With regard to Abraham it is written, 'And there was a famine in the land' (Gen. 12:10). In connection with Israel: 'For these two years has the famine been in the land" (Gen. 45:6).

F.   "With regard to Abraham: 'And Abram went down into Egypt' (Gen. 12:10).

G.   "With regard to Israel: 'And our fathers went down into Egypt' (Num. 20:15).

H.   "With regard to Abraham: 'To sojourn there' (Gen. 12:10).

I.   "With regard to Israel: 'To sojourn in the land we have come' (Gen. 47:4).

J.   "With regard to Abraham: 'For the famine is heavy in the land' (Gen. 12:10).

K.   "With regard to Israel: 'And the famine was heavy in the land' (Gen. 43:1).

L.   "With regard to Abraham: 'And it came to pass, when he drew near to enter into Egypt' (Gen. 12:11: 'When he was about to enter Egypt').

M.   "With regard to Israel: 'And when Pharaoh drew near' (Ex. 14:10).

N.   "With regard to Abraham: 'And they will kill me but you will they keep alive' (Gen. 12:12).

O.   "With regard to Israel: 'Every son that is born you shall cast into the river, and every daughter you shall save alive' (Ex. 1:22).

P.   "With regard to Abraham: 'Say you are my sister, that it may go well with me because of you' (Gen. 12:13).

Q.   "With regard to Israel: 'And God dealt well with the midwives' (Ex. 1:20).

R.   "With regard to Abraham: 'And when Abram had entered Egypt' (Gen. 12:14).

S.   "Israel: 'Now these are the names of the sons of Israel, who came into Egypt' (Ex. 1:1).

T.   "With regard to Abraham: 'And Abram was very rich in cattle, in silver, and in gold' (Gen. 13:23).

U.   "With regard to Israel: 'And he brought them forth with silver and gold' (Ps. 105:37).

V.   "With regard to Abraham: And Pharaoh gave men orders concerning him and they set him on the way' (Gen. 12:20).

W.   "Israel: 'And the Egyptians were urgent upon the people to send them out' (Ex. 12:33).

X.   "With regard to Abraham: 'And he went on his journeys' (Gen. 13:3).

Y.   "With regard to Israel: 'These are the journeys of the children of Israel' (Num. 33:1)."

Not only so, but the deeds of the patriarchs prefigure the history of Israel, and actions they took shaped the future history of their descendants:

XLIV

XV.1   A.   Another matter: "Bring me a heifer three years old, [a she-goat three years old, a ram three years old, a turtledove, and a young pigeon]" (Gen. 15:9):

B. "Bring me a heifer three years old" refers to Babylonia, that produced three [kings important in Israel's history], Nebuchadnezzar, Evil Merodach, and Balshazzar.

C. "...a she-goat three years old" refers to Media, that also produced three kings, Cyrus, Darius, and Ahasuerus.

D. "...a ram three years old" refers to Greece.

E. R. Eleazar and R. Yohanan:

F. R. Eleazar said, "Greece conquered every point on the compass except for the east."

G. R. Yohanan said to him, "And indeed so, for is it not written, 'I saw the ram pushing westward and northward and southward, and no beasts could stand before him' (Dan. 8:4)?"

H. That indeed is the view of R. Eleazar, for the verse at hand does not refer to the east.

I. "...a turtledove, and a young pigeon" (Gen. 15:9) refers to Edom. It was a turtledove that would rob.

God informed Abraham about what would happen in the future history of Israel. Abraham in fact formulated what would happen to Israel in the future, making choices about his descendants' fate:

XLIV

XVIII.1 A. "Then the Lord said to Abram, 'Know of a surety [that your descendants will be sojourners in a land that is not theirs, and they will be slaves there, and they will be oppressed for four hundred years; but I will bring judgment on the nation which they serve, and afterward they shall come out with great possessions']" (Gen. 15:13-14):

B. "Know" that I shall scatter them.

C. "Of a certainty" that I shall bring them back together again.

D. "Know" that I shall put them out as a pledge [in expiation of their sins].

E. "Of a certainty" that I shall redeem them.

F. "Know" that I shall make them slaves.

G. "Of a certainty" that I shall free them.

XXI.2 A. "...behold a smoking fire pot and a flaming torch passed between these pieces" (Gen. 15:17):

B. Simeon bar Abba in the name of R. Yohanan: "He showed him four things, Gehenna, the [four] kingdoms, the giving of the Torah, and the sanctuary. He said to him, 'So long as your descendants are occupied with these latter two, they will be saved from the former two. If they abandon two of them, they will be judged by the other two.'

C. "He said to him, 'What is your preference? Do you want your children to go down into Gehenna or to be subjugated to the four kingdoms?'"

D. R. Hinena bar Pappa said, "Abraham chose for himself the subjugation to the four kingdoms."

E. R. Yudan and R. Idi and R. Hama bar Hanina: "Abraham chose for himself Gehenna, but the Holy One, blessed be He, chose the subjugation to the four kingdoms for him."

F. That [statement of Hinena b. Papa] is in line with the following: "How should one chase a thousand and two put ten thousand to flight, except their rock had given them over"" (Deut. 32:30). That statement refers to Abraham.

G. "But the Lord delivered them up" (Deut. 32:30) teaches that God then approved what he had chosen.

XXI.3   A. R. Huna in the name of R. Aha: "Now Abraham sat and puzzled all that day, saying, 'Which should I choose?'

B. "Said the Holy One, blessed be He, to him, 'Choose without delay.' That is in line with this verse: 'On that day the Lord made a covenant with Abram' (Gen. 15:18)."

C. This brings us to the dispute of R. Hinena bar Pappa with R. Yudan and R. Idi and R. Hama bar Haninah.

D. R. Hinena bar Pappa said, "Abraham chose for himself the subjugation to the four kingdoms."

E. R. Yudan and R. Idi and R. Hama bar Haninah said in the name of a single sage in the name of Rabbi: "The Holy One, blessed be He, chose the subjugation to the four kingdoms for him, in line with the following verse of Scripture: 'You have caused men to ride over our heads' (Ps. 66:12). That is to say, you have made ride over our heads various nations, and it is as though 'we went through fire and through water' (Ps. 66:21)."

F. R. Joshua said, "Also the splitting of the Red Sea he showed him, as it is written, 'That passed between these pieces' (Gen. 15:17), along the lines of the verse, 'O give thanks to him who divided the Red Sea in two' [in which the same word, the letters for pieces, occurs as 'in two'] (Ps. 86:13)."

2. Israel is eternal and is subject to God's providence:

XLI

IX.1   A. "I will make your descendants as the dust of the earth" (Gen. 13:16):

B. Just as the dust of the earth is from one end of the world to the other, so your children will be from one end of the world to the other.

C. Just as the dust of the earth is blessed only with water, so your children will be blessed only through the merit attained by study of the Torah, which is compared to water [hence: through water].

D. Just as the dust of the earth wears out metal utensils and yet endures forever, so Israel endures while the nations of the world come to an end.

E. Just as the dust of the world is treated as something on which to trample, so your children are treated as something to be trampled upon by the government.

F. That is in line with this verse: "And I will put it into the hand of them that afflict you" (Isa. 51:23), that is to say, those who make your wounds flow [Freedman].

G. Nonetheless, it is for your good that they do so, for they cleanse you of guilt, in line with this verse: "You make her soft with showers" (Ps. 65:11). [Freedman, p. 339, n. 33: "Words of the same root are used for 'make soft' and 'who afflict you.' The passage understands the former in the sense of making the rain flow and hence the latter, too – to make the wounds flow."]

H. "That have said to your soul, 'Bow down, that we may go over'" (Isa. 51:23):

I. What did they do to them? They made them lie down in the streets and drew ploughs over them."

J. R. Azariah in the name of R. Aha: "That is a good sign. Just as the street wears out those who pass over it and endures forever, so your children will wear out all the nations of the world and will live forever."

3. Study of the Torah is what sustains Israel, and through study of the Torah Israel meets God:

XLII

III.2 A. "And it came to pass in the days of Ahaz" (Isa. 7:1):

B. "The Aramaeans on the east and the Philistines on the west devour Israel with open mouth" (Isa. 9:12):

C. The matter [of Israel's position] may be compared to the case of a king who handed over his son to a tutor, who hated the son. The tutor thought, "If I kill him now, I shall turn out to be liable to the death penalty before the king. So what I'll do is take away his wet nurse, and he will die on his own."

D. So thought Ahaz, "If there are no kids, there will be no he-goats. If there are no he-goats, there will be no flock. If there is no flock, there will be no Shepherd, if there is no Shepherd, there will be no world."

E. So did Ahaz plan, "If there are no children, there will be no adults. If there are no adults, there will be no disciples. If there are no disciples, there will be no sages. If there are no sages, there will be no elders. If there are no elders, there will be no prophets. If there are no prophets, the Holy One, blessed be He, will not allow his presence to come to rest in the world." [Lev. R.: ...Torah. If there is no Torah, there will be no synagogues and schools. If there are no synagogues and schools, then the Holy One, blessed be He, will not allow his presence to come to rest in the world.]

F. That is in line with the following verse of Scripture: "Bind up the testimony, seal the Torah among my disciples" (Isa. 8:16).

4. The status of Israel depends upon Israel's acceptance of the commandments of the Torah. If Israel does what God commands, they then are Israel, and if not, they are not; all depends upon accepting the divinity of God:

XLVI

IX.1 A. "And I will give to you and to your descendants after you [the land of your sojournings, all the land of Canaan, for an everlasting possession; and I will be their God]" (Gen. 17:8):

B. In this connection R. Yudan made five statements [imputing to God five propositions, which are now spelled out].

C.   R. Yudan said, "[God said,] 'If your descendants accept my divinity,
     I shall be their patron God, and if not, I shall not be their patron
     God.

D.   "'If your children enter the land, they will receive my divinity, and
     if they do not enter the land, they will not receive my divinity.

E.   "'If your descendants accept circumcision, they will receive my
     divinity, and if not, they will not receive my divinity.

F.   "'If your descendants accept circumcision, they will enter the land,
     and if not, they will not enter the land.' [So the cited verse yields a
     number of distinct conditions.]"

III. Matters of Philosophy, Natural Science and Metaphysics

This category remains irrelevant.

4

Genesis Rabbah to Parashat Vayere (XLVIII-LVII)

I. Unarticulated Premises: The Givens of Religious Conduct

1. The laws express in prescribed gestures what the Torah tells of the actions of the patriarchs and matriarchs:

XLIX

XI.2   A. We have learned in the Mishnah: **What is the rite for the conduct of a fast? People bring the ark out into the public square and put burned ashes on the ark [M. Ta. 2:1].**

B. R. Yudan bar Menasseh and R. Samuel bar Nahman:

C. One of them said, "It is on account of the merit attained by Abraham, as it is said, 'I who am but dust and ashes' (Gen. 18:27)."

D. The other said, "It is on account of the merit attained by Isaac." But the latter memorized the statement of the Mishnah so that it referred only to ashes and not dust.

E. A ruling of R. Yudan b. Pazzi stands at issue with this formulation [of C].

F. For R. Yudan b. Pazzi would announce in the community, saying, "Whoever has not been reached by the leader of the congregation for the pouring of ashes on his head should take ashes and pour them on his head on his own." [Hence he did not require both dust and ashes, but only ashes.]

G. The ruling of R. Yudan b. Pazzi treats dust and ashes as the same thing [so it does not prove that he differs from C's position].

II. Unarticulated Premises: The Givens of Religious Conviction

1. Abraham's descendants, Israel, derived *zekhut* from each of his actions in due course:

XLVIII

X.2   A. "Let a little water be brought" (Gen. 18:4):

B.   Said to him the Holy One, blessed be He, "You have said, 'Let a
     little water be brought' (Gen. 18:4). By your life, I shall pay your
     descendants back for this: 'Then sang Israel this song, "spring up, O
     well, sing you to it"' (Num. 21:7)."
C.   That recompense took place in the wilderness. Where do we find
     that it took place in the Land of Israel as well?
D.   "A land of brooks of water" (Deut. 8:7).
E.   And where do we find that it will take place in the age to come?
F.   "And it shall come to pass in that day that living waters shall go out
     of Jerusalem" (Zech. 14:8).
G.   ["And wash your feet" (Gen. 18:4)]: [Said to him the Holy One,
     blessed be He,] "You have said , 'And wash your feet.' By your life,
     I shall pay your descendants back for this: 'Then I washed you in
     water' (Ezek. 16:9)."
H.   That recompense took place in the wilderness. Where do we find
     that it took place in the Land of Israel as well?
I.   "Wash you, make you clean" (Isa. 1:16).
J.   And where do we find that it will take place in the age to come?
K.   "When the Lord will have washed away the filth of the daughters of
     Zion" (Isa. 4:4).
L.   [Said to him the Holy One, blessed be He,] "You have said, 'And
     rest yourselves under the tree' (Gen. 18:4). By your life, I shall pay
     your descendants back for this: 'He spread a cloud for a screen' (Ps.
     105:39)."
M.   That recompense took place in the wilderness. Where do we find
     that it took place in the Land of Israel as well?
N.   "You shall dwell in booths for seven days" (Lev. 23:42).
O.   And where do we find that it will take place in the age to come?
P.   "And there shall be a pavilion for a shadow in the daytime from the
     heat" (Isa. 4:6).
Q.   [Said to him the Holy One, blessed be He,] "You have said, 'While I
     fetch a morsel of bread that you may refresh yourself' (Gen. 18:5).
     By your life, I shall pay your descendants back for this: 'Behold I
     will cause to rain bread from heaven for you' (Ex. 16:45)."
R.   That recompense took place in the wilderness. Where do we find
     that it took place in the Land of Israel as well?
S.   "A land of wheat and barley" (Deut. 8:8).
T.   And where do we find that it will take place in the age to come?
U.   "He will be as a rich cornfield in the land" (Ps. 82:16).
V.   [Said to him the Holy One, blessed be He,] "You ran after the herd
     ['And Abraham ran to the herd' (Gen. 18:7)]. By your life, I shall
     pay your descendants back for this: 'And there went forth a wind
     from the Lord and brought across quails from the sea' (Num.
     11:27)."
W.   That recompense took place in the wilderness. Where do we find
     that it took place in the Land of Israel as well?
X.   "Now the children of Reuben and the children of Gad had a very
     great multitude of cattle" (Num. 32:1).
Y.   And where do we find that it will take place in the age to come?
Z.   "And it will come to pass in that day that a man shall rear a young
     cow and two sheep" (Isa. 7:21).

AA. [Said to him the Holy One, blessed be He,] "You stood by them: 'And he stood by them under the tree while they ate' (Gen. 18:8). By your life, I shall pay your descendants back for this: 'And the Lord went before them' (Ex. 13:21)."

BB. That recompense took place in the wilderness. Where do we find that it took place in the Land of Israel as well?

CC. "God stands in the congregation of God" (Ps. 82:1).

DD. And where do we find that it will take place in the age to come?

EE. "The breaker is gone up before them...and the Lord at the head of them" (Mic. 2:13).

2. That same rule may bear negative consequences as well:

LIV

IV.1   A. "Abraham set seven ewe lambs of the flock apart" (Gen. 21:28):

B. Said the Holy One, blessed be He, to him, "You have given him seven ewe lambs. By your life I shall postpone the joy of your descendants for seven generations.

C. "You have given him seven ewe lambs. By your life, matching them his descendants [the Philistines] will kill seven righteous men among your descendants, and these are they: Hofni, Phineas, Samson, Saul and his three sons.

D. "You have given him seven ewe lambs. By your life, matching them the seven sanctuaries of your descendants will be destroyed, namely, the tent of meeting, the altars at Gilgal, Nob, Gibeon, Shiloh, and the two eternal houses of the sanctuary.

E. "You have given him seven ewe lambs. [By your life, matching them] my ark will spend seven months in the fields of the Philistines."

3. The same rule, that the actions of the patriarchs prefigure the future life of Israel, pertains also to the redemption of Israel and the resurrection of the dead:

LVI

I.1   A. "On the third day Abraham lifted up his eyes and saw the place afar off" (Gen. 22:4):

B. "After two days he will revive us, on the third day he will raise us up, that we may live in his presence" (Hos.16:2).

C. On the third day of the tribes: "And Joseph said to them on the third day, 'This do and live'" (Gen. 42:18).

D. On the third day of the giving of the Torah: "And it came to pass on the third day when it was morning" (Ex. 19:16).

E. On the third day of the spies: "And hide yourselves there for three days" (Josh. 2:16).

F. On the third day of Jonah: "And Jonah was in the belly of the fish three days and three nights" (Jonah 2:1).

G. On the third day of the return from the Exile: "And we abode there three days" (Ezra 8:32).

H. On the third day of the resurrection of the dead: "After two days he will revive us, on the third day he will raise us up, that we may live in his presence" (Hos. 16:2).

I. On the third day of Esther: "Now it came to pass on the third day that Esther put on her royal apparel" (Est. 5:1).

J. She put on the monarchy of the house of her fathers.

K. On account of what sort of merit?

L. Rabbis say, "On account of the third day of the giving of the Torah."

M. R. Levi said, "It is on account of the merit of the third day of Abraham: 'On the third day Abraham lifted up his eyes and saw the place afar off' (Gen. 22:4)."

II.5   A. Said R. Isaac, "And all was on account of the merit attained by the act of prostration.

B. "Abraham returned in peace from Mount Moriah only on account of the merit owing to the act of prostration: '...and we will worship [through an act of prostration] and come [then, on that account] again to you' (Gen. 22:5).

C. "The Israelites were redeemed only on account of the merit owing to the act of prostration: 'And the people believed...then they bowed their heads and prostrated themselves' (Ex. 4:31).

D. "The Torah was given only on account of the merit owing to the act of prostration: 'And worship [prostrate themselves] you afar off' (Ex. 24:1).

E. "Hannah was remembered only on account of the merit owing to the act of prostration: 'And they worshipped before the Lord' (1 Sam. 1:19).

F. "The exiles will be brought back only on account of the merit owing to the act of prostration: 'And it shall come to pass in that day that a great horn shall be blown and they shall come that were lost...and that were dispersed...and they shall worship the Lord in the holy mountain at Jerusalem' (Isa. 27:13).

G. "The Temple was built only on account of the merit owing to the act of prostration: 'Exalt you the Lord our God and worship at his holy hill' (Ps. 99:9).

H. "The dead will live only on account of the merit owing to the act of prostration: 'Come let us worship and bend the knee, let us kneel before the Lord our maker' (Ps. 95:6)."

4. In the Temple in particular Abraham's descendants benefit in a direct way from the binding of Isaac:

LVI

X.1   A. "So Abraham called the name of that place 'The Lord will provide,' [as it is said to this day, 'On the mount of the Lord it shall be provided']" (Gen. 22:14):

B. R. Bibi the Elder in the name of R. Yohanan: "He said before him, 'Lord of all ages, from the time that you said to me, "Take your son, your only son" (Gen. 22:2), I could have replied to you, "Yesterday you said to me, 'For in Isaac shall seed be called to you' (Gen. 21:12), and now you say, 'Take your son, your only son' (Gen.

22:2)." God forbid, did I not do it? But I suppressed my love so as to carry out your will. May it always please you, Lord our God, that, when the children of Isaac will come into trouble, you remember in their behalf that act of binding and be filled with mercy for them.'"

X.4   A. ["So Abraham called the name of that place 'The Lord will provide,' as it is said to this day, 'On the mount of the Lord it shall be provided'" (Gen. 22:14)]: This teaches that the Holy One, blessed be He, showed him the house of the sanctuary as it was built, wiped out, and built once more:

B. "So Abraham called the name of that place 'The Lord will provide'" refers to the house of the sanctuary when it was built, in line with this verse: "Three times in the year will all your males be seen...in the place where he shall choose" (Gen. 16:16).

C. "As it is said to this day, 'On the mount of the Lord'" refers to the Temple in its hour of destruction, in line with this verse: "For the mountain of Zion, which is desolate" (Lam. 5:18).

D. "...it shall be provided" [refers to the Temple] rebuilt and restored in the coming age, in line with this verse: "When the Lord has built up Zion, when he has been seen in his glory" (Ps. 102:17).

III. Matters of Philosophy, Natural Science and Metaphysics

This category really does not apply.

5

Genesis Rabbah to Parashat Hayye Sarah (LVIII-LXII)

I. Unarticulated Premises: The Givens of Religious Conduct

1. The law realizes the practices of the patriarch:

LVIII

VI.2   A. Said R. Yohanan, "From whence do we derive scriptural support for that which we have learned in the Mishnah: **He who has yet to bury his deceased is exempt from the requirement of reciting the Shema [M. Ber. 3:1]**?

      B. "It is from this passage: 'And Abraham rose up from upon the face of his dead and [without reciting his prayers, he turned directly to the business of the burial, for] he said...' (Gen. 23:3)."

LX

V.1   A. "The maiden was very fair to look upon, a virgin, whom no man had known" (Gen. 24:16):

      B. We have learned in the Mishnah:

      C. **"The marriage settlement owing to a girl who had lost her virginity by the blow of a piece of wood is two hundred,"** the words of R. Meir.

      D. **And sages say, "As to a girl who had lost her virginity by the blow of a piece of wood, it is a maneh [one hundred]"** [M. Ket. 1:3].

      E. R. Abbahu in the name of R. Eleazar: "The scriptural basis for the position of R. Meir is as follows: '...whom no man had known.' Lo, if she had lost her virginity by the blow of a piece of wood, she remains a virgin.

      F. "The scriptural basis for the position of sages is as follows: '...a virgin.' Lo, if she had lost her virginity by the blow of a piece of wood, she would not have been regarded as a virgin."

II. Unarticulated Premises: The Givens of Religious Conviction
I find nothing relevant.

III. Matters of Philosophy, Natural Science and Metaphysics
There is nothing that qualifies.

6

Genesis Rabbah to
Parashat Toledot (LXIII-LXVII)

I. Unarticulated Premises: The Givens of Religious Conduct

1.   The laws of the Mishnah correspond to the narratives of Scripture:

LXV

XX.6   A.   "The voice is Jacob's voice": In the incident of the concubine of Gibeah.

B.   "Cursed is he who gives a wife to Benjamin" (Judg. 21:18).

C.   "The voice is Jacob's voice":

D.   In the days of Jeroboam: "Neither did Jeroboam recover strength again in the days of Abijah, and the Lord smote him and he died" (2 Chr. 13:20).

E.   Said R. Samuel bar Nahman, "Do you think that Jeroboam was smitten? But in fact Abijah was smitten."

F.   Why was Abijah smitten?

G.   Said R. Abba b. Kahana, "Because he removed the identifying marks of the faces of the Israelites, as it is written, 'The show of their countenance does witness for them' (Isa. 3:9)."

H.   Said R. Assi, "Because he set up guards over them for three days until the features of their faces were disfigured.

I.   "For so we have learned in the Mishnah: **People give testimony to the identity of a corpse only through the features of the face together with the nose, and that is the case even if there are other marks of identification on the body and the garments; and one may give testimony only within three days of death [beyond which point the face is disfigured] [M. Yeb. 16:3].**

II. Unarticulated Premises: The Givens of Religious Conviction

1.   Israel and Rome are brothers and enemies, and they are comparable opposites:

LXIII

VII.2   A.   "Two nations are in your womb, [and two peoples, born of you, shall be divided; the one shall be stronger than the other, and the elder shall serve the younger]" (Gen. 25:23):

B.   There are two proud nations in your womb, this one takes pride in his world, and that one takes pride in his world.

C.   This one takes pride in his monarchy, and that one takes pride in his monarchy.

D.   There are two proud nations in your womb.

E.   Hadrian represents the nations, Solomon, Israel.

F.   There are two who are hated by the nations in your womb. All the nations hate Esau, and all the nations hate Israel.

G.   [Following Freedman's reading:] The one whom your creator hates is in your womb: "And Esau I hated" (Mal. 1:3).

2.   The actions of the patriarchs correspond to the components of the Written Torah:

LXIV

VIII.1   A.   "And Isaac dug again the wells of water [which had been dug in the days of Abraham his father; for the Philistines had stopped them after the death of Abraham; and he gave them the names which his father had given them. But when Isaac's servants dug in the valley and found there a well of springing water, the herdsmen of Gerar quarreled with Isaac's herdsmen, saying, 'The water is ours.' So he called the name of the well Esek, because they contended with him. Then they dug another well, and they quarreled over that also, so he called its name Sitnah. And he moved from there and dug another well and over that they did not quarrel, so he called its name Rehoboth, saying 'For now the Lord has made room for us, and we shall be fruitful in the land'" (Gen. 26:18-22). "That same day Isaac's servants came and told him about the well which they had dug and said to him, 'We have found water.' He called it Shibah, therefore the name of the city is Beer Sheba to this day" (Gen. 26:32-33)]:

B.   How many wells did our father Isaac dig in Beer Sheba?

C.   R. Judah bar Simon said, "Four, corresponding to the four standards in the wilderness that marked off his descendants."

D.   And rabbis said, "Five, corresponding to the five scrolls of the Torah."

E.   "'So he called the name of the well Esek, because they contended with him': this one corresponds to the scroll of Genesis, in which the Holy One, blessed be He, is contending in the creation of his world.

F.   "'Then they dug another well, and they quarreled over that also, so he called its name Sitnah': this one corresponds to the scroll of Exodus, on the count that they embittered their lives with harsh labor.

G.   "'But when Isaac's servants dug in the valley and found there a well of springing water': this corresponds to the book of Leviticus, which is full of many laws.

H.   "'He called it Shibah': this one corresponds to the book of Numbers, which completes the number of the seven scrolls of the Torah."

I.   But are they not only five, not seven?!

J.   [No, indeed there were seven, as will now be explained:] Bar Qappara treated the first part of the book of Numbers until the verse, "And it came to pass, when the ark set forward" (Num. 10:35), as one book. [And the portion beginning with the verse,] "And it came to pass, when the ark set forward" until the end of the book of Numbers, he treated as another book.

3.   Old age, sickness, and death are gifts from God to humanity, brought about through the prayers of the patriarchs:

LXV

IX.1   A.   "When Isaac was old, and his eyes were dim, so that he could not see, he called Esau his older son, and said to him, 'My son,' and he answered, 'Here I am'" (Gen. 27:1):

B.   Said R. Judah bar Simon, "Abraham sought [the physical traits of] old age [so that from one's appearance, people would know that he was old]. He said before him, 'Lord of all ages, when a man and his son come in somewhere, no one knows whom to honor. If you crown a man with the traits of old age, people will know whom to honor.'

C.   "Said to him the Holy One, blessed be He, 'By your life, this is a good thing that you have asked for, and it will begin with you.'

D.   "From the beginning of the book of Genesis to this passage, there is no reference to old age. But when Abraham our father came along, the traits of old age were given to him, as it is said, 'And Abraham was old' (Gen. 24:1).

E.   "Isaac asked God for suffering. He said before him, 'Lord of the age, if someone dies without suffering, the measure of strict justice is stretched out against him. But if you bring suffering on him, the measure of strict justice will not be stretched out against him. [Suffering will help counter the man's sins, and the measure of strict justice will be mitigated through suffering by the measure of mercy.]'

F.   "Said to him the Holy One, blessed be He, 'By your life, this is a good thing that you have asked for, and it will begin with you.'

G.   "From the beginning of the book of Genesis to this passage, there is no reference to suffering. But when Isaac came along, suffering was given to him: his eyes were dim.

H.   "Jacob asked for sickness. He said before him, 'Lord of all ages, if a person dies without illness, he will not settle his affairs for his children. If he is sick for two or three days, he will settle his affairs with his children.'

I.   "Said to him the Holy One, blessed be He, 'By your life, this is a good thing that you have asked for, and it will begin with you.'

J. "That is in line with this verse: 'And someone said to Joseph, "Behold, your father is sick"' (Gen. 48:1)."
K. Said R. Levi, "Abraham introduced the innovation of old age, Isaac introduced the innovation of suffering, Jacob introduced the innovation of sickness.
L. "Hezekiah introduced the innovation of chronic illness. He said to him, 'You have kept a man in good condition until the day he dies. But if someone is sick and gets better, is sick and gets better, he will carry out a complete and sincere act of repentance for his sins.'
M. "Said to him the Holy One, blessed be He, 'By your life, this is a good thing that you have asked for, and it will begin with you.'
N. "'The writing of Hezekiah, king of Judah, when he had been sick and recovered of his sickness' (Isa. 38:9)."
O. Said R. Samuel b. Nahman, "On the basis of that verse we know that between one illness and another there was an illness more serious than either one."

III. Matters of Philosophy, Natural Science and Metaphysics

Nothing qualifies here.

7

Genesis Rabbah to Parashat Vayese (LXVIII-LXXIV)

I. Unarticulated Premises: The Givens of Religious Conduct

1. The law realizes in general rules the precepts of the patriarchs and matriarchs, expressed through their deeds:

LXXII

IV.1   A.   "[Rachel said, 'Then he may lie with you tonight for your son's mandrakes.'] When Jacob came from the field in the evening, [Leah went out to meet him and said, 'You must come in to me, for I have hired you with my son's mandrakes.' So he lay with her that night]" (Gen. 30:15-17):

      B.   We have learned in the Mishnah: **He who hired workers and made an agreement with them to get up for work earlier than is the norm or to work later in the evening than is the norm – in a place in which it is not customary to get up early or to stay late, he cannot force them to do so [M. B.M. 7:1].**

      C.   Said R. Mana, "In a place in which there is no customary practice, the rule is covered by the generally applicable stipulation of the court. This requires that going forth to work is on the householder's time, and coming home from work is on the worker's time, as it is said, 'The sun rises, they [animals] slink away and couch in their dens,' and then: 'Man goes forth to his work, and to his labor until the evening' (Ps. 104:22-23)."

      D.   Said R. Ammi in the name of R. Simeon b. Laqish, "If it is a Friday afternoon, they have placed on the householder the burden, so that the return from work is on his time.

      E.   "To what extent [must the householder allow the workers on Friday to come home early]? To such an extent that each one has the time to fill a jug of water and to roast a fish for himself and to light a candle."

II. Unarticulated Premises: The Givens of Religious Conviction

1. Jacob's dream encompassed principal components of Israel's existence, past and future, the Temple, Sinai, the lives of the patriarchs, and the exile; Israel's salvific life is covered by the dream; here are some of the components:

LXVIII

XII.4 A. Rabbis interpreted the matter to prefigure Sinai: "'And he dreamed:

   B. "'...that there was a ladder': this refers to Sinai.

   C. "'...set up on the earth': 'And they stood at the lower part of the mountain' (Ex. 19:17).

   D. "'...and the top of it reached to heaven': 'And the mountain burned with fire into the heart of heaven' (Deut. 4:11).

   E. "'...and behold, the angels of God': these are Moses and Aaron.

   F. "'...were ascending': 'And Moses went up to God' (Ex. 19:3).

   G. "'...and descending on it': 'And Moses went down from the mount' (Ex. 19:14).

   H. "'...And behold, the Lord stood above it': 'And the Lord came down upon Mount Sinai' (Ex. 19:20)."

XIII.1 A. [Resuming the discourse of LXVIII:XII.3-4,] R. Joshua b. Levi interpreted the verse at hand to speak of the Exiles of Israel [symbolized in Jacob's exile from the Land]:

   B. "'And Jacob went out from Beer Sheba': 'Cast them out of my sight and let them go forth' (Jer. 15:1).

   C. "'...and went toward Haran': 'Wherewith the Lord has afflicted me in the day of his fierce anger' (Lam. 1:1) ["anger" using letters shared with the word for Haran].

   D. "'And he lighted on a certain place': 'Til there be no place' (Isa. 5:8).

   E. "'...and stayed there that night because the sun had set': 'She who has borne seven languishes, her spirit droops, her sun has set' (Jer. 15:9).

   F. "'...Taking one of the stones of the place': 'The hallowed stones are poured out at the head of every street' (Lam. 4:1).

   G. "'...he put it under his head': 'For your headtires are come down' (Jer. 13:18).

   H. "'...and lay down in that place to sleep': 'Let us lie down in our shame and let our confusion cover us' (Jer. 3:25).

   I. "'And he dreamed': this alludes to the dream of Nebuchadnezzer.

   J. "'...that there was a ladder': this alludes to Nebuchadnezzar's image, for the word for image shares the same letters as the word for ladder.

   K. "'...set up on the earth': 'He set it up in the plain of Dura' (Dan. 3:1).

   L. "'...and the top of it reached to heaven': 'Whose height was three score cubits' (Dan. 3:1).

   M. "'...and behold, the angels of God': Hananiah, Mishael, and Azariah.

   N. "'...were ascending and descending on it': they were raising him up and dragging him down, dancing on him, leaping on him, abusing him: 'Be it known to you, O king, that we will not serve your gods' (Dan. 3:18).

O.   "'And behold, the Lord stood beside him and said': 'You servants of God, most high, come forth and come hither' (Dan. 3:26)."

2.   Israel's humility toward the nations is a mark of their humility toward God, and in this way they cleanse their guilt and atone for their sins, so leading to reconciliation and a restoration of their fortunes:

LXIX

V.1   A.   "...and your descendants shall be like the dust of the earth, and you shall spread abroad to the west and to the east and to the north, and to the south; and by you and your descendants shall all the families of the earth bless themselves'" (Gen. 28:13-14):

B.   [Lacking here: Just as the dust of the earth is from one end of the world to the other, so your children will be from one end of the world to the other.]

C.   Just as the dust of the earth is blessed only with water, so your children will be blessed only through the merit attained by study of the Torah, which is compared to water [hence: through water].

D.   Just as the dust of the earth wears out metal utensils and yet endures forever, so Israel endures while the nations of the world come to an end.

E.   Just as the dust of the world is treated as something on which to trample, so your children are treated as something to be trampled upon by the government.

F.   That is in line with this verse: "And I will put it into the hand of them that afflict you" (Isa. 51:23), that is to say, those who make your wounds flow [Freedman].

G.   Nonetheless, it is for your good that they do so, for they cleanse you of guilt, in line with this verse: "You make her soft with showers" (Ps. 65:11). [Freedman, p. 339, n. 33: "Words of the same root are used for 'make soft' and 'who afflict you.' The passage understands the former in the sense of making the rain flow and hence the latter, too – to make the wounds flow."]

H.   "That have said to your soul, Bow down, that we may go over" (Isa. 51:23):

I.   What did they do to them? They made them lie down in the streets and drew ploughs over them."

J.   R. Azariah in the name of R. Aha: "That is a good sign. Just as the street wears out those who pass over it and endures forever, so your children will wear out all the nations of the world and will live forever."

3.   The proselyte becomes fully an Israelite, and his daughter may marry into the priesthood, if he studies the Torah and otherwise attains merit, like any other Israelite:

LXX

V.1   A.   "...will give me bread to eat and clothing to wear":

B. Aqilas the proselyte came to R. Eliezer and said to him, "Is all the gain that is coming to the proselyte going to be contained in this verse: '...and loves the proselyte, giving him food and clothing' (Deut. 10:18)?"

C. He said to him, "And is something for which the old man [Jacob] beseeched going to be such a small thing in your view namely, '...will give me bread to eat and clothing to wear'? [God] comes and hands it over to [a proselyte] on a reed [and the proselyte does not have to beg for it]."

D. He came to R. Joshua, who commenced by saying words to appease him: "'Bread' refers to Torah, as it is said, 'Come, eat of my bread' (Prov. 9:5). 'Clothing' refers to the cloak of a disciple of sages.

E. "When a person has the merit of studying the Torah, he has the merit of carrying out a religious duty. [So the proselyte receives a great deal when he gets bread and clothing, namely, entry into the estate of disciples].

F. "And not only so, but his daughters may be chosen for marriage into the priesthood, so that their sons' sons will offer burnt-offerings on the altar. [So the proselyte may also look forward to entry into the priests' caste. That statement will now be spelled out.]

G. "'Bread' refers to the showbread.'

H. "'Clothing' refers to the garments of the priesthood.'

I. "So lo, we deal with the sanctuary.

J. "How do we know that the same sort of blessing applies in the provinces? 'Bread' speaks of the dough-offering [that is separated in the provinces], while 'clothing' refers to the first fleece [handed over to the priest]."

4. The entire structure of Judaism was foreseen by Jacob in the well in the field, that is, the events of the exodus and the wandering in the wilderness; Zion; the Temple; the history of Israel under the three kingdoms; the disciples of sages in God's presence; the synagogue; Sinai; the Presence of God:

LXX

VIII.2 A. "As he looked, he saw a well in the field":

B. R. Hama bar Hanina interpreted the verse in six ways [that is, he divides the verse into six clauses and systematically reads each of the clauses in light of the others and in line with an overriding theme:

C. "'As he looked, he saw a well in the field': this refers to the well [of water in the wilderness, Num. 21:17].

D. "'...and lo, three flocks of sheep lying beside it': specifically, Moses, Aaron, and Miriam.

E. "'...for out of that well the flocks were watered': from there each one drew water for his standard, tribe, and family."

F. "And the stone upon the well's mouth was great":

G. Said R. Hanina, "It was only the size of a little sieve."

H. [Reverting to Hama's statement:] "'...and put the stone back in its place upon the mouth of the well': for the coming journeys. [Thus the first interpretation applies the passage at hand to the life of Israel in the wilderness.]

VIII.3   A.   "'As he looked, he saw a well in the field': refers to Zion.

B.   "'...and lo, three flocks of sheep lying beside it': refers to the three festivals.

C.   "'....for out of that well the flocks were watered': from there they drank of the Holy Spirit.

D.   "'...The stone on the well's mouth was large': this refers to the rejoicing of the house of the water drawing."

E.   Said R. Hoshaiah, "Why is it called 'the house of the water drawing'? Because from there they drink of the Holy Spirit."

F.   [Resuming Hama b. Hanina's discourse:] "'...and when all the flocks were gathered there': coming from 'the entrance of Hamath to the brook of Egypt' (1 Kgs. 8:66).

G.   "'...the shepherds would roll the stone from the mouth of the well and water the sheep': for from there they would drink of the Holy Spirit.

H.   "'...and put the stone back in its place upon the mouth of the well': leaving it in place until the coming festival. [Thus the second interpretation reads the verse in light of the Temple celebration of the Festival of Tabernacles.]

VIII.4   A.   "'...As he looked, he saw a well in the field': this refers to Zion.

B.   "'...and lo, three flocks of sheep lying beside it': this refers to the three courts, concerning which we have learned in the Mishnah: **There were three courts there, one at the gateway of the Temple mount, one at the gateway of the courtyard, and one in the chamber of the hewn stones [M. San. 11:2].**

C.   "'...for out of that well the flocks were watered': for from there they would hear the ruling.

D.   "The stone on the well's mouth was large': this refers to the high court that was in the chamber of the hewn stones.

E.   "'...and when all the flocks were gathered there': this refers to the courts in session in the Land of Israel.

F.   "'...the shepherds would roll the stone from the mouth of the well and water the sheep': for from there they would hear the ruling.

G.   "'...and put the stone back in its place upon the mouth of the well': for they would give and take until they had produced the ruling in all the required clarity." [The third interpretation reads the verse in light of the Israelite institution of justice and administration.]

VIII.5   A.   "'As he looked, he saw a well in the field': this refers to Zion.

B.   "'...and lo, three flocks of sheep lying beside it': this refers to the first three kingdoms [Babylonia, Media, Greece].

C.   "'...for out of that well the flocks were watered': for they enriched the treasures that were laid up in the chambers of the Temple.

D.   "'...The stone on the well's mouth was large': this refers to the merit attained by the patriarchs.

E.   "'...and when all the flocks were gathered there': this refers to the wicked kingdom, which collects troops through levies over all the nations of the world.

F. "'...the shepherds would roll the stone from the mouth of the well and water the sheep': for they enriched the treasures that were laid up in the chambers of the Temple.

G. "'...and put the stone back in its place upon the mouth of the well': in the age to come the merit attained by the patriarchs will stand [in defense of Israel].' [So the fourth interpretation interweaves the themes of the Temple cult and the domination of the four monarchies.]

VIII.6 A. "'As he looked, he saw a well in the field': this refers to the sanhedrin.

B. "'...and lo, three flocks of sheep lying beside it': this alludes to the three rows of disciples of sages that would go into session in their presence.

C. "for out of that well the flocks were watered': for from there they would listen to the ruling of the law.

D. "'...The stone on the well's mouth was large': this refers to the most distinguished member of the court, who determines the law decision.

E. "'...and when all the flocks were gathered there': this refers to disciples of the sages in the Land of Israel.

F. "'...the shepherds would roll the stone from the mouth of the well and water the sheep': for from there they would listen to the ruling of the law.

G. "'...and put the stone back in its place upon the mouth of the well': for they would give and take until they had produced the ruling in all the required clarity." [The fifth interpretation again reads the verse in light of the Israelite institution of legal education and justice.]

VIII.7 A. "'As he looked, he saw a well in the field': this refers to the synagogue.

B. "'...and lo, three flocks of sheep lying beside it': this refers to the three who are called to the reading of the Torah on weekdays.

C. "'...for out of that well the flocks were watered': for from there they hear the reading of the Torah.

D. "'...The stone on the well's mouth was large': this refers to the impulse to do evil.

E. "'...and when all the flocks were gathered there': this refers to the congregation.

F. "'...the shepherds would roll the stone from the mouth of the well and water the sheep': for from there they hear the reading of the Torah.

G. "'...and put the stone back in its place upon the mouth of the well': for once they go forth [from the hearing of the reading of the Torah] the impulse to do evil reverts to its place." [The sixth and last interpretation turns to the twin themes of the reading of the Torah in the synagogue and the evil impulse, temporarily driven off through the hearing of the Torah.]

IX.1 A. R. Yohanan interpreted the statement in terms of Sinai:

B. "'As he looked, he saw a well in the field': this refers to Sinai.

C. "'...and lo, three flocks of sheep lying beside it': these stand for the priests, Levites, and Israelites.

D.   "'...for out of that well the flocks were watered': for from there they heard the Ten Commandments.

E.   "'...The stone on the well's mouth was large': this refers to the Presence of God."

F.   "...and when all the flocks were gathered there":

G.   R. Simeon b. Judah of Kefar Akum in the name of R. Simeon: "All of the flocks of Israel had to be present, for if any one of them had been lacking, they would not have been worthy of receiving the Torah."

H.   [Returning to Yohanan's exposition:] "'...the shepherds would roll the stone from the mouth of the well and water the sheep': for from there they heard the Ten Commandments.

I.   "'...and put the stone back in its place upon the mouth of the well': 'You yourselves have seen that I have talked with you from heaven' (Ex. 20:19)."

III. Matters of Philosophy, Natural Science and Metaphysics

I find nothing that belongs here.

8

Genesis Rabbah to Parashat Vayishlah (LXXV-LXXXIII)

I. Unarticulated Premises: The Givens of Religious Conduct

I observe nothing pertinent.

II. Unarticulated Premises: The Givens of Religious Conviction

1. Jacob's conduct with Esau shaped the future history of Israel:

LXXV

XI.2 A. At the moment that Jacob referred to Esau as "my lord," the Holy One, blessed be He, said to him, "You have lowered yourself and called Esau 'my Lord' no fewer than eight times.

B. "I shall produce out of his descendants eight kings before your children [have any]: 'And these are the kings that reigned in the land of Edom before any king ruled the children of Israel' (Gen. 36:31)."

2. The righteous in this world already enjoy the benefits of the world to come, and what God is going to do later he has already done now through them:

LXXVII

I.1 A. "And Jacob was left alone" (Gen. 32:24):

B. "There is none like unto God, O Jeshurun" (Deut. 33:26):

C. R. Berekhiah in the name of R. Judah bar Simon, "The sense of the verse is this: 'There is none like God. But who is like God? It is Jeshurun, specifically, the proudest and the noblest among you. [Freedman, p. 710, n. 2: Jeshurun is derived from the word for upright or noble.]'

D. "You find that everything that the Holy One, blessed be He, is destined to do in the age to come he has already gone ahead and done through the righteous in this world.

> E. "The Holy One, blessed be He, will raise the dead, and Elijah raised the dead.
>
> F. "The Holy One, blessed be He, will hold back rain, and Elijah held back rain.
>
> G. "The Holy One, blessed be He, made what was little into a blessing [and so increased it in volume], and Elijah made what was little into a blessing.
>
> H. "The Holy One, blessed be He, visits barren women [and makes them fruitful], and Elijah visits barren women [and makes them fruitful].
>
> I. "The Holy One, blessed be He, made what was little into a blessing [and so increased it in volume], and Elijah made what was little into a blessing.
>
> J. "The Holy One, blessed be He, made the bitter sweet, and Elijah made the bitter sweet.
>
> K. "The Holy One, blessed be, made the bitter sweet through something that was bitter, and Elijah made the bitter sweet through something that was bitter."

3. Israel's rule will follow that of Rome; the Messiah will come when Rome falls, and Israel will take over:

LXXXIII

IV.3 A. "Magdiel and Iram: these are the chiefs of Edom, that is Esau, the father of Edom, according to their dwelling places in the land of their possession" (Gen. 36:42):

B. On the day on which Litrinus came to the throne, there appeared to R. Ammi in a dream this message: "Today Magdiel has come to the throne."

C. He said, "One more king is required for Edom [and then Israel's turn will come]."

IV.4 A. Said R. Hanina of Sepphoris, "Why was he called Iram? For he is destined to amass [a word using the same letters] riches for the king messiah."

B. Said R. Levi, "There was the case of a ruler in Rome who wasted the treasuries of his father. Elijah of blessed memory appeared to him in a dream. He said to him, 'Your fathers collected treasures and you waste them.'

C. "He did not budge until he filled the treasuries again."

III. Matters of Philosophy, Natural Science and Metaphysics

This category remains inert.

9

Genesis Rabbah to Parashat Vayesheb (LXXXIV-LXXXVIII)

I. Unarticulated Premises: The Givens of Religious Conduct

1. The patriarchs founded certain legal institutions:

LXXXV

V.1
A. "Then Judah said to Onan, 'Go in to your brother's wife and perform the duty of a brother-in-law to her, and raise up offspring for your brother'" (Gen. 38:9):

B. Judah began the practice of levirate marriage.

C. It has been taught on Tannaite authority: Any matter which had been in the category of what was permitted and then was forbidden and still later was permitted again, when permitted the second time does not revert to the status of what was permitted the first time around, but only to its status as it was ultimately permitted.

D. Thus a deceased childless brother's widow was once permitted [before she was married to the brother], then she was prohibited [while she was married to the brother] and now she is permitted again [as the deceased childless brother's widow, but, as we shall see, the way in which she is permitted at the end is not the same as the way in which she was permitted at the outset].

E. Might one suppose that she reverts to the original status of availability?

F. Scripture states, "Her husband's brother shall go in to her" (Deut. 25:5), as a matter of carrying out a religious duty. [The marriage is not one of choice or love, but only to carry out a religious duty.]

II. Unarticulated Premises: The Givens of Religious Conviction

1. The most important thing that the patriarchs and matriarchs did was to proselytize; the proselyte is newborn into Israel and a full Israelite:

LXXXIV

IV.1   A.   "Jacob dwelt in the land of his father's sojournings, in the land of Canaan":

        B.   [Since the word "sojournings" contains the consonants for the word for "proselyte," it is as if we read, "in the land in which his ancestors had made proselytes, and so we note:] Abraham made proselytes, for its is written, "And Abraham took Sarai his wife...and the souls that they had made in Haran" (Gen. 12:5).

        C.   R. Eleazar in the name of R. Yosé b. Zimra: "If all of the nations of the world should come together to try to create a single mosquito, they could not put a soul into it, and yet you say, 'And the soul that they had made'? But this refers to the proselytes."

        D.   Then why should not the text say, "The proselytes whom they had converted"? Why stress, "whom they had made"?

        E.   This serves to teach you that whoever brings a gentile close [to the worship of the true God] is as if he had created him anew.

        F.   And why not say, "That he had made"? Why, "That they had made"?

        G.   Said R. Huniah, "Abraham converted the men and Sarah the women."

        H.   Jacob likewise made converts: "Then Jacob said to his household and to all that were with him, 'Put away the strange gods that are among you'.... And they gave to Jacob all the foreign gods" (Gen. 35:2ff.).

        I.   In regard to Isaac we have no explicit statement of the same matter. Yet where do we find that Isaac did so?

        J.   It has been taught by R. Hoshaia in the name of R. Judah bar Simon, "Here it is said, 'Jacob dwelt in the land of his father's sojournings, in the land of Canaan.' [Since the word "sojournings" contains the consonants for the word for "proselyte," it is as if we read, "in the land in which his ancestors had made proselytes:] 'among the proselytes of his father.'"

2.   God reveals himself in various specific settings involving acts of justice:

LXXXV

XII.1   A.   "Then Judah acknowledged them and said, 'She is more righteous than I, inasmuch as I did not give her to my son Shelah.' And he did not lie with her again" (Gen. 38:26):

        B.   R. Jeremiah in the name of R. Samuel bar R. Isaac: "The Holy One, blessed be He, revealed himself in three settings: in the court of Shem, of Samuel, and of Solomon.

        C.   "In the court of Shem: 'Then Judah acknowledged them and said, "She is more righteous than I."'"

        D.   R. Jeremiah in the name of R. Samuel bar R. Isaac: "The Holy Spirit said, 'From me [which is the same word as 'than I'] have these things come.'"

        E.   [Continuing the original statement, B:] "In the court of Samuel: 'And he said to them, "The Lord is witness against you, and his anointed is witness this day,"...and he said, "He is witness"' (1 Sam. 12:5)."

F. Who said, "He is witness"?

G. R. Jeremiah in the name of R. Samuel bar R. Isaac: "The Holy Spirit said, 'He is witness.'"

H. [Continuing where E left off:] "In the court of Solomon: 'Give her the living child, and in no way slay it, she is its mother' (1 Kgs. 3:27)."

I. Who said "she is its mother"?

J. R. Jeremiah in the name of R. Samuel bar R. Isaac: "The Holy Spirit said, 'She is its mother.'"

3. It was the perfect faith of Joseph that sustained him in his trials:

LXXXVII

X.1   A. "But the Lord was with Joseph and showed him steadfast love and gave him favor in the sight of the keeper of the prison. [And the keeper of the prison committed to Joseph's care all the prisoners who were in the prison; and whatever was done there, he was the doer of it; the keeper of the prison paid no heed to anything that was in Joseph's care, because the Lord was with him; and whatever he did, the Lord made it prosper]" (Gen. 39:21-23):

B. R. Huna in the name of R. Hana: "His service pleased his master.

C. "When he would go out, Joseph would wash the dishes, lay out the tables, and make the beds. [But in trying to entice him, Potiphar's wife] said to him, 'In this matter I made your life miserable. By your life! I shall make your life miserable in other ways.'

D. "He would say to her, '"The Lord executes justice for the persecuted. [He gives bread to the hungry, the Lord looses those who are bound, the Lord raises up those who are bowed down, the Lord opens the eyes of the blind]" (Ps. 146:7).' [We shall now see how, by his faith in God's justice and mercy as described in the verse of Psalms, Joseph found an answer to each of her threats.]

E. "She said to him, 'I shall have your rations cut in half.' He said to her, '"He gives bread to the hungry."'

F. "She said to him, 'I shall have you put into chains.' He said to her, '"...the Lord looses those who are bound."'

G. "She said to him, 'I shall have you bowed down.' He said to her, '"...the Lord raises up those who are bowed down."'

H. "She said to him, 'I shall have you blinded.' He said to her, '"...the Lord opens the eyes of the blind."'"

I. To what extent [did she go]?

J. R. Huna in the name of R. Aha: "To such an extent that [Freedman:] she put an iron fork under his neck, so that he would have to cast his eyes on her.

K. "Even so, he would not look at her. That is in line with this verse: 'His feet they hurt with fetters, his person was laid in iron' (Ps. 105:18)."

4. Israel's future history and salvation are prefigured in the actions of
    Joseph in Egypt and in Joseph's redemption from Egypt:

LXXXVIII

V.1   A. ["So the chief butler told his dream to Joseph and said to him, 'In
           my dream there was a vine before me, and on the vine there were
           three branches; as soon as it budded, its blossoms shot forth, and
           the clusters ripened into grapes. Pharaoh's cup was in my hand,
           and I took the grapes and pressed them into Pharaoh's cup and
           placed the cup in Pharaoh's hand. And I took the grapes and
           pressed them into Pharaoh's cup and placed the cup in Pharaoh's
           hand'" (Gen. 49:11-13)]. "...there was a vine before me": this refers
           to Israel: "You plucked up a vine out of Egypt" (Ps. 80:9).
       B. "...and on the vine there were three branches": this refers to Moses,
           Aaron, and Miriam.
       C. "...as soon as it budded, its blossoms shot forth": specifically, the
           blossoming of the redemption of Israel.
       D. "...and the clusters ripened into grapes": as soon as the vine
           budded, it blossomed, and as soon as the grapes blossomed, the
           clusters ripened.
V.2   A. "'Pharaoh's cup was in my hand, and I took the grapes and pressed
           them into Pharaoh's cup and placed the cup in Pharaoh's hand.
           And I took the grapes and pressed them into Pharaoh's cup and
           placed the cup in Pharaoh's hand.' '...you shall place Pharaoh's cup
           in his hand'":
       B. On what basis did sages ordain that there should be four cups of
           wine for Passover?
       C. R. Hunah in the name of R. Benaiah: "They correspond to the four
           times that redemption is stated with respect to Egypt: 'I will bring
           you out...and I will deliver you...and I will redeem you...and I will
           take you' (Ex. 6:6-7)."
       D. R. Samuel b. Nahman said, "They correspond to the four times that
           'cups' are mentioned here: 'Pharaoh's *cup* was in my hand, and I
           took the grapes and pressed them into Pharaoh's *cup* and placed the
           cup in Pharaoh's hand. And I took the grapes and pressed them
           into Pharaoh's *cup*.'"
       E. R. Levi said, "They correspond to the four kingdoms."
       F. R. Joshua b. Levi said, "They correspond to the four cups of fury
           that the Holy One, blessed be He, will give the nations of the world
           to drink: 'For thus says the Lord, the God of Israel, to me, "Take this
           cup of the wine of fury"' (Jer. 25:15). 'Babylon has been a golden
           cup in the Lord's hand' (Jer. 51:7). 'For in the hand of the Lord
           there is a cup' (Ps. 75:9). 'And burning wind shall be the portion of
           their cup' (Ps. 11:6).
       G. "And in response to these, the Holy One, blessed be He, will give
           Israel four cups of salvation to drink in the age to come: 'O Lord,
           the portion of my inheritance and of my cup, you maintain my lot'
           (Ps. 16:5). 'You prepare a table before me in the presence of my
           enemies, you have anointed my head with oil, my cup runs over'
           (Ps. 23:5). 'I will lift up the cup of salvations and call upon the
           name of the Lord' (Ps. 116:13).

H. "What is said is not 'cup of salvation' but 'cup of salvations,' one in the days of the Messiah, the other in the time of Gog and Magog."

III. Matters of Philosophy, Natural Science and Metaphysics

Nothing pertains.

10

Genesis Rabbah to Parashat Miqqes (LXXXIX-XCII)

I. Unarticulated Premises: The Givens of Religious Conduct

There is nothing relevant.

II. Unarticulated Premises: The Givens of Religious Conviction

1. Divine justice is exact, corresponding to the virtues of the person at hand; reward is worked out in precise, appropriate ways, so, too, punishment:

XC

III.1 A. "And Pharaoh said to Joseph, 'Behold I have set you over all the land of Egypt.' Then Pharaoh took his signet ring from his hand and put it on Joseph's hand and arrayed him in garments of fine linen and put a gold chain about his neck and he made him to ride in his second chariot, and they cried before him, 'Abrech [Bow the knee]!' Thus he set him over all the land of Egypt" (Gen. 41:43-44):

B. R. Yudan in the name of R. Benjamin bar Levi: "Joseph was given what belonged to him.

C. "The mouth that had not kissed sin, 'That no one will kiss me [in obeisance] except for your authority for him to do so.'

D. "The neck, which did not cleave to transgression: '...and put a gold chain about his neck.'

E. "The hands, that did not reach out in transgression: 'Then Pharaoh took his signet ring from his hand and put it on Joseph's hand.'

F. "The body, which did not cleave in transgression: '...and arrayed him in garments of fine linen.'

G. "The feet, which did not take a step in transgression, will step aboard the royal chariot: '...and he made him to ride in his second chariot.'

H. "The intellect, which did not obsess about transgression, will come and gain the title of wisdom: 'And they cried before him, Abrech,

Abrech,' meaning [reading its consonants as two distinct words,] 'a father' (*ab*) in wisdom but young (*rach*) in years.

I. "But Nebuchadnezzar was called *tafsar,* a word that yields through its consonants fool in wisdom but a prince only in years."

III. Matters of Philosophy, Natural Science and Metaphysics

Nothing pertains.

11

Genesis Rabbah to Parashat Vayiggash (XCIII-XCLV) and Parashah Vayehi (XCLVI-C)

I. Unarticulated Premises: The Givens of Religious Conduct

Apart from familiar premises on the origin of law in the practices of patriarchs and matriarchs, nothing here is remarkable.

II. Unarticulated Premises: The Givens of Religious Conviction

1. All will be healed, the blind, deaf, dumb, but all return as they had been. In the coming age Israel will be restored to life as it had been before, but then God will heal Israel. In the age to come, God will restore all things to their proper condition; people will come back to life as they left life:

XCV

I.1
    A. "He sent Judah before him to Joseph, to appear before him in Goshen, and they came into the land of Goshen" (Gen. 46:28):

    B. "The wolf and the lamb shall feed together" (Isa. 65:25).

    C. Come and see how every wound that the Holy One, blessed be He, inflicts in this world he heals in the age to come. [At issue is the following intersecting verse: "Then the eyes of the blind shall be opened, then shall the lame man leap as a hart, and the tongue of the dumb shall sing" (Isa. 35:5).]

    D. The blind are healed: "Then the eyes of the blind shall be opened."

    E. The lame are healed: "...then shall the lame man leap as a hart."

    F. The dumb are healed: "...and the tongue of the dumb shall sing."

    G. All are healed, but just as a person goes out, so he comes back to life.

    H. If he goes out blind, he comes back blind, if he goes out deaf, he comes back deaf, if he goes out dumb, he comes back dumb, if he goes out lame, he comes back lame.

I. Just as he is garbed when he goes out, so he is garbed when he comes back: "It is changed as clay under the seal, and they stand as in a garment" (Job 38:14).

J. From whom do you learn that lesson? It is from Samuel the Ramathite. When Saul brought him up, what did he say to the woman? "'What form is he of?' And she said, 'An old man comes up, and he is covered with a robe'" (1 Sam. 28:14).

K. For that is what he had been wearing: "Moreover his mother made him a little robe" (1 Sam. 2:19).

L. And why is it the case that just as a person goes out, so he comes back to life?

M. It is so that the wicked of the world will not claim that, after they have died the Holy One, blessed be He, will heal them and afterward bring them back to life. It then would appear that these are not the ones who died, but others.

N. Accordingly, the Holy One, blessed be He, says, "If so, let them rise up out of the dust just as they went, and afterward I shall heal them."

O. Why so? "That you may know that...before me there was no God formed, neither shall any be after me" (Isa. 43:10).

P. And afterward even the wild beasts are healed, as it is said, "The wolf and the lamb shall feed together." All are healed.

Q. But the one who brought [the ultimate] injury [of death] on all will not be healed: "And dust shall be the serpent's food" (Isa. 45:28).

R. Why? Because he brought all of life down to the dust.

1.2 A. Another interpretation of the verse: "The wolf and the lamb shall feed together, the lion like the ox shall eat straw" (Isa. 65:25):

B. "The wolf": this refers to Benjamin: "Benjamin is a wolf that tears at prey" (Gen. 49:27).

C. "...and the lamb": this speaks of the tribal fathers: "Israel is a scattered sheep" (Jer. 50:17).

D. "...shall feed together": When is this the case? When Benjamin went down with them.

E. Jacob said to them, "My son shall not go down with you" (Gen. 42:38).

F. But when the time came and they went down, and Benjamin went down with them, they watched over him and kept good care of him.

G. So it says with regard to Joseph, "And he lifted up his eyes and saw his brother Benjamin...and said, 'God be gracious to you...'" (Gen. 43:29).

H. "...the lion": this refers to Judah: "Judah is a lion's whelp" (Gen. 49:9).

I. "...like the ox": "this speaks of Joseph: "And of Joseph he said, 'His beauty is that of his firstling bullock'" (Deut. 33:13, 17).

J. They turned out to eat together: "And they sat before him, the firstborn according to his birthright and the youngest according to his youth...portions were taken to them..." (Gen. 43:33-34).

K. "and the lion like the ox shall eat straw": therefore: "He sent Judah before him to Joseph, to appear before him in Goshen, and they came into the land of Goshen" (Gen. 46:28).

2.   Israel will not require that the Messiah teach them Torah, but only gather them together into the Land of Israel:

XCVIII

IX.2   A.   Said R. Hanin, "Israel does not require the learning of the king messiah in the age to come, as it is said, 'Unto him shall *the nations* seek' (Isa. 11:1) – but not Israel.

B.   "If so, why will the king messiah come? And what will he come to do? It is to gather together the exiles of Israel and to give them thirty religious duties: 'And I said to them, If you think good, give me my hire, and if not, forbear. So they weighed for my hire thirty pieces of silver' (Zech. 11:12)."

C.   Rab said, "These refer to thirty heroes."

D.   R. Yohanan said, "These refer to thirty religious duties."

E.   They said to R. Yohanan, "Have you not accepted the view of Rab that the passage speaks only of the nations of the world?"

F.   In the view of Rab, "And I said to them" speaks of Israel, and in the view of Israel, "And I said to them" speaks of the nations of the world.

G.   In the view of Rab, when the Israelites have sufficient merit, the greater number of the thirty heroes are in the Land of Israel, and the lesser number in Babylonia, and when the Israelites do not have sufficient merit, the greater number are in Babylonia and the smaller number in the Land of Israel.

3.   Israel's salvation depends upon its keeping the hope alive:

XCVIII

XIV.1   A.   "Dan shall be a serpent in the way, [a viper by the path, that bites the horse's heels, so that his rider falls backward]" (Gen. 49:16-17):

B.   Just as the serpent found his place among women [beginning with Eve], so Samson the son of Manoah found his place among women.

C.   Just as the snake was bound by an oath, so Samson the son of Manoah was bound by an oath: "And Samson said to them, 'Swear to me'" (Judg. 15:12).

D.   Just as in the case of a snake all of its strength is only in its head, so Samson: "If I am shaved, then my strength will go from me" (Judg. 16:17).

E.   Just as in the case of a snake, its eyelid quivers after it is dead, so with Samson: "So the dead that he killed at his death were more than they whom he slew in his life" (Judg. 16:30).

XIV.2   A.   "Dan shall be a serpent in the way, a viper by the path, that bites the horse's heels, so that his rider falls backward":

B.   "Call for Samson, that he may play for us" (Judg. 16:25).

C.   Said R. Levi, "It is written, 'And there were upon the roof about three thousand men and women' (Judg. 16:27).

D.   "These were the ones on the edge of the roof, but as to the number of those behind them and behind those, no one knows how many they were. Yet: 'Then his brethren and all the house of his father came down and took him and brought him up and buried him in the burying place of Manoah his father' (Judg. 16:31).

E. "Our father Jacob sought mercy for this matter: 'so that his rider falls backward.' Let matters go back to the way they had been."

XIV.4   A. "I hope for your salvation, O Lord" (Gen. 49:18):

B. Said R. Isaac, "All things depend on hope, suffering depends on hope, the sanctification of God's name depends on hope, the merit attained by the fathers depends on hope, the lust for the age to come depends on hope.

C. "That is in line with this verse: 'Yes, in the way of your judgments, O Lord, we have hoped for you, to your name, and to your memorial, is the desire of our soul' (Isa. 26:8). 'The way of your judgments' refers to suffering.

D. "'...to your name': this refers to the sanctification of the divine name.

E. "'...and to your memorial': this refers to the merit of the fathers.

F. "'...is the desire of our soul': this refers to the lust for the age to come.

G. "Grace depends on hope: 'O Lord, be gracious to us, we have hoped for you' (Isa. 33:2).

H. "Forgiveness depends on hope: 'For with you is forgiveness' (Ps. 133:4), then: 'I hope for the Lord' (Ps. 130:5)."

XIV.5   A. It is because our father saw [Samson] and thought that through him the redemption would come in his days.

B. When he saw that he, too, died, he said, "I hope for your salvation, O Lord" (Gen. 49:18).

III. Matters of Philosophy, Natural Science and Metaphysics

The category does not pertain.

Part Two

LEVITICUS RABBAH

12

Leviticus Rabbah Parashah One

I The Character of Leviticus Rabbah

The framers of Leviticus Rabbah, closed in the mid-fifth century, set forth, in the thirty-seven chapters (*parashiyyot*) into which their document is divided, thirty-seven well-crafted propositions. They made no pretense at a systematic exegesis of sequences of verses of Scripture, abandoning the verse by verse mode of organizing discourse They struck out on their own to compose a means of expressing their propositions in a more systematic and cogent way. Each of the thirty-seven chapters proves cogent, and all of them spell out their respective statements in an intellectually economical, if rich, manner. Each *parashah* makes its own point, but all of them together furthermore form a single statement.

The message of Leviticus Rabbah – congruent with that of Genesis Rabbah – is that the laws of history may be known, and that these laws, so far as Israel is concerned, focus upon the holy life of the community. If Israel then obeys the laws of society aimed at Israel's sanctification, then the foreordained history, resting on the merit of the ancestors, will unfold as Israel hopes. So there is no secret to the meaning of the events of the day, and Israel, for its part, can affect its destiny and effect salvation. The authorship of Leviticus Rabbah has thus joined the two great motifs, sanctification and salvation, by reading a biblical book, Leviticus, that is devoted to the former in the light of the requirements of the latter. In this way they made their fundamental point, which is that salvation at the end of history depends upon sanctification in the here and now.

To prove these points, the authors of the compositions make lists of facts that bear the same traits and show the working of rules of history. It follows that the mode of thought brought to bear upon the theme of history remains exactly the same as in the Mishnah: list making, with data exhibiting similar taxonomic traits drawn together into lists based on common monothetic traits or definitions. These lists then through the power of repetition make a single enormous point or prove a social law of history. The catalogues of exemplary heroes and historical events serve a further purpose. They provide a model of how contemporary events are to be absorbed into the biblical paradigm. Since biblical events exemplify recurrent happenings, sin and redemption, forgiveness and atonement, they lose their one-time character. At the same time and in the same way, current events find a place within the ancient, but eternally present, paradigmatic scheme. So no new historical events, other than exemplary episodes in lives of heroes, demand narration because, through what is said about the past, what was happening in the times of the framers of Leviticus Rabbah would also come under consideration.

This mode of dealing with biblical history and contemporary events produces two reciprocal effects. The first is the mythicization of biblical stories, their removal from the framework of ongoing, unique patterns of history and sequences of events and their transformation into accounts of things that happen all the time. The second is that contemporary events, too, lose all of their specificity and enter the paradigmatic framework of established mythic existence. So (1) the Scripture's myth happens every day, and (2) every day produces re-enactment of the Scripture's myth.

The focus of Leviticus Rabbah's laws of history is upon the society of Israel, its national fate and moral condition. Indeed, nearly all of the *parashiyyot* of Leviticus Rabbah turn out to deal with the national, social condition of Israel, and this in three contexts: (1) Israel's setting in the history of the nations, (2) the sanctified character of the inner life of Israel itself, (3) the future, salvific history of Israel. So the biblical book that deals with the holy Temple now is shown to address the holy people. That is no paradox, rather a logical next step in the exploration of sanctification. Leviticus really discusses not the consecration of the cult but the sanctification of the nation – its conformity to God's will laid forth in the Torah, and God's rules. Leviticus Rabbah executes the paradox of shifting categories, applying to the nation – not a locative category – and its history the category that in the book subject to commentary pertained to the holy place – a locative category – and its eternal condition. The nation now is like the cult then, the ordinary Israelite now like the priest then. The holy way of life lived now, through acts to which merit accrues, corresponds to the holy rites then. The process of metamorphosis is full, rich, complete. When everything stands for something else, the something else repeatedly turns out to be the nation. This is what our document spells out in exquisite detail, yet never missing the main point.

The message of Leviticus Rabbah paradoxically attaches itself to the book of Leviticus, as if that book had come from prophecy and addressed the issue of salvation. But it came from the priesthood and spoke of sanctification. The paradoxical syllogism – the as-if reading, the opposite of how things seem – of the composers of Leviticus Rabbah therefore reaches simple formulation. In the very setting of sanctification the authors find the promise of salvation. In the topics of the cult and the priesthood they uncover the national and social issues of the moral life and redemptive hope of Israel. The repeated comparison and contrast of priesthood and prophecy, sanctification and salvation, turn out to produce a complement, which comes to most perfect union in the text at hand.

What we have in Leviticus Rabbah is the result of the mode of thought not of prophets or historians, but of philosophers and scientists. The framers propose not to lay down, but to discover, rules governing Israel's life. As we find the rules of nature by identifying and classifying facts of natural life, so we find rules of society by identifying and classifying the facts of Israel's social life. In both modes of inquiry we make sense of things by bringing together like specimens and finding out whether they form a species, then bringing together like species and finding out whether they form a genus – in all, classifying data and identifying the rules that make possible the classification. That sort of thinking lies at the deepest level of list making, which is work of offering a proposition and facts (for social rules) as much as a genus and its species (for rules of nature). Once discovered, the social rules of Israel's national life of course yield explicit statements, such as that God hates the arrogant and loves the humble. The logical status of these statements, in context, is as secure and unassailable as the logical status of statements about physics, ethics, or politics, as these emerge in philosophical thought. What differentiates the statements is not their logical status – as sound, scientific philosophy – but only their subject matter, on the one side, and distinctive rhetoric, on the other.

FROM COMMENTARY TO PROPOSITIONAL STATEMENTS: The framers of Leviticus Rabbah treat topics, not particular verses. They make generalizations that are free-standing. They express cogent propositions through extended compositions, not episodic ideas. Earlier, in Genesis Rabbah, as we have seen, things people wished to say were attached to predefined statements based on an existing text, constructed in accord with an organizing logic independent of the systematic expression of a single, well-framed idea. That is to say, the sequence of verses of Genesis and their contents played a massive role in the larger-scale organization of Genesis Rabbah and expression of its propositions. Now the authors of Leviticus Rabbah so collected and arranged their materials that an abstract proposition emerges. That proposition is not expressed only or mainly through episodic restatements, assigned, as I said, to an order established by a base text (whether Genesis or Leviticus, or a Mishnah tractate, for that matter). Rather it emerges through a logic of its own.

What is new is the move from an essentially exegetical mode of logical discourse to a fundamentally philosophical one. It is the shift from discourse framed around an established (hence old) text to syllogistic argument organized around a proposed (hence new) theorem or proposition. What changes, therefore, is the way in which cogent thought takes place, as people moved from discourse contingent on some prior principle of organization to discourse autonomous of a ready-made program inherited from an earlier paradigm. When they read the rules of sanctification of the priesthood, the sages responsible for Leviticus Rabbah heard the message of the salvation of all Israel. Leviticus became the story of how Israel, purified from social sin and sanctified, would be saved.

The authors of Leviticus Rabbah express their ideas, first, by selecting materials already written for other purposes and using them for their own, second, by composing materials, and third, by arranging both in *parashiyyot* into an order through which propositions may reach expression. This involves both the modes of thought, and the topical program, and also the unifying proposition of the document as a whole. To summarize:

1. The principal mode of thought required one thing to be read in terms of another, one verse in light of a different verse (or topic, theme, symbol, idea), one situation in light of another.

2. The principal subject is the moral condition of Israel, on the one side, and the salvation of Israel, on the other.

3. The single unifying proposition – the syllogism at the document's deepest structure – is that Israel's salvation depends upon its moral condition.

It follows that Leviticus Rabbah constitutes not merely diverse thoughts but a single, sustained composition. The authors do so through a rich tapestry of unstated propositions that only are illustrated, delineated at the outset, by the statement of some propositions that also are illustrated. It is, in a word, a syllogism by example – that is, by repeated appeal to facts – rather than by argument alone. For in context, an example constitutes a fact. The source of many examples or facts is Scripture, the foundation of all reality. Accordingly, in the context of Israelite life and culture, in which Scripture recorded facts, we have a severely logical, because entirely factual, statement of how rightly organized and classified facts sustain a proposition. In context that proposition is presented as rigorously and critically as the social rules of discourse allowed.

The authors of the document's compositions and composites transformed scriptural history from a sequence of one-time events, leading from one place to some other, into an ever-present mythic world. No longer does Scripture speak of only one Moses, one David, one set of happenings of a distinctive and never-to-be-repeated character. Now whatever happens of which the thinkers propose to take account must enter and be absorbed into that established and ubiquitous pattern and structure founded in Scripture. It is not that biblical history repeats itself. Rather, biblical history no longer constitutes history at all, that is, history as a linear, purposeful, continuous story of things that happened once, long ago, and pointed to some one moment in the future. Rather it becomes an account of things that happen every day – hence, an ever-present mythic world. In this way the basic trait of history in the salvific framework, its one-timeness and linearity, is reworked into the generative quality of sanctification, its routine and everyday, ongoing reality. When history enters a paradigm, it forms an exercise within philosophy, the search for the rules and regularities of the world. That is the profound achievement of the document before us.

And that is why, in Leviticus Rabbah, Scripture – the book of Leviticus – as a whole does not dictate the order of discourse, let alone its character. In this document the authorship at hand chose in Leviticus itself an isolated verse here, an odd phrase there. These then presented the pretext for propositional discourse commonly quite out of phase with the cited passage. The verses that are quoted ordinarily shift from the meanings they convey to the implications they contain, speaking about something, anything, other than what they seem to be saying. So the *as-if* frame of mind brought to Scripture precipitates renewal of Scripture, requiring the seeing of everything with fresh eyes. And the result of the new vision was a re-imagining of the social world envisioned by the document at hand, I mean, the everyday world of Israel in its Land in that same difficult time at which Genesis Rabbah was taking shape, sometime in the fifth century and the first century of the Christian West. For what the sages now proposed was a reconstruction of existence along the lines of the ancient design of Scripture as they read it. What that meant was that, from a sequence of one-time and linear events, everything that happened was turned into a repetition of known and already experienced paradigms, hence, once more, a mythic being. The source and core of the myth, of course, derive from Scripture – Scripture reread, renewed, reconstructed along with the society that revered Scripture.

Rhetoric

While Leviticus Rabbah focuses the discourse of each of its thirty-seven *parashiyyot* on a verse of the book of Leviticus, these verses in no way are sequential, for example, Leviticus 1:1, then Leviticus 1:2, in the way in which the structure of Genesis Rabbah dictates exegesis of the verses of the book of Genesis, read in sequence. The document's chapters work out theses on a sequence of themes, for example, the evils of gossip or of drink, the unique character of Moses, and the like. But the respective themes cover a variety of propositions, and a *parashah* ordinarily displays and demonstrates more than a single cogent syllogism.

The single most striking recurrent literary structure of Leviticus Rabbah is the base verse/intersecting verse construction, already familiar from Genesis Rabbah, and to be repeated in Pesiqta deRab Kahana. In such a construction, a base verse, drawn from the book of Leviticus, is juxtaposed to an intersecting verse, drawn from any book other than a Pentateuchal one. Then this intersecting verse is subjected to systematic exegesis. On the surface the exegesis is out of all relationship with the base verse. But in a stunning climax, all of the exegeses of the intersecting verse are shown to relate to the main point the exegete wishes to make about the base verse. What that means is that the composition as a whole is so conceived as to impose meaning and order on all of the parts, original or ready-made parts, of which the author of the whole has made use.

Another classification of rhetorical pattern, familiar from Sifra and Sifré to Numbers as well as from Genesis Rabbah, derives from the clause-by-clause type of exegesis of the base verse, with slight interest in intersecting verses or in illustrative materials deriving from other books of the Scripture. The base verse in this classification defines the entire frame of discourse, either because of its word choices or because of its main point. Where verses of other passages are quoted, they serve not as the focus of discourse but only as prooftexts or illustrative texts. They therefore function in a different way from the verses adduced in discourse in the first two classifications, for, in those former cases, the intersecting verses form the center of interest. The categories of units of discourse also explain the order of arrangement of types of units of discourse. First will come the base verse/intersecting verse construction; then will come intersecting verse/base verse construction; finally we shall have clause-by-clause exegetical constructions.

In the base verse/intersecting verse exegesis characteristic of Leviticus Rabbah, exegetes read one thing in terms of something else. To begin with, it is the base verse in terms of the intersecting verse. It also is the intersecting verse in other terms as well – a multiple layered construction of analogy and parable. The intersecting verse's elements always turn out to stand for, to signify, to speak of, something other than that to which they openly refer. If water stands for Torah, the skin disease for evil speech, the reference to something for some other thing entirely, then the mode of thought at hand is simple. One thing symbolizes another, speaks not of itself but of some other thing entirely. It is as if a common object or symbol really represented an uncommon one. Nothing says what it means. All statements carry deeper meaning, which inheres in other statements altogether. The profound sense, then, of the base verse emerges only through restatement within and through the intersecting verse – as if the base verse spoke of things that, on the surface, we do not see at all. Accordingly, if we ask the single prevalent literary construction to testify to the prevailing frame of mind, its message is that things are never what they seem.

Logic of Coherent Discourse

The paramount logic that imposes coherence on the *parashiyyot* and their subdivisions is not only propositional but syllogistic. The syllogistic argument of Leviticus Rabbah rests on the simple equation: if X, then Y; if not X, then not Y. If Israel carries out its moral obligations, then God will redeem Israel. If Israel does not, then God will punish Israel. This simple statement is given innumerable illustrations, for example, Israel in times past repented, therefore God saved them. Israel in times past sinned, therefore God punished them. Other sorts of statements follow suit. God loves the humble and despises the haughty. Therefore God saves the humble and punishes the haughty. In the same terms, if one is humble, then God will save him, and if one is haughty, then God will punish him. Accordingly, if one condition is met, then another will come about. And the opposite also is the fact.

True, the document does not express these syllogisms in the form of arguments at all. Rather they come before us as lists of statements of fact, and the facts upon which numerous statements rest derive from Scripture. So, on the surface, there is not a single statement in the document that a Greco-Roman logician would have understood, since the formal patterns of Greco-Roman logic do not make an appearance. Yet once we translate the statements the authors do make into the language of abstract discourse, we find exact correspondences between the large-scale propositions of the document and the large-scale syllogisms of familiar logic. Along these same lines, we may find numerous individual examples in which, in exquisite detail, the syllogistic mode at hand – if X, then Y; if not X, then not Y – defines the pattern of discourse. We find both brief and simple propositions that make sense of large-scale compositions, for example, on humility and arrogance, and also an overall scheme of proposition and argument.

The Mishnah makes its principal points by collecting three or five examples of a given rule. The basic rule is not stated, but it is exemplified through the several statements of its application. The reader then may infer the generalization from its specific exemplifications. Sometimes, but not often, the generalization will be made explicit. The whole then constitutes an exercise in rhetoric and logic carried out through list making. And the same is true in Leviticus Rabbah. But it makes lists of different things from those of the Mishnah: events, not everyday situations. The framers of Leviticus Rabbah revert to sequences of events, all of them exhibiting the same definitive traits and the same ultimate results, for example, arrogance, downfall, not one time but many; humility, salvation, over and over again, and so throughout. Indeed, if we had to select a single paramount trait of argument in Leviticus Rabbah, it would be the theorem stated by the making of a list of similar examples. The search for the rules lies through numerous instances that, all together, yield the besought rule.

In context, therefore, we have in Leviticus Rabbah the counterpart to the list making that defined the labor of the philosophers of the Mishnah. Through composing lists of items joined by a monothetic definitive trait, the framers produce underlying or overriding rules always applicable. Here, too, through lists of facts of history, the foundations of social life rise to the surface. All of this, we see, constitutes a species of a molecular argument, framed in very definite terms, for example, Nebuchadnezzar, Sennacherib, David, Josiah did so-and-so with such-and-such result. So, as we said, the mode of argument at hand is the assembly of instances of a common law. The argument derives from the proper construction of a statement of that law in something close to a syllogism. The syllogistic statement often, though not invariably, occurs at the outset, all instances of so-and-so produce such-and-such a result, followed by the required catalogue.

The conditional syllogisms of our composition over and over again run through the course of history. The effort is to demonstrate that the rule at hand applies at all times, under all circumstances. Why so? It is because the conditional syllogism must serve under all temporal circumstances. The recurrent listing of events subject to a single rule runs as often as possible through the course of all of human history, from creation to the fourth monarchy (Rome), which, everyone knows, is the end of time prior to the age that is coming. Accordingly, the veracity of Rabbinic conditional arguments depends over and over again on showing that the condition holds at all times.

Accordingly, when we listen to the framers of Leviticus Rabbah, we see how statements in the document at hand thus become intelligible not contingently, that is, on the strength of an established text, but a priori, that is, on the basis of a deeper logic of meaning and an independent principle of rhetorical intelligibility. Leviticus Rabbah is topical, not exegetical in any received sense. Each of its thirty-seven *parashiyyot* pursues its given topic and develops points relevant to that topic. It is logical, in that (to repeat) discourse appeals to an underlying principle of composition and intelligibility, and that logic inheres in what is said. Logic is what joins one sentence to the next and forms the whole into paragraphs of meaning, intelligible propositions, each with its place and sense in a still larger, accessible system. Because of logic one mind connects to another, public discourse becomes possible, debate on issues of general intelligibility takes place, and an anthology of statements about a single subject becomes a composition of theorems about that subject.

In this sense, after the Mishnah, Leviticus Rabbah constitutes the next major logical composition in the Rabbinic canon. Accordingly, with Leviticus Rabbah rabbis take up the problem of saying what they wish to say not in an exegetical, but in a syllogistic and freely discursive logic and rhetoric. It was a pioneering document, but the next set of successors, those associated with the Talmud of Babylonia, reverted to the received form of verse-by-verse commentary, even while accomplishing the same goal of a broad-ranging syllogistic discourse – a synthesis of the form of verse-by-verse exegesis and sustainedly propositional presentation.

Topical Program

The recurrent message of the document may be stated briefly. God loves Israel, so gave them the Torah, which defines their life and governs their welfare. Israel is alone in its category (*sui generis*), so what is a virtue to Israel is a vice to the nation, life giving to Israel, poison to the gentiles. True, Israel sins, but God forgives that sin, having punished the nation on account of it. Such a process has yet to come to an end, but it will culminate in Israel's complete regeneration. Meanwhile, Israel's assurance of God's love lies in the many expressions of special concern, for even the humblest and most ordinary aspects of the national life: the food the nation eats, the sexual practices by which it procreates. These life sustaining, life transmitting activities draw God's special interest, as a mark of his general love for Israel. Israel then is supposed to achieve its life in conformity with the marks of God's love.

These indications moreover also signify the character of Israel's difficulty, namely, subordination to the nations in general, but to the fourth kingdom, Rome, in particular. Both food laws and skin diseases stand for the nations. There is yet another category of sin, also collective and generative of collective punishment, and that is social. The moral character of Israel's life, the treatment of people by one another, the practice of gossip and small-scale thuggery – these, too, draw down divine penalty. The nation's fate therefore corresponds to its moral condition. The moral condition, however, emerges not only from the current generation. Israel's richest hope lies in the merit of the ancestors, thus in the scriptural record of the merits attained by the founders of the nation, those who originally brought it into being and gave it life.

The world to come will right all presently unbalanced relationships. What is good will go forward, what is bad will come to an end. The simple message is that the things people revere, the cult and its majestic course through the year, will go on; Jerusalem will come back, so, too, the Temple, in all their glory. Israel will be saved through the merit of the ancestors, atonement, study of Torah, practice of religious duties. The prevalence of the eschatological dimension at the formal structures, with its messianic and other expressions, here finds its counterpart in the repetition of the same few symbols in the expression of doctrine.

The theme of the moral life of Israel produces propositions concerning not only the individual but, more important, the social virtues that the community as a whole must exhibit. First of all, the message to the individual constitutes a revision, for this context, of the address to the nation: humility as against arrogance, obedience as against sin, constant concern not to follow one's natural inclination to do evil or to overcome the natural limitations of the human condition. Israel must accept its fate, obey and rely on the merits accrued through the ages and God's special love. The individual must conform, in ordinary affairs, to this same paradigm of patience and submission. Great men and women, that is, individual heroes within the established paradigm, conform to that same pattern, exemplifying the national virtues. Among these, of course, Moses stands out; he has no equal. The special position of the humble Moses is complemented by the patriarchs and by David, all of whom knew how to please God and left as an inheritance to Israel the merit they had thereby attained.

If we now ask about further recurring themes or topics, there is one so commonplace that we should have to list the majority of paragraphs of discourse in order to provide a complete list. It is the list of events in Israel's history, meaning, in this context, Israel's history solely in scriptural times, down through the return to Zion. The one-time events of the generation of the flood, Sodom and Gomorrah, the patriarchs and the sojourn in Egypt, the exodus, the revelation of the Torah at Sinai, the golden calf, the Davidic monarchy and the building of the Temple, Sennacherib, Hezekiah, and the destruction of northern Israel, Nebuchadnezzar and the destruction of the Temple in 586, the life of Israel in Babylonian captivity, Daniel and his associates, Mordecai and Haman – these events occur over and over again. They turn out to serve as paradigms of sin and atonement, steadfastness and divine intervention, and equivalent lessons.

We find, in fact, a fairly standard repertoire of scriptural heroes or villains, on the one side, and conventional lists of Israel's enemies and their actions and downfall, on the other. The boastful, for instance, include the generation of the flood, Sodom and Gomorrah, Pharaoh, Sisera, Sennacherib, Nebuchadnezzar, the wicked empire (Rome) – contrasted to Israel, "despised and humble in this world." The four kingdoms recur again and again, always ending, of course, with Rome, with the repeated message that after Rome will come Israel. But Israel has to make this happen through its faith and submission to God's will. Lists of enemies ring the changes on Cain, the Sodomites, Pharaoh, Sennacherib, Nebuchadnezzar, Haman.

At the center of the pretense, that is, the as-if mentality of Leviticus Rabbah and its framers, we find a simple proposition. Israel is God's special love. That love is shown in a simple way. Israel's present condition of subordination derives from its own deeds. It follows that God cares, so Israel may look forward to redemption on God's part in response to Israel's own regeneration through repentance. When the exegetes proceeded to open the scroll of Leviticus, they found numerous occasions to state that proposition in concrete terms and specific contexts. The sinner brings on his own sickness. But God heals through that very ailment. The nations of the world govern in heavy succession, but Israel's lack of faith guaranteed their rule and its moment of renewal will end it. Israel's leaders – priests, prophets, kings – fall into an entirely different category from those of the nations, as much as does Israel. In these and other concrete allegations, the same classical message comes forth. Israel's sorry condition in no way testifies to Israel's true worth – the grandest pretense of all. All of the little evasions of the primary sense in favor of some other testify to this, the great denial that what is, is what counts. Leviticus Rabbah makes that statement with art and imagination. But it is never subtle about saying so.

Salvation and sanctification join together in Leviticus Rabbah. The laws of the book of Leviticus, focused as they are on the sanctification of the nation through its cult, in Leviticus Rabbah indicate the rules of salvation as well. The message of Leviticus Rabbah attaches itself to the book of Leviticus, as if that book had come from prophecy and addressed the issue of the meaning of history and Israel's salvation. But the book of Leviticus came from the priesthood and spoke of sanctification. The paradoxical syllogism – the as-if reading, the opposite of how things seem – of the composers of Leviticus Rabbah therefore reaches simple formulation. In the very setting of sanctification we find the promise of salvation. In the topics of the cult and the priesthood we uncover the national and social issues of the moral life and redemptive hope of Israel. The repeated comparison and contrast of priesthood and prophecy, sanctification and salvation, turn out to produce a complement, which comes to most perfect union in the text at hand.

The focus of Leviticus Rabbah and its laws of history is upon the society of Israel, its national fate and moral condition. Indeed, nearly all of the *parashiyyot* of Leviticus Rabbah turn out to deal with the national, social condition of Israel, and this in three contexts: (1) Israel's setting in the history of the nations, (2) the sanctified character of the inner life of Israel itself, (3) the future, salvific history of Israel. So the biblical book that deals with the holy Temple now is shown to address the holy people. Leviticus really discusses not the consecration of the cult but the sanctification of the nation – its conformity to God's will laid forth in the Torah, and God's rules. So when we review the document as a whole and ask what is that something else that the base text is supposed to address, it turns out that the sanctification of the cult stands for the salvation of the nation. So the nation now is like the cult then, the ordinary Israelite now like the priest then. The holy way of life lived now, through acts to which merit accrues, corresponds to the holy rites then. The process of metamorphosis is full, rich, complete. When everything stands for something else, the something else repeatedly turns out to be the nation. This is what our document spells out in exquisite detail, yet never missing the main point.

II. Unarticulated Premises: The Givens of Religious Conduct

There is nothing here of legal interest.

III. Unarticulated Premises: The Givens of Religious Conviction

1. Moses is the greatest of the prophets, God's messenger par excellence; the humble man is called upon to take up the exalted position and leadership of Israel:

I

I.1   A. "The Lord called Moses [and spoke to him from the tent of meeting, saying, 'Speak to the children of Israel and say to them, "When any man of you brings an offering to the Lord, you shall bring your offering of cattle from the herd or from the flock.'"'

B. R. Tanhum bar Hanilai opened [discourse by citing the following verse: "'Bless the Lord, you his messengers, you mighty in strength, carrying out his word, obeying his word' (Ps. 103:20)....

I.6 A. [Continuing the same exercise:] "Harkening to his word" (Ps. 103:20):

B. Said R. Tanhum bar Hanilai, "Under ordinary circumstances a burden which is too heavy for one person is light for two, or too heavy for two is light for four.

C. "But is it possible to suppose that a burden that is too weighty for six hundred thousand can be light for a single individual?

D. "Now the entire people of Israel were standing before Mount Sinai and saying, 'If we hear the voice of the Lord our God any more, then we shall die' (Deut. 5:22). But, [for his part], Moses heard the sound of the [Divine] word himself and lived.

E. "You may find evidence that that is the case, for, among all [the Israelites], the [act of] speech [of the Lord] called only to Moses, on which account it is stated, 'The Lord called Moses'" (Lev. 1:1).

V.2 A. Said to him the Holy One, blessed be He, "And now, go (LKH), I am sending you to Pharaoh" (Ex. 3:10).

B. Said R. Eleazar, "[Taking the word 'Go,' LK, not as the imperative, but to mean, 'to you,' and spelled LKH, with an H at the end, I may observe that] it would have been sufficient to write, 'You (LK),' [without adding] an H at the end of the word. [Why then did Scripture add the H?] To indicate to you, 'If you are not the one who will redeem them, no one else is going to redeem them.'

C. "At the Red Sea, Moses stood aside. Said to him the Holy One, blessed be He, 'Now you, raise your rod and stretch out your hand [over the sea and divide it]' (Ex. 14:16).

D. "This is to say, 'If you do not split the sea, no one else is going to split it.'

E. "At Sinai Moses stood aside. Said to him the Holy One, blessed be He, 'Come up to the Lord, you and Aaron' (Ex. 24:1).

F. "This is to say, 'If you do not come up, no one else is going to come up.'

G. "At the [revelation of the instructions governing sacrifices at] the tent of meeting, [Moses] stood to the side. Said to him the Holy One, blessed be He, 'How long are you going to humble yourself? For the times demand only you.'

H. "You must recognize that that is the case, for among them all, the Word [of God] called only to Moses, as it is written, 'And [God] called to Moses'" (Lev. 1:1).

Not only so, but Moses was unique among the prophets; God spoke to him in ways in which he did not speak to others:

I

IX.1 A. "And [the Lord] called to Moses" (Lev. 1:1) [bearing the implication, to Moses in particular].

B.   Now did he not call Adam? [But surely he did:] "And the Lord God called Adam" (Gen. 3:9).

C.   [He may have called him, but he did not speak with him, while at Lev. 1:1, the Lord "called Moses and spoke to him"], for is it not undignified for a king to speak with his tenant farmer [which Adam, in the Garden of Eden, was]?

D.   "...and the Lord spoke to him" (Lev. 1:1) [to him in particular].

E.   Did he not speak also with Noah? [But surely he did:] "And God spoke to Noah" (Gen. 8:15).

F.   [He may have spoken to him, but he did not call him,] for is it not undignified for a king to speak with [better: call] his ship's captain [herding the beasts into the ark]?

G.   "And [the Lord] called to Moses" (Lev. 1:1) [in particular].

H.   Now did he not call Abraham? [But surely he did:] "And the angel of the Lord called Abraham a second time from heaven" (Gen. 22:15).

I.   [He may have called him, but he did not speak with him,] for is it not undignified for a king to speak with his host (Gen. 18:1)?

J.   "And the Lord spoke with him" (Lev. 1:1) [in particular].

K.   And did he not speak with Abraham? [Surely he did:] "And Abram fell on his face, and [God] spoke with him" (Gen. 17:3).

L.   But is it not undignified for a king to speak with his host?

IX.2   A.   "And the Lord called Moses" (Lev. 1:1), but not as in the case of Abraham.

B.   [How so?] In the case of Abraham, it is written, "And an angel of the Lord called Abraham a second time from heaven" (Gen. 22:15). The angel did the calling, the Word [of God] then did the speaking.

C.   "Here, [by contrast,]" said R. Abin, "the Holy One, blessed be He, said, 'I am the one who does the calling, and I am the one who does the speaking.'

D.   "'I, even I, have spoken, yes, I have called him, I have brought him and he shall prosper in his way'" (Isa. 48:15).

XIV.1   A.   What is the difference between Moses and all the other [Israelite] prophets?

B.   R. Judah b. R. Ilai and rabbis:

C.   R. Judah said, "All the other prophets saw [their visions] through nine lenses [darkly], in line with the following verse of Scripture: 'And the appearance of the vision which I saw was like the vision that I saw when I came to destroy the city; and the visions were like the vision that I saw by the River Chebar, and I fell on my face' [Ex. 43:3] [with the root RH occurring once in the plural, hence two, and seven other times in the singular, nine in all].

D.   "But Moses saw [his vision] through a single lense: 'in [one vision] and not in dark speeches'" (Num. 12:8).

E.   Rabbis said, "All other [Israelite] prophets saw [their visions] through a dirty lens. That is in line with the following verse of Scripture: 'And I have multiplied visions, and by the ministry of the angels I have used similitudes' (Hos. 12:11).

F.   "But Moses saw [his vision] through a polished lens: 'And the image of God does he behold'" (Num. 12:8).

XIV.2   A.   R. Phineas in the name of R. Hoshaia: "[The matter may be compared] to a king who makes his appearance to his courtier in his informal garb [as an intimate].

        B.   "For in this world the Indwelling Presence makes its appearance only to individuals [one by one], while concerning the age to come, what does Scripture say? 'The glory of the Lord shall be revealed, and all flesh shall see [it together, for the mouth of the Lord has spoken]'" (Isa. 40:5).

2.   The prophets sent to Israel, for example, Moses, were of a different order entirely from those sent to the gentiles, and, from Moses forward, prophecy was taken away from the nations altogether:

I

XIII.1   A.   What is the difference between the prophets of Israel and those of the nations [= Gen. R. 52:5]?

        B.   R. Hama b. R. Haninah and R. Issachar of Kepar Mandi:

        C.   R. Hama b. R. Haninah said, "The Holy One, blessed be He, is revealed to the prophets of the nations of the world only in partial speech, in line with the following verse of Scripture: 'And God called Balaam' (Num. 23:16). On the other hand, [he reveals himself] to the prophets of Israel in full and complete speech, as it is said, 'And [the Lord] called to Moses'" (Lev. 1:1).

        D.   Said R. Issachar of Kepar Mandi, "Should that [prophecy, even in partial form] be [paid to them as their] wage? [Surely not, in fact there is no form of speech to gentile prophets, who are frauds]. [The connotation of] the language, 'And [God] called (WYQR) to Balaam' (Num. 23:16) is solely uncleanness. That is in line with the usage in the following verse of Scripture: 'That is not clean, by that which happens (MQRH) by night' (Deut. 23:11). [So the root is the same, with the result that YQR at Num. 23:16 does not bear the meaning of God's calling to Balaam. God rather declares Balaam unclean.]

        E.   "But the prophets of Israel [are addressed] in language of holiness, purity, clarity, in language used by the ministering angels to praise God. That is in line with the following verse of Scripture: 'And they called (QR) one to another and said'" (Isa. 6:3).

IV. Matters of Philosophy, Natural Science and Metaphysics

Nothing pertains.

13

Leviticus Rabbah Parashah Two

I. Unarticulated Premises: The Givens of Religious Conduct

The general valuation of laws of religious conduct as marks of divine love and grace does not spill over into any particular proposition concerning specific laws.

II. Unarticulated Premises: The Givens of Religious Conviction

1. Israel, the priesthood, Levites, offerings, sanhedrin, Land of Israel, Jerusalem, sanctuary, anointing oil, and the like will endure not only in this world but in the world to come:

II

II.1
A. "[Is Ephraim a precious son] to me" (Jer. 31:20).
B. Wherever in Scripture the words, "to me," are written, [that to which the words refer] is not to be moved either in this world or in the world to come [see Sifre Deut. 92].
C. In reference to the priests, it is written, "And they shall serve as priests to me" (Ex. 40:15).
D. The Levites: "And they shall take heave-offering for me" (Ex. 25:2).
E. Israel: "For to me belong the children of Israel" (Lev. 25:45).
F. Heave-offering: "And they shall take up heave-offering for me" (Ex. 25:2).
G. Firstlings: "For to me belongs every firstborn" (Num. 3:13).
H. The Sanhedrin: "Gather to me [seventy elders]" (Num. 11:16).
I. The Land of Israel: "For to me belongs the land" (Lev. 25:23).
J. Jerusalem: "The city which I have chosen for me" (1 Kgs. 11:36).
K. "For I have seen for myself a king among his sons" (1 Sam. 16:1).
L. The sanctuary: "And they shall make a sanctuary for me" (Ex. 25:8).
M. The altar: "An altar of dirt you will make for me" (Ex. 20:21).
N. To the offerings: "You shall watch to offer to me" (Num. 25:2).
O. The anointing oil: "This will be for me a holy oil of anointing" (Ex. 30:31).

P. Lo, every reference in Scripture to "to me" means that that to which reference is made will not be moved either in this world or in the world to come.

2. The mark of God's special love for Israel is the proliferation of the commandments, and that is because at the Sea Israel sanctified God's name:

II

IV.1 A. Returning to the matter (GWPH): "Speak to the children of Israel" (Lev. 1:2).

B. R. Yudan in the name of R. Samuel b. R. Nehemiah [B-P = Pesiqta de R. Kahana Sheqalim 15:2-17]: "The matter may be compared to the case of a king who had an undergarment, concerning which he instructed his servant, saying to him, 'Fold it, shake it out, and be careful about it!'

C. "He said to him, 'My lord, O king, among all the undergarments that you have, [why] do you give me such instructions only about this one?'

D. "He said to him, 'It is because this is the one that I keep closest to my body.'

E. "So, too, did Moses say before the Holy One, blessed be He, Lord of the Universe: 'Among the seventy distinct nations that you have in your world, [why] do you give me instructions only concerning Israel? [For instance,] "Command the children of Israel" (Num. 28:2), "Say to the children of Israel" (Ex. 33:5), "Speak to the children of Israel"' (Lev. 1:2).

F. "He said to him, 'The reason is that they stick close to me, in line with the following verse of Scripture: "For as the undergarment cleaves to the loins of a man, so have I caused to cleave unto me the whole house of Israel"'" (Jer. 13:11).

G. Said R. Abin, "[The matter may be compared] to a king who had a purple cloak, concerning which he instructed his servant, saying, 'Fold it, shake it out, and be careful about it!'

H. "He said to him, 'My Lord, O king, among all the purple cloaks that you have, [why] do you give me such instructions only about this one?'

I. "He said to him, 'That is the one that I wore on my coronation day.'

J. "So, too, did Moses say before the Holy One, blessed be He, Lord of the Universe: 'Among the seventy distinct nations that you have in your world, [why] do you give instructions to me only concerning Israel? [For instance,] "Say to the children of Israel," "Command the children of Israel," "Speak to the children of Israel."'

K. "He said to him, 'They are the ones who at the [Red] Sea declared me to be king, saying, 'The Lord will be king'" (Ex. 15:18).

L. Said R. Berekhiah, "[The matter may be compared to an elder, who had a hood [signifying his office as Elder], concerning which he instructed his disciple, saying to him, 'Fold it, shake it out, and be careful about it!'

M. "He said to him, 'My lord, Elder, among all the hoods that you have, [why] do you give me such instructions only about this one?'

N. "He said to him, 'It is because that is the one that I wore on the day on which I was officially named an Elder.'

O. "So, too, did Moses say before the Holy One, blessed be He, Lord of the Universe: 'Among the seventy distinct nations that you have in your world, [why] do you give instructions to me only concerning Israel?'

P. He said to him, "[It is because] they accepted my dominion on them at Mount Sinai, saying, 'Whatever the Lord has spoken we shall do and we shall hear'" (Ex. 24:7).

III. Matters of Philosophy, Natural Science and Metaphysics

Nothing enters consideration.

14

Leviticus Rabbah Parashah Three

I. Unarticulated Premises: The Givens of Religious Conduct

The references to legal practice all are particular to the case and none contains a premise of broad consequence except the rather familiar notion that the offerings of the poor are accepted as much as those of the rich, since all depends upon the attitude of the one who brings the offering:

III

V.4   A. M^cSH B: A woman brought a handful of fine flour [for a cereal-offering, in line with Lev. 2:1]. But the priest ridiculed her and said, "See what these women are bringing as their offerings! In such a paltry thing what is there to eat? And what is there to offer up?"

        B. The priest saw a message in his dream: "Do not ridicule her on such an account, for it is as if she was offering up her own soul."

        C. Now is it not a matter of an argument a fortiori? If concerning someone who doesn't offer up a living soul [of a beast] Scripture uses the word, "Soul" [When any soul (RSV: one) brings a cereal-offering], if someone brings a [contrite] soul, how much the more is it as if this one has offered her own soul.

II. Unarticulated Premises: The Givens of Religious Conviction

1. God prefers offerings that expiate sin, however modest, over offerings that have other purposes altogether:

III

I.6   A. Another possibility [for interpreting Qoh. 4:6]: "Better is a handful of quietness" – this refers to the handful of cereal-offering brought as a freewill-offering by a poor person, [the handful of cereal sufficing].

        B. "...than both hands full of labor" – this refers to the finely ground incense of spices [Lev. 16:12] brought by the community as a whole.

C. [How so?] Said the Holy One, blessed be He, "I prefer the handful of cereal-offering brought as a freewill-offering by a poor person than the two hands full of finely ground incense of spices brought by the community as a whole,

D. "for the former bears with it expiation [for sin] while the latter does not bear with it expiation [for sin]."

E. And what is [the measure of the handful of cereal-offering]? It is a tenth of an ephah.

F. "When anyone brings a cereal-offering..." (Lev. 2:1).

III.3   A. "And let him return to the Lord, that he may have mercy on him" (Isa. 55:7).

B. Rabbis and R. Simeon b. Yohai:

C. Rabbis say, "All forms of atonement-[offerings] did the Holy One, blessed be He, show to Abraham, our father, [at the covenant 'between the pieces,' Gen. 15] except for the form of atonement gained through offering a tenth of an ephah of fine flour [Lev. 2:1]."

D. R. Simeon b. Yohai said, "Also the form of atonement-offering of the tenth of an ephah of fine flour did the Holy One, blessed be He, show to Abraham, our father.

E. "The word, 'these' is used here [with reference to the meal-offering, at Lev. 2:8: 'The meal-offering that is made out of these'], and the same word occurs elsewhere [with reference to the account of the covenant 'between the pieces': 'And he took him all these' (Gen. 15:10)].

F. "Just as the word, 'these,' used in the present context refers to the tenth of an ephah of fine flour, so the word, 'these' used with reference to [the modes of expiatory-offering described at Gen. 15] likewise encompasses the tenth of an ephah of fine flour."

III. Matters of Philosophy, Natural Science and Metaphysics

Nothing pertains.

15

Leviticus Rabbah Parashah Four

I. Unarticulated Premises: The Givens of Religious Conduct

There is nothing of legal interest here.

II. Unarticulated Premises: The Givens of Religious Conviction

1. The soul and the body are equally responsible for the sin that a person does, but the soul bears the burden of guilt, having the obligation to know better:

IV

IV.1
- A. "Speak to the children of Israel, 'A soul...'" ["If any one sins unwittingly in any of the things which the Lord has commanded not to be done"] (Lev. 4:1) –
- B. [B. San. 91a-b:] Why [does Scripture make explicit reference to] a soul, [rather than speaking of "a man"]?
- C. [The intent is to] punish the soul.

IV.2
- A. R. Ishmael taught, "[The matter of the soul's and body's guilt for sin may be] compared to the case of a king, who had an orchard, in which were excellent early figs. So he set up two guards to keep watch [over the orchard], one lame, one blind. He told them, 'Keep watch over the early figs.' He left them there and went his way.
- B. "The lame guard said to the blind one, 'I spy some wonderful figs.'
- C. "The other said, 'Come on, let's eat.'
- D. "The lame one said, 'Now can I walk around?'
- E. "The blind one said, 'And can I see a thing?'
- F. "What did they do? The lame one rode on the blind one and they picked the figs and ate them. Then they went back and each one took his original place.
- G. "After a while the king came back and said to them, 'Where are my figs?'
- H. "The blind one said to him, 'Can I see a thing?'
- I. "The lame one said, 'And can I walk around?'
- J. "Since the king was smart, what did he do? He had the lame one climb onto the blind one, and he judged the two of them as a single

105

defendant. He said to them, 'This is how you did it when you went and ate the figs.'

K.   "So in time to come, the Holy One will say to the soul, 'Why did you sin before me?'

L.   "And the soul will say before him, 'Lord of the age[s], am I the one that sinned before you? It is the body that sinned. From the day that I left it, have I committed a single sin?'

M.   "So the [Holy One] will say to the body, 'Why did you sin?'

N.   "And it will say before him, 'Lord of the ages, it is the soul that committed the sin. From the day on which it left me, have I not been cast down before you like a shard on a garbage dump?'

O.   "What will the Holy One, blessed be He, do? He will put the soul back into the body and judge them as a single defendant.

P.   "That is in line with the following verse of Scripture: 'He calls to the earth above, heavens above, and to the earth, that he may judge his people' (Ps. 50:4).

Q.   "'He calls to the heaven' – to produce the soul.

R.   "'And to the earth' – to bring forth the body.

S.   "And then: 'To judge with him' [all together, reading as if it read not *amo* but *imo*]."

IV.3   A.   R. Hiyya taught, "[The matter of the soul's guilt for sin may be compared] to the case of a priest who had two wives, one the daughter of a priest, the other the daughter of an Israelite.

B.   "He gave them a piece of dough in the status of heave-offering [which was to be kept in conditions of cultic cleanness], but they rendered it cultically unclean.

C.   "He went and remonstrated with the daughter of the priest, but he left the daughter of the Israelite alone.

D.   "She said to him, 'Our lord, priest, you gave it to both of us simultaneously. Why do you remonstrate with me and leave that one alone?'

E.   "He said to her, 'You are a priest's daughter and experienced [on account of growing up] in your father's house [in dealing with the rules of cultic cleanness], but that one is an Israelite's daughter and not experienced from her upbringing in her father's house.

F.   "'Therefore I remonstrate with you.'

G.   "So in time to come, the Holy One, blessed be He, will say to the soul, 'Why have you sinned before me?'

H.   "And the soul will say before him, 'Lord of the age[s], the body and I sinned simultaneously. Why then are you remonstrating with me but leaving that one alone?'

I.   "He will then say to the soul, 'You come from the upper world, a place in which people do not sin, while the body comes from the lower world, a place in which people sin. Therefore I remonstrate with you.'"

III. Matters of Philosophy, Natural Science and Metaphysics

This category hardly serves any longer.

16

Leviticus Rabbah Parashah Five

I. Unarticulated Premises: The Givens of Religious Conduct
There is nothing of legal interest here.

II. Unarticulated Premises: The Givens of Religious Conviction
1. Tranquility and prosperity cause people to sin, but misfortune brings about repentance:

V

I.1 A. "If it is the anointed priest who sins, [thus bringing guilt on the people, then let him offer to the Lord for the sin which he has committed a young bull without blemish]" (Lev. 4:3).

I.2 A. Another interpretation: "When he is quiet, who can condemn? When he hides his face, who can set him right?" (Job 34:29).

    B. When he gave tranquillity to the generation of the flood, who could come and condemn them?

II.1 A. Another interpretation: "When he is quiet, who can condemn" (Job 34:29).

    B. When he gave tranquillity to the Sodomites, who could come and condemn them?

II.3 A. "When he hides his face, who can put him right?" –

    B. When he hid his face from them, who comes to say to him, "You did not do rightly"?

    C. And when did he hide his face from them?

    D. When he made brimstone and fire rain down on them.

    E. That is in line with the following verse of Scripture: "Then the Lord made brimstone and fire rain on Sodom and Gomorrah" (Gen. 19:24).

III.1 A. Another interpretation of "When he is quiet, who can condemn? When he hides his face, who can set him right?" (Job 34:29).

    B. When he gave tranquillity to the ten tribes, who could come and condemn them?

III.2 A. "Woe to those who are at ease in Zion" refers to the tribe of Judah and Benjamin.

B.   "Those who feel secure on the mountain of Samaria" refers to the ten tribes.

C.   "The notable men of the first of the nations" who derive from the two noteworthy names, Shem and Eber.

D.   When the nations of the world eat and drink, they pass the time in nonsense talk, saying, "Who is a sage, like Balaam! Who is a hero, like Goliath! Who is rich, like Haman!"

E.   And the Israelites come after them and say to them, "Was not Ahitophel a sage, Samson a hero, Korah rich?"

III.13 A. [Margulies: What follows treats "...whether it be a nation or a man together" (Job 34:29):] Now the justice of the Holy One, blessed be He, is not like man's justice.

B.   A mortal judge may show favor to a community, but he will never show favor to an individual.

C.   But the Holy One, blessed be He, is not so. Rather: "If it is the anointed priest who sins, [thus bringing guilt on the people,] then let him offer [for the sin which he has committed] a young bull [without blemish to the Lord as a sin-offering]" (Lev. 4:3-4).

D.   "[If the whole congregation of Israel commits a sin unwittingly, and the thing is hidden from the eyes of the assembly, and they do any one of the things which the Lord has commanded not to be done and are guilty, when the sin which they have committed becomes known,] the assembly shall offer a young bull for a sin-offering" (Lev. 4:13-14). [God exacts the same penalty from an individual and from the community and does not distinguish the one from the other. The anointed priest and the community both become subject to liability for the same offering, a young bull.]

2.   Israel and the nations of the world are comparable, but when a word applies to Israel, it serves to praise, and when the same word applies to the nations, it underlines their negative character. Both are called congregation, but the nations' congregation is desolate, and so throughout, as the context of the passage cited concerning the nations repeatedly indicates. The nations' sages are wiped out; the unblemished nations go down to the pit; the nations, called men, only work iniquity:

V

V.1 A. "[If the whole congregation of Israel commits a sin unwittingly and the thing is hidden from the eyes of the assembly, and they do any one of the things which the Lord has commanded not to be done and are guilty, when the sin which they have committed becomes known, the assembly shall offer a young bull for a sin-offering and bring it before the tent of meeting;] and the elders of the congregation shall lay their hands [upon the head of the bull before the Lord]" (Lev. 4:13-15).

B.   [Since, in laying their hands (SMK) on the head of the bull, the elders sustain (SMK) the community by adding to it the merit they enjoy,] said R. Isaac, "The nations of the world have none to sustain them, for it is written, 'And those who sustain Egypt will fall' (Ezek. 30:6).

C. "But Israel has those who sustain it, as it is written: 'And the elders of the congregation shall lay their hands [and so sustain Israel]'" (Lev. 4:15).

V.2   A. Said R. Eleazar, "The nations of the world are called a congregation, and Israel is called a congregation.

B. "The nations of the world are called a congregation: 'For the congregation of the godless shall be desolate' (Job 15:34).

C. "And Israel is called a congregation: 'And the elders of the congregation shall lay their hands' (Lev. 4:15).

D. "The nations of the world are called sturdy bulls and Israel is called sturdy bulls.

E. "The nations of the world are called sturdy bulls: 'The congregation of [sturdy] bulls with the calves of the peoples' (Ps. 68:31).

F. "Israel is called sturdy bulls, as it is said, 'Listen to me, you sturdy [bullish] of heart' (Isa. 46:13).

G. "The nations of the world are called excellent, and Israel is called excellent.

H. "The nations of the world are called excellent: 'You and the daughters of excellent nations' (Ex. 32:18).

I. "Israel is called excellent: 'They are the excellent, in whom is all my delight' (Ps. 16:4).

J. "The nations of the world are called sages, and Israel is called sages.

K. "The nations of the world are called sages: 'And I shall wipe out sages from Edom' (Ob. 1:8).

L. "And Israel is called sages: 'Sages store up knowledge' (Prov. 10:14).

M. "The nations of the world are called unblemished, and Israel is called unblemished.

N. "The nations of the world are called unblemished: 'Unblemished as are those that go down to the pit' (Prov. 1:12).

O. "And Israel is called unblemished: 'The unblemished will inherit goodness' (Prov. 28:10).

P. "The nations of the world are called men, and Israel is called men.

Q. "The nations of the world are called men: 'And you men who work iniquity' (Ps. 141:4).

R. "And Israel is called men: 'To you who are men I call' (Prov. 8:4).

S. "The nations of the world are called righteous, and Israel is called righteous.

T. "The nations of the world are called righteous: 'And righteous men shall judge them' (Ezek. 23:45).

U. "And Israel is called righteous: 'And your people – all of them are righteous' (Isa. 60:21).

V. "The nations of the world are called mighty, and Israel is called mighty.

W. "The nations of the world are called mighty: 'Why do you boast of evil, O mighty man' (Ps. 52:3).

X. "And Israel is called mighty: 'Mighty in power, those who do his word' (Ps. 103:20).

III. Matters of Philosophy, Natural Science and Metaphysics

This category is irrelevant.

17

Leviticus Rabbah Parashah Six

I. Unarticulated Premises: The Givens of Religious Conduct

There is nothing that pertains.

II. Unarticulated Premises: The Givens of Religious Conviction

1. Israel took an oath at Sinai but sinned through the golden calf; nonetheless, God did not abandon them:

VI

V.1   A. R. Phineas interpreted the verses (Lev. 5:1) to speak of Israel at Mount Sinai:

B. "'If any soul sins' (Lev. 5:1). 'And I saw, and lo, you had sinned against the Lord your God' (Deut. 9:16).

C. "'And heard the sound of a public adjuration' (Deut. 5:1). 'His sound did we hear from the midst of the fire'" (Deut. 5:21).

V.2   A. Said R. Yohanan, "They made a mutual agreement between them,

B. "that [God] would not reject them, and that they would not reject him."

III. Matters of Philosophy, Natural Science and Metaphysics

No candidates present themselves for consideration here.

18

Leviticus Rabbah Parashah Seven

I. Unarticulated Premises: The Givens of Religious Conduct
There is nothing of legal interest here.

II. Unarticulated Premises: The Givens of Religious Conviction
1. Though God hates Israel for their idolatry in Egypt, he ultimately forgave them because of his love for them:

VII

I.1   A. "[The Lord said to Moses,] 'Command Aaron [and his sons, saying, This is the law of the burnt-offering']" (Lev. 6:2 [RSV: 6:9]).

B. "Hatred stirs up strife, but love covers all offenses" (Prov. 10:12).

C. The hatred that Israel brought between themselves and their father in heaven "stirs up strife" (MDNYM), [that is to say,] provoked judgments (DYNY\DYNYM).

D. Said R. Ishmael b. R. Nehemiah, "For nearly nine hundred years hatred was pent up between Israel and their father in heaven [because of their idolatry in Egypt] from the time that they went forth from Egypt until Ezekiel arose. That is in line with the following verse of Scripture: '[On that day I swore to them that I would bring them out of the land of Egypt into a land that I had searched out for them, a land flowing with milk and honey, and most glorious of all lands,] and I said to them, "Cast away the detestable things your eyes feast on, [everyone of you, and do not defile yourselves with the idols of Egypt; I am the Lord your God." But they rebelled against me and would not listen to me; they did not every man cast away the detestable things their eyes feasted on, nor did they forsake the idols of Egypt]' (Ezek. 20:8).

E. "'But I dealt with them for the sake of my great name, that it not be profaned.' That is in line with the following verse of Scripture: 'But I acted for the sake of my name, that it should not be profaned in the sight of the nations among whom they dwelt in whose sight I made myself known to them in bringing them out of the land of Egypt' (Ezek. 20:9).

  F. "'But love covers all offenses' (Prov. 10:12).

  G. "It is the love with which the Holy One, blessed be He, loved Israel: 'I have loved you, said the Lord'" (Mal. 1:2).

2. Study of the Torah is equivalent to offering sacrifices and attains the same goal:

VII

III.2 A. R. Aha in the name of R. Hanana bar Pappa, "Since when the Temple was standing, Israel would offer all of the offerings that are required in the Torah, what is the rule as to taking account of them at this time [at which there is no Temple]?

  B. "Said to them the Holy One, blessed be He, 'Since you engage in studying their rules, I credit it to you as if you actually offered them.'"

III.3 A. R. Huna made two statements.

  B. R. Huna said, "All of the communities of exiles will be gathered back into the land only on account of the merit of the passages of the Mishnah [that they have memorized].

  C. "That is in line with the following verse of Scripture: 'Especially when they repeat [Mishnah traditions and memorize them] among the gentiles, then will I gather them back'" (Hos. 8:10).

  D. R. Huna made yet a second statement.

  E. R. Huna said, "It is written, 'For from the rising of the sun even to the setting of the sun, my name is great among the nations, and in every place incense is offered to my name' (Mal. 1:11). Now in Babylonia is there [an incense-offering accomplished by] the taking of a handful of incense and burning it up?

  F. "Rather, the Holy One, blessed be He, has said, 'Since you engage in studying them, I credit it to you as if you offered them up.'"

III.4 A. Samuel said, "'[And you, son of man, describe to the house of Israel the temple and its appearance and plan, that they may be ashamed of their iniquities.] And if they are ashamed of all that they have done, [portray the temple, its arrangements, its exits and its entrances, and its whole form, and make known to them all its ordinances and all its laws; and write it down in their sight, so that they may observe and perform all the laws and all its ordinances]' (Ezek. 43:10-11).

  B. "Now at this time was the form of the temple house available?

  C. "But the Holy One, blessed be He, has said, 'Since you engage in studying them, I credit it to you as if you built the Temple.'"

III.5 A. Said R. Issi, "What account do they start children's education in the Torah of the Priests [the book of Leviticus]? It would make more sense for them to start at Genesis.

  B. "Said the Holy One, blessed be He, 'Since the sacrifices are pure and children are pure, let the pure come and engage in the study of the pure.'"

3. Boastfulness and arrogance are punished, but humility is rewarded; if Israel is humble and accepts its status, God will restore its condition:

    A. Said R. Levi, "It is an ordinance and a decree that whoever is boastful before the Omnipresent is punished only by fire, [just as the fire-offering, *olah*, goes up on the fire and is burned up (Margulies)].

    B. "As to the generation of the flood, because they were boastful and said, 'Who is the Almighty, that we should serve him' (Job 21:15), they were punished only by fire, as it is said, 'In time of heat they disappear, when it is hot, they vanish from their place'" (Job 6:17).

    C. What is the meaning of the word "when it is hot?" When it is boiling.

    D. Said R. Yohanan, "Every drop [of rain] which the Holy One, blessed be He, brought down on them, did he heat up in Gehenna.

    E. "That is indicated by the statement, 'When it is hot, they vanish from their place'" (Job 6:17).

    F. [Levi resumes,] "As to the Sodomites, because they were boastful and said, 'Let us go and cause the laws of hospitality to be forgotten from our midst,' they were punished only by fire.

    G. "That is in line with the following verse of Scripture: 'And he made to rain on Sodom and Gomorrah brimstone and fire' (Gen. 19:24).

    H. "As to Pharaoh, because he was boastful and said, 'And who is the Lord, that I should listen to his voice' (Ex. 5:2), he was punished only in fire, as it is written, 'So there was hail and fire flashing up amidst the hail' (Ex. 9:24).

    I. "As to Sisera, because he was boastful and oppressed the Israelites, as it is written, 'And he oppressed the children of Israel forcefully' (Jud. 4:3) –

    J. (what does "forcefully" mean? Said R. Isaac, "It means with blasphemy and cursing" –)

    K. "'he was punished only with fire.'

    L. "That is in line with the following verse of Scripture: 'From heaven they fought [against Sisera]' (Jud. 5:20).

    M. "As to Sennacherib, because he was boastful and said, 'Who are among the gods of these countries, who have delivered their country out of my hand' (Isa. 36:20), he was punished only by fire.

    N. "That is in line with the following verse of Scripture: 'And under his glory there shall be kindled a burning like the burning of fire' (Isa. 10:16).

    O. "As to Nebuchadnezzar, because he was boastful and said, 'And who is God, that he will deliver you out of my hands?' (Dan. 3:15), he was punished only by fire.

    P. "That is in line with the following verse of Scripture: 'The flame of the fire slew those men that took up Shadrach, Meshach, and Abed-nego' (Dan. 3:22).

    Q. "As to the wicked empire, because it is boastful and arrogant, saying, 'Whom have I in heaven, and Whom have I in heaven but you? And there is nothing on earth that I want besides you' (Ps. 73:25), it is destined to be punished by fire.

R. "That is in line with the following verse of Scripture: '[As to the fourth beast], as I looked, the beast was slain, and its body destroyed and given over to be burned with fire' (Dan. 7:11).

S. "But as to Israel, because they are despised and humble in this world, they will be comforted only with fire.

T. "That is in line with the following verse of Scripture: 'For I [Jerusalem shall be inhabited as villages without walls...], for I will be to her a wall of fire round about'" (Zech. 2:9 [RSV: 2:5]).

III. Matters of Philosophy, Natural Science and Metaphysics

This category is irrelevant to our data.

19

Leviticus Rabbah Parashah Eight

I find nothing noteworthy in this parashah.

20

Leviticus Rabbah Parashah Nine

Apart from some commonplaces, the parashah contains nothing that requires cataloguing among governing premises.

21

Leviticus Rabbah Parashah Ten

I. Unarticulated Premises: The Givens of Religious Conduct

1. The laws of the priestly garment correspond to the theology attached thereto, and this is spelled out; the point then is that the laws realize in concrete ways the abstract truths of theology:

X

VI.1   A. "[The Lord said to Moses, 'Take Aaron and his sons with him,] and the garments [and the anointing oil and the bull of the sin-offering, the two rams, and the basket of unleavened bread, and assemble all the congregation at the door of the tent of meeting]'" (Lev. 8:1-3).

       B. R. Simon said, "Just as the sacrifices effect atonement, so [wearing of the] garments effects atonement.

       C. "This is in accord with the following teaching, which we have learned in the Mishnah [M. Yoma 7:5]: '**The high priest serves in eight garments, and an ordinary priest in four: tunic, underpants, headcovering, and girdle. The high priest in addition wears the breastplate, apron, upper garment, and frontlet.**'

       D. "The tunic serves to effect atonement for those who wear garments made up of mixed fabrics [deriving from both vegetable matter and animal matter, such as linen and wool].

       E. "That is in line with the following verse of Scripture: 'And he made from him a tunic of many colors' (Gen. 37:3).

       F. "Underpants serve to effect atonement for licentiousness.

       G. "That is in line with the following verse of Scripture: 'And you shall make linen underpants for them to cover the flesh of nakedness' (Ex. 28:42).

       H. "The headcovering serves to effect atonement for arrogance.

       I. "That is in line with the following verse of Scripture: 'And you will set the headcovering on his head' (Ex. 29:6).

       J. "The girdle: There is he who maintains that it is on account of deceivers, and he who holds it is on account of thieves."

K. Said R. Levi, "The girdle was thirty-two cubits, and he wound it toward the front and the back."

L. [Simon continues:] "The breastplate serves to effect atonement for those who corrupt justice.

M. "This is in line with the following verse of Scripture: 'And you shall put in the breastplate of judgment' (Ex. 28:30).

N. "The apron serves to effect atonement for idolatry.

O. "This is in line with the following verse of Scripture: '[For the children of Israel shall dwell many days without king or prince, without sacrifice or pillar,] without apron or teraphim. [Afterward the children of Israel shall return and seek the Lord]'" (Hos. 3:4).

P. The upper garment: R. Simon in the name of R. Nathan said, "For two matters there is no possibility of atonement, yet the Torah has [still] assigned a mode of atonement to them, and these are they: gossip and unintentional manslaughter.

Q. "What is it that serves as atonement in the view of him who maintains that while there is no real possibility of atonement for gossip, yet the Torah has assigned to it a mode of atonement?

R. "It is the little bells of the priest's robe.

S. "That is in line with the following verse of Scripture: 'A golden bell and a pomegranate, a golden bell and a pomegranate, round about on the skirts of the robe. And it shall be upon Aaron when he ministers, and its voice shall be heard when he goes into the holy place before the Lord, and when he comes out, lest he die' (Ex. 28:34-5).

T. "Said the Holy One, blessed be He, 'Let the voice come and effect atonement for what the voice has done.'

U. "He who commits unintentional manslaughter has no means of atonement, yet the Torah has assigned atonement to such a deed. And what is that means of atonement? It is the death of the high priest.

V. "That is in line with the following verse of Scripture: 'But after the death of the high priest the one guilty of manslaughter may return to the land of his possession' (Num. 35:28).

W. "The frontlet:

X. "There is he who maintains that it serves to make atonement for those who are shameless, and there is he who holds that it serves to make atonement for those who blaspheme.

Y. "He who holds that it serves to make atonement for those who are shameless derives evidence from the case of the daughters of Zion.

Z. "Here it is written, 'It shall be upon Aaron's forehead' (Ex. 28:38).

AA. "There it is written, 'You [daughters of Zion] had a harlot's forehead, but you refused to be ashamed' (Jer. 3:3).

BB. "He who maintains that it serves to attain atonement for those who blaspheme draws evidence from the case of Goliath.

CC. "Here it is written, 'It will be on his forehead forever' (Ex. 28:38).

DD. "And in regard to Goliath it is written, 'and the stone sank into his forehead'" (1 Sam. 17:49).

II. Unarticulated Premises: The Givens of Religious Conviction

1. God respected Aaron and forgave him for the sin of the golden calf, because he knew Aaron's real motive in making the calf; hence it is not the deed, but the motive for doing the deed, that is determinative, even in the worst possible case:

X

III.1   A.   R. Berekhiah in the name of R. Abba bar Kahana interpreted the verse to speak of Aaron ["You love righteousness and hate wickedness, therefore God, your God, has anointed you with oil of gladness above your fellows" (Ps. 45:7)].

        B.   "When the Israelites did that dreadful deed, first of all they went to Hur. They said to him, 'Come, make a God for us' (Ex. 32:1). When he would not listen to them, they ganged up on him and killed him.

        C.   "That is in line with the following verse of Scripture: 'Also on your skirts is found the lifeblood of guiltless poor. You did not find them breaking in, yet in spite of all these things, [you say, "I am innocent"]' (Jer. 2:34). It was because [Hur and the elders] did not do [what they wanted and said], 'These are your Gods' (Ex. 32:2).

        D.   "Then they went to Aaron. They said to him, 'Come, make a god for us.'

        E.   "When Aaron heard this, he was frightened. That is in line with the following verse of Scripture: 'And Aaron was frightened and he understood from the slaughtering' (Ex. 33:5). He was afraid when he saw the slaughtered man before him.

        F.   "So Aaron said, 'What shall I do? Lo, they have killed Hur, who was a prophet. Now if they kill me, too, and I am a priest, then the verse of Scripture will be fulfilled in their deed: "Should priest and prophet be slain in the sanctuary of the Lord" (Lam. 2:20), and then the Israelites will forthwith go into exile [as penalty for their deed. Better build the cow]'" (see B. San. 7a).

III.2   A.   Another interpretation of, "And Aaron saw this and built an altar before it" (Ex. 32:5).

        B.   What did he see? "If they build it, this one will bring a stone, and that one will bring a stone, and the work will be done all at once. If I build it, I shall drag the work on, and during that time, Moses, our lord, will come down."

        C.   "[Furthermore, if they build it,] the acts of service on it will be for the purpose of idolatry. But if I build it, I shall build it for the sake of the Holy One, blessed be He."

        D.   "And Aaron proclaimed and said, 'Tomorrow there will be a feast to the Lord'" (Ex. 32:5). It is not written "Tomorrow there will be a feast to the calf" but "to the Lord."

III.3   A.   Another interpretation of, "And Aaron saw this and built an altar before it" (Ex. 32:5):

        B.   What did he see? He said, "If they built it, the [guilt for this terrible] sin will be assigned to them. It is better that it should be assigned to me and not to all Israel."

C. R. Abba bar Yudan in the name of R. Aha, "The matter may be compared to a prince who became very arrogant and took a sword to slice up his father.

D. "His tutor said to him, 'Don't you trouble yourself. Let me do it, and I'll slice him up.'

E. "The king looked at him and said to him, 'I know full well the real intent of your plan. You thought it is better that the guilt for the sin apply to yourself and not to my son. By your life, you will never set foot outside of my palace, and the best food of my table you will eat, and twenty-four taxes you will collect.'"

F. "'You will not set foot outside my palace': 'From the sanctuary he will not go forth' (Lev. 21:12).

G. "'And the best food of my table you will eat': 'That which is left of the meal-offering will belong to Aaron and his sons' (Lev. 2:3).

H. "'Twenty-four taxes you will collect': this refers to the twenty-four gifts that are owing to the priesthood, which were assigned to Aaron and his sons."

III.4 A. "He said to Aaron, 'You love righteousness.' You love to show my children to be righteous.

B. "'You hate wickedness.' You hate declaring them to be guilty.

C. "'Therefore God, your God, has anointed you with the oil of gladness above your fellows.'

D. "What is the meaning of 'above your fellows'?

E. "He said to him, 'By your life! Of the entire tribe of Levi, only you will be selected to serve as high priest: Take Aaron and his sons with him'" (Lev. 8:2).

III. Matters of Philosophy, Natural Science and Metaphysics

Nothing fits here.

22

Leviticus Rabbah Parashah Eleven

I find nothing of broad, general interest here, though there are of course many premises that we should expect; but the richness of the parashah derives from its exegetical power, not its theological or legal premises.

23

Leviticus Rabbah Parashah Twelve

The main point here is that wine is the source of most evil. That is of neither theological nor legal interest.

24

Leviticus Rabbah Parashah Thirteen

I. Unarticulated Premises: The Givens of Religious Conduct

The dietary laws yield apocalpytic history but no important premises on law.

II. Unarticulated Premises: The Givens of Religious Conviction

1. The excellence of Israel is shown by God's giving the Torah to Israel; so, too, the excellence of Mount Moriah, Jerusalem, Sinai, the Land of Israel:

XIII

II.1   A.   R. Simeon b. Yohai opened [discourse by citing the following verse:] "'He stood and measured the earth; he looked and shook [YTR = released] the nations; [then the eternal mountains were scattered as the everlasting hills sank low. His ways were as of old]' (Hab. 3:6).

     B.   "The Holy One, blessed be He, took the measure of all the nations and found no nation but Israel that was truly worthy to receive the Torah.

     C.   "The Holy One, blessed be He, further took the measure of all generations and found no generation but the generation of the wilderness that was truly worthy to receive the Torah.

     D.   "The Holy One, blessed be He, further took the measure of all mountains and found no mountain but Mount Moriah that was truly worthy for the Presence of God to come to rest upon it.

     E.   "The Holy One, blessed be He, further took the measure of all cities and found no city but Jerusalem that was truly worthy in which to have the house of the sanctuary built.

     F.   "The Holy One, blessed be He, further took the measure of all mountains and found no mountain but Sinai that was truly worthy for the Torah to be given upon it.

    G.   "The Holy One, blessed be He, further took the measure of all lands and found no land but the Land of Israel that was truly worthy for Israel.

    H.   "That is in line with the following verse of Scripture: 'He stood and took the measure of the earth.'"

2.   The purpose of the religious duties, or commandments, is only to refine or purify people through them:

XIII

III.1   A.   "Every word of God is refined; he is a shield to those who take refuge in him" (Prov. 30:5).

    B.   Rab said, "The religious duties were handed over only to refine human beings through them."

    C.   Why so much [engagement]?

    D.   "He is a shield to those who take refuge in him" (Prov. 30:5) [and through the practice of religious duties gives people the opportunity to gain merit].

3.   The history of Israel among the nations is foreseen by prophecy and conveyed apocalyptically. The nations at hand are Babylonia, Media, Greece, and Rome, time and again differentiated from the first three. The matter unfolds rather majestically, introducing first one theme – the nations' role in the history of Israel, their hostile treatment of Israel – and then the next, the food taboos, finally bringing the two themes together. We can identify each of the successive kingdoms with the four explicitly tabooed animals of Leviticus 11:1-8: camel, rock badger, hare, pig. Then, as we see, the reasons for the taboo assigned to each of them are worked out, in a triple sequence of plays on words, with special reference to the secondary possibilities presented by the words for "chew the cud," "bring up GRH." So while the first impression is that a diverse set of materials has been strung together, upon a closer glance we see quite the opposite: a purposive and careful arrangement of distinct propositions, each leading to, and intensifying the force of, the next. That is why at the climax comes the messianic reference to Israel's ultimate inheritance of the power and dominion of Rome.

XIII

V.1   A.   Said R. Ishmael b. R. Nehemiah, "All the prophets foresaw what the pagan kingdoms would do [to Israel].

    B.   "The first man foresaw what the pagan kingdoms would do [to Israel].

    C.   "That is in line with the following verse of Scripture: 'A river flowed out of Eden [to water the garden, and there it divided and became four rivers]' (Gen. 2:10). [The four rivers stand for the four kingdoms, Babylonia, Media, Greece, and Rome]."

V.2   A.   R. Tanhuma said it, [and so did] R. Menahema [in the name of] R. Joshua b. Levi: "The Holy One, blessed be He, will give the cup of reeling to the nations of the world to drink in the world to come.

        B.   "That is in line with the following verse of Scripture: 'A river flowed out of Eden (YDN)' (Gen 2:10), the place from which justice [DYN] goes forth."

V.3   A.   "[There it divided] and became four rivers" (Gen 2:10) – this refers to the four kingdoms.

        B.   "The name of the first is Pishon (PSWN); [it is the one which flows around the whole land of Havilah, where there is gold; and the gold of that land is good; bdellium and onyx stone are there]" (Gen. 2:11-12).

        C.   This refers to Babylonia, on account [of the reference to Babylonia in the following verse:] "And their [the Babylonians'] horsemen spread themselves (PSW)" (Hab. 1:8).

        D.   [It is further] on account of [Nebuchadnezzar's being] a dwarf, shorter than ordinary men by a handbreadth.

        E.   "It is the one which flows around the whole land of Havilah" (Gen. 2:11).

        F.   This [reference to the river's flowing around the whole land] speaks of Nebuchadnezzar, the wicked man, who came up and surrounded the entire Land of Israel, which places its hope in the Holy One, blessed be He.

        G.   That is in line with the following verse of Scripture: "Hope in God, for I shall again praise him" (Ps. 42:5).

        H.   "Where there is gold" (Gen. 2:11) – this refers to the words of Torah, "which are more to be desired than gold, more than much fine gold" (Ps. 19:11).

        I.   "And the gold of that land is good" (Gen. 2:12).

        J.   This teaches that there is no Torah like the Torah that is taught in the Land of Israel, and there is no wisdom like the wisdom that is taught in the Land of Israel.

        K.   "Bdellium and onyx stone are there" (Gen. 2:12) –Scripture, Mishnah, Talmud, and lore.

V.4   A.   "The name of the second river is Gihon; [it is the one which flows around the whole land of Cush]" (Gen. 2:13).

        B.   This refers to Media, which produced Haman, that wicked man, who spit out venom like a serpent.

        C.   It is on account of the verse: "On your belly will you go" (Gen. 3:14).

        D.   "It is the one which flows around the whole land of Cush" (Gen. 2:13).

        E.   [We know that this refers to Media, because it is said:] "Who rules from India to Cush" (Est. 1:1).

V.5   A.   "And the name of the third river is Tigris (HDQL), [which flows east of Assyria]" (Gen. 2:14).

        B.   This refers to Greece [Syria], which was sharp (HD) and frivolous (QL) in making its decrees, saying to Israel, "Write on the horn of an ox [= announce publicly] that you have no portion in the God of Israel."

        C.   "Which flows east (QDMT) of Assyria" (Gen. 2:14).

D. Said R. Huna, "In three aspects the kingdom of Greece was in advance (QDMH) of the present evil kingdom [Rome]: in respect to shipbuilding, the arrangement of camp vigils, and language."

E. Said R. Huna, "Any and every kingdom may be called 'Assyria' ('SR = powerful), on account of all of their making themselves powerful (MTSRYM) at Israel's expense."

F. Said R. Yosé b. R. Hanina, "Any and every kingdom may be called Nineveh (NNWH), on account of their adorning (NWY) themselves at Israel's expense."

G. Said R. Yosé b. R. Hanina, "Any and every kingdom may be called Egypt (MSRYM), on account of their oppressing (MSRYM) Israel."

V.6 A. "And the fourth river is the Euphrates (PRT)" (Gen. 2:14).

B. This refers to Edom [Rome], since it was fruitful (PRT), and multiplied through the prayer of the elder [Isaac at Gen. 27:39].

C. Another interpretation: "It was because it was fruitful and multiplied, and so cramped his world."

D. Another explanation: Because it was fruitful and multiplied and cramped his son.

E. Another explanation: Because it was fruitful and multiplied and cramped his house.

F. Another explanation: "Parat" – because in the end, "I am going to exact a penalty (PR) from it."

G. That is in line with the following verse of Scripture: "I have trodden (PWRH) the winepress alone" (Isa. 63:3).

V.7 A. [Gen. R. 42:2:] Abraham foresaw what the evil kingdoms would do [to Israel].

B. "[As the sun was going down,] a deep sleep fell on Abraham; [and lo, a dread and great darkness fell upon him]" (Gen. 15:12).

C. "Dread" (YMH) refers to Babylonia, on account of the statement, "Then Nebuchadnezzer was full of fury (HMH)" (Dan. 3:19).

D. "Darkness" refers to Media, which brought darkness to Israel through its decrees: "to destroy, to slay, and to wipe out all the Jews" (Est. 7:4).

E. "Great" refers to Greece.

F. Said R. Judah b. R. Simon, "The verse teaches that the kingdom of Greece set up one hundred twenty-seven governors, one hundred and twenty-seven hyparchs, and one hundred twenty-seven commanders."

G. And rabbis say, "They were sixty in each category."

H. R. Berekhiah and R. Hanan in support of this position taken by rabbis: "'Who led you through the great terrible wilderness, with its fiery serpents and scorpions [and thirsty ground where there was no water]' (Deut. 8:15).

I. "Just as the scorpion produces eggs by sixties, so the kingdom of Greece would set up its administration in groups of sixty."

J. "Fell on him" (Gen. 15:12).

K. This refers to Edom, on account of the following verse: "The earth quakes at the noise of their [Edom's] fall" (Jer. 49:21).

L. There are those who reverse matters.

M. "Fear" refers to Edom, on account of the following verse: "And this I saw, a fourth beast, fearful, and terrible" (Dan. 7:7).

N. "Darkness" refers to Greece, which brought gloom through its decrees. For they said to Israel, "Write on the horn of an ox that you have no portion in the God of Israel."

O. "Great" refers to Media, on account of the verse: "King Ahasuerus made Haman [the Median] great" (Est. 3:1).

P. "Fell on him" refers to Babylonia, on account of the following verse: "Fallen, fallen is Babylonia" (Isa. 21:9).

V.8   A. Daniel foresaw what the evil kingdoms would do [to Israel].

B. "[Daniel said], I saw in my vision by night, and behold, the four winds of heaven were stirring up the great sea. And four great beasts came up out of the sea, [different from one another. The first was like a lion and had eagles' wings. Then as I looked, its wings were plucked off.... And behold, another beast, a second one, like a bear.... After this I looked, and lo, another, like a leopard.... After this I saw in the night visions, and behold, a fourth beast, terrible and dreadful and exceedingly strong; and it had great iron teeth]" (Dan. 7:3-7).

C. If you enjoy sufficient merit, it will emerge from the sea, but if not, it will come out of the forest.

D. The animal that comes up from the sea is not violent, but the one that comes up out of the forest is violent.

E. Along these same lines: "The boar out of the wood ravages it" (Ps. 80:14).

F. If you enjoy sufficient merit, it will come from the river, and if not, from the forest.

G. The animal that comes up from the river is not violent, but the one that comes up out of the forest is violent.

H. "Different (SNYN) from one another" (Dan. 7:3).

I. Hating (SNN) one another.

J. This teaches that every nation that rules in the world hates Israel and reduces them to slavery.

K. "The first was like a lion [and had eagles' wings]" (Dan. 7:4).

L. This refers to Babylonia.

M. Jeremiah saw [Babylonia] as a lion. Then he went and saw it as an eagle.

N. He saw it as a lion: "A lion has come up from his thicket" (Jer. 4:7).

O. And [as an eagle:] "Behold, he shall come up and swoop down as the eagle" (Jer. 49:22).

P. [People] said to Daniel, "What do you see?"

Q. He said to them, "I see the face like that of a lion and wings like those of an eagle: 'The first was like a lion and had eagles' wings. Then, as I looked, its wings were plucked off, and it was lifted up from the ground [and made to stand upon two feet like a man and the heart of a man was given to it]'" (Dan. 7:4).

R. R. Eleazar and R. Ishmael b. R. Nehemiah:

S. R. Eleazar said, "While the entire lion was smitten, its heart was not smitten.

T. "That is in line with the following statement: 'And the heart of a man was given to it'" (Dan. 7:4).

U. And R. Ishmael b. R. Nehemiah said, "Even its heart was smitten, for it is written, 'Let his heart be changed from a man's'" (Dan. 4:17).

V. "And behold, another beast, a second one, like a bear. [It was raised up one side; it had three ribs in its mouth between its teeth, and it was told, Arise, devour much flesh]" (Dan. 7:5).

W. This refers to Media.

X. Said R. Yohanan, "It is like a bear."

Y. It is written, "Similar to a wolf" (DB); thus, "And a wolf was there."

Z. That is in accord with the view of R. Yohanan, for R. Yohanan said, "'Therefore a lion out of the forest [slays them]' (Jer. 5:6) – this refers to Babylonia.

AA. "'A wolf of the deserts spoils them' (Jer. 5:6) refers to Media.

BB. "'A leopard watches over their cities' (Jer. 5:6) refers to Greece.

CC. "'Whoever goes out from them will be savaged' (Jer. 5:6) refers to Edom.

DD. "Why so? 'Because their transgressions are many, and their backslidings still more'" (Jer. 5:6).

EE. "After this, I looked, and lo, another, like a leopard [with four wings of a bird on its back; and the beast had four heads; and dominion was given to it]" (Dan. 7:6).

FF. This [leopard (NMR)] refers to Greece, which persisted (MNMRT) impudently in making harsh decrees, saying to Israel, "Write on the horn of an ox that you have no share in the God of Israel."

GG. "After this I saw in the night visions, and behold, a fourth beast, terrible and dreadful and exceedingly strong; [and it had great iron teeth; it devoured and broke in pieces and stamped the residue with its feet. It was different from all the beasts that were before it; and it had ten horns]" (Dan. 7:7).

HH. This refers to Edom [Rome].

II. Daniel saw the first three visions on one night, and this one he saw on another night. Now why was that the case?

JJ. R. Yohanan and R. Simeon b. Laqish:

KK. R. Yohanan said, "It is because the [terror caused by the fourth beast, that is, Rome] would be greater than [the terror caused by] the other three [together]."

LL. And R. Simeon b. Laqish said, "It outweighed them."

MM R. Yohanan objected to R. Simeon b. Laqish, "'Prophesy, therefore, son of man, clap your hands [and let the sword come down twice; yea, thrice. The sword for those to be slain; it is the sword for the great slaughter, which encompasses them]' (Ezek. 21:14-15). [So the single sword of Rome weighs against the three others]."

NN. And how does R. Simeon b. Laqish interpret the same passage? He notes that [the threefold sword] is doubled (Ezek. 21:14), [thus outweighs the three swords, equaling twice their strength].

V.9 A. Moses foresaw what the evil kingdoms would do [to Israel].

B. "The camel, rock badger, and hare" (Deut. 14:7). [Compare: "Nevertheless, among those that chew the cud or part the hoof, you shall not eat these: the camel, because it chews the cud but does not part the hoof, is unclean to you. The rock badger, because it chews the cud but does not part the hoof, is unclean to you. And the hare,

the cud but does not part the hoof, is unclean to you. And the hare, because it chews the cud but does not part the hoof, is unclean to you, and the pig, because it parts the hoof and is cloven-footed, but does not chew the cud, is unclean to you" (Lev. 11:4-8).]

C. The camel (GML) refers to Babylonia, [in line with the following verse of Scripture: "O daughter of Babylonia, you who are to be devastated!] Happy will be he who requites (GML) you, with what you have done to us" (Ps. 147:8).

D. "The rock badger" (Deut. 14:7) – this refers to Media.

E. Rabbis and R. Judah b. R. Simon.

F. Rabbis say, "Just as the rock badger exhibits traits of uncleanness and traits of cleanness, so the kingdom of Media produced both a righteous man and a wicked one."

G. Said R. Judah b. R. Simon, "The last Darius was Esther's son. He was clean on his mother's side and unclean on his father's side."

H. "The hare" (Deut. 14:7) – this refers to Greece. The mother of King Ptolemy was named "Hare" [in Greek: *lagos*].

I. "The pig" (Deut. 14:7) – this refers to Edom [Rome].

J. Moses made mention of the first three in a single verse and the final one in a verse by itself (Deut. 14:7, 8). Why so?

K. R. Yohanan and R. Simeon b. Laqish.

L. R. Yohanan said, "It is because [the pig] is equivalent to the other three."

M. And R. Simeon b. Laqish said, "It is because it outweighs them."

N. R. Yohanan objected to R. Simeon b. Laqish, "'Prophesy, therefore, son of man, clap your hands [and let the sword come down twice, yea thrice]'" (Ezek. 21:14).

O. And how does R. Simeon b. Laqish interpret the same passage? He notes that [the threefold sword] is doubled (Ezek. 21:14).

V.10 A. [Gen. R. 65:1:] R. Phineas and R. Hilqiah in the name of R. Simon: "Among all the prophets, only two of them revealed [the true evil of Rome], Assaf and Moses.

B. "Assaf said, 'The pig out of the wood ravages it' (Ps. 80:14).

C. "Moses said, 'And the pig, [because it parts the hoof and is cloven-footed but does not chew the cud]' [Lev. 11:7].

D. "Why is [Rome] compared to a pig?

E. "It is to teach you the following: Just as, when a pig crouches and produces its hooves, it is as if to say, 'See how I am clean [since I have a cloven hoof],' so this evil kingdom acts arrogantly, seizes by violence, and steals, and then gives the appearance of establishing a tribunal for justice."

F. There was the case of a ruler in Caesarea, who put thieves, adulterers, and sorcerers to death, while at the same time telling his counselor, "That same man [I] did all these three [crimes] on a single night."

V.11 A. Another interpretation: "The camel" (Lev. 11:4).

B. This refers to Babylonia.

C. "Because it chews the cud (MLH\GRH) [but does not part the hoof]" (Lev. 11:4).

D. For it brings forth praises [(MQLS) with its throat] of the Holy One, blessed be He. [The Hebrew words for "chew the cud" – bring up cud – are now understood to mean "give praise." GRH is connected with GRWN, throat, hence, "bring forth (sounds of praise through) the throat."]

E. R. Berekhiah and R. Helbo in the name of R. Ishmael b. R. Nahman: "Whatever [praise of God] David [in writing a psalm] treated singly [item by item], that wicked man [Nebuchadnezzar] lumped together in a single verse.

F. "'Now I, Nebuchadnezzar, praise and extol and honor the King of heaven, [for all his works are right and his ways are just, and those who walk in pride he is able to abase' (Dan. 4:37).

G. [Nebuchadnezzar said only the word], "'Praise' – [but David devoted the following entire Psalm to praise]: 'O Jerusalem, praise the Lord' (Ps. 147:12).

H. "'Extol' – 'I shall extol you, O Lord, for you have brought me low' (Ps. 30:2).

I. "'Honor the king of heaven' – 'The Lord reigns, let the peoples tremble! [He sits enthroned upon the cherubim, let the earth quake]' (Ps. 99:1).

J. "'For all his works are right' – 'For the sake of thy steadfast love and thy faithfulness' (Ps. 115:1).

K. "'And his ways are just' – 'He will judge the peoples with equity' (Ps. 96:10).

L. "'And those who walk in pride' – 'The Lord reigns, he is robed in majesty, [the Lord is robed, he is girded with strength]' (Ps. 93:1).

M. "'He is able to abase' – 'All the horns of the wicked he will cut off'" (Ps. 75:11).

N. "The rock badger" (Lev. 11:5) – this refers to Media.

O. "For it chews the cud" – for it gives praise to the Holy One, blessed be He: "Thus says Cyrus, king of Persia, 'All the kingdoms of the earth has the Lord, the God of the heaven, given me'" (Ezra 1:2).

P. "The hare" – this refers to Greece.

Q. "For it chews the cud" – for it gives praise to the Holy One, blessed be He.

R. Alexander the Macedonian, when he saw Simeon the Righteous, said, "Blessed be the God of Simeon the Righteous."

S. "The pig" (Lev. 11:7) – this refers to Edom.

T. "For it does not chew the cud" – for it does not give praise to the Holy One, blessed be He.

U. And it is not enough that it does not give praise, but it blasphemes and swears violently, saying, "Whom do I have in heaven, and with you I want nothing on earth" (Ps. 73:25).

V.12   A. Another interpretation [of GRH, cud, now with reference to GR, stranger:]

B. "The camel" (Lev. 11:4) – this refers to Babylonia.

C. "For it chews the cud" [now: brings up the stranger] – for it exalts righteous men: "And Daniel was in the gate of the [Babylonian] king" (Dan. 2:49).

D. "The rock badger" (Lev. 11:5) – this refers to Media.

E. "For it brings up the stranger" – for it exalts righteous men: "Mordecai sat at the gate of the king [of Media]" (Est. 2:19).

F. "The hare" (Lev. 11:6) – this refers to Greece.

G.   "For it brings up the stranger" – for it exalts the righteous.

H.   When Alexander of Macedonia, [a Greek,] saw Simeon the Righteous, he would rise up on his feet. They said to him, "Can't you see Jews [elsewhere], that you stand up before this Jew [and honor him]?"

I.   He said to them, "When I go forth to battle, I see something like this man's visage, and I conquer."

J.   "The pig" (Lev. 11:7) – this refers to Rome.

K.   "But it does not bring up the stranger" – for it does not exalt the righteous.

L.   And it is not enough that it does not exalt them, but it kills them.

M.   That is in line with the following verse of Scripture: "I was angry with my people, I profaned my heritage; I gave them into your hand, [you showed them no mercy; on the aged you made your yoke exceedingly heavy]" (Isa. 47:6).

N.   This refers to R. Aqiba and his colleagues.

V.13   A.   Another interpretation [now treating "bring up the cud" (GR) as "bring along in its train" (GRR)]:

B.   "The camel" (Lev. 11:4) – this refers to Babylonia.

C.   "Which brings along in its train" – for it brought along another kingdom after it.

D.   "The rock badger" (Lev. 11:5) – this refers to Media.

E.   "Which brings along in its train" – for it brought along another kingdom after it.

F.   "The hare" (Lev. 11:6) – this refers to Greece.

G.   "Which brings along in its train" – for it brought along another kingdom after it.

H.   "The pig" (Lev. 11:7) – this refers to Rome.

I.   "Which does not bring along in its train" – for it did not bring along another kingdom after it.

J.   And why is it then called "pig" (HZYR)? For it restores (MHZRT) the crown to the one who truly should have it [namely, Israel, whose dominion will begin when the rule of Rome ends].

K.   That is in line with the following verse of Scripture: "And saviors will come up on Mount Zion to judge the Mountain of Esau [Rome], and the kingdom will then belong to the Lord" (Ob. 1:21).

III. Matters of Philosophy, Natural Science and Metaphysics

This category is useless.

25

Leviticus Rabbah Parashah Fourteen

This parashah yields nothing for our inquiry.

26

Leviticus Rabbah Parashah Fifteen

I. Unarticulated Premises: The Givens of Religious Conduct

1. Authoritative law derives from the actions of principal authorities:

XV

IV.2 A. [Y. Shab. 16:1:] Rabbi and R. Ishmael b. R. Yosé were in session and dealing with the scroll of Lamentations on the eve of the ninth of Ab [that fell on a Friday] at dark.

   B. They omitted one alphabet [of the scroll, that is, a chapter], saying, "Tomorrow we shall complete it."

   C. When Rabbi got up, he stubbed his little toe. In his own regard he recited the following verse: "Many are the pangs of the wicked" (Ps. 32:10).

   D. Said to him R. Ishmael b. R. Yosé, "My lord, even if we were not dealing with that passage [I should have reason to cite, now all the more so:] 'The breath of our nostrils, the anointed of the Lord, [was seized for their corrupt deeds]' (Lam. 4:20). Now that we are in fact dealing with that exact passage, all the more so [does it apply that] 'the breath of our nostrils, the anointed of the Lord' [that is, Rabbi, suffers on account of our sins]."

   E. When Rabbi reached home [on the Sabbath, the sun having set], he put a dry sponge on his sore toe and wrapped reed grass around it on the outside.

   F. Said R. Ishmael, "On the basis of these deeds of his, we have learned three things:

   G. "[1] sponge does not draw out the blood but only protects the wound [absorbing liquid is forbidden on the Sabbath];

   H. "[2] they wrap reed grass available at home around it because that is regarded as ready [in advance of the holy day, hence available for use on that day];

   I. "[3] they do not recite passages of the Holy Scriptures from the time of the late afternoon prayer onward, but they do repeat and expound them.

134

    J.   "Still, if it is necessary to look up a passage, one may take the scroll and examine it."

    K.   And Samuel said, "[It is permitted to handle in the house] a tiny sherd or a tiny piece of reed grass."

    L.   R. Yudan taught in the name of Samuel, "It is permitted on the Sabbath to handle the stopper of a jar and its shards, but if one already has tossed them into the rubbish heap, it is forbidden to carry them about on the Sabbath."

II. Unarticulated Premises: The Givens of Religious Conviction

1.   Providence will provide in every detail for all concerns:

XV

III.1   A.   "Who has cleft a channel for the torrents of rain [and a way for the thunderbolt, to bring rain on a land where no man is, on the desert in which there is no man]" (Job 38:25).

    B.   [As to the meaning of the word STP, cleave a channel], said R. Berekhiah, "There are places in which they call a hair a follicle [*shitfa*]."

    C.   There is the case of a pious man who went into session and expounded as follows: "You have no hair for which the Holy One, blessed be He, did not create its own channel [follicle] [so that each should draw sustenance from its own source and not from that of any other hair]."

    D.   The next day he intended to go [out of the Holy Land] to make a living. His wife said to him, "Yesterday you went into session and expounded as follows: 'You have no hair for which the Holy One, blessed be He, did not create its own hole [follicle], so that not one of them should derive sustenance from any other.' And now do you intend to go [abroad] to seek your living? Stay home [in the Holy Land] and let your Creator provide for you."

    E.   He obeyed her and stayed home, and his Creator provided for him.

III. Matters of Philosophy, Natural Science and Metaphysics

The category is inert.

27

Leviticus Rabbah Parashah Sixteen

I. Unarticulated Premises: The Givens of Religious Conduct

I see nothing that pertains.

II. Unarticulated Premises: The Givens of Religious Conviction

1. God hates gossip and punishes the gossip with leprosy:

XVI

I.6   A. "A lying tongue" (Prov. 6:17).
     B. The proof [that one who lies is smitten by leprosy derives] from Miriam.
     C. "And Miriam and Aaron spoke against Moses" (Num. 12:1).
     D. And how do we know that she was smitten with leprosy?
     E. As it is said, "And the cloud departed from on the tent" (Num. 12:10).

The same point is stated in the following:

XVI

VI.1   A. Said R. Joshua b. Levi, "The word 'torah' [law] occurs with regard to the leper on five different occasions:
     B. "'This is the Torah governing a spot of leprosy' (Lev. 13:59).
     C. "'This is the Torah governing him on whom is a spot of leprosy' (Lev. 14:32).
     D. "'This is the Torah governing every spot of leprosy and itch' (Lev. 14:54).
     E. "'This is the Torah governing leprosy' (Lev. 14:57).
     F. "And the encompassing reference: 'This will be the Torah governing the leper' (Lev. 14:2) – the Torah governing the common gossip.
     G. "This teaches you that whoever repeats gossip violates all five scrolls of the Torah."

VI.2 A. Therefore Moses admonished the Israelites, saying to them, "This will be the Torah governing the leper (mesora)" (Lev. 14:2) – the Torah governing the gossip.

But uncleanness forms a punishment for various other sins as well, as is demonstrated here, for example, murder:

VI.7 A. "And hands that shed blood" (Prov. 6:17).

  B. [We learn that God hates such a person] from Joab.

  C. For it is said, "And the Lord will return his blood upon his [Joab's] own head" (1 Kgs. 2:32).

  D. And how do we know that he was smitten with leprosy?

  E. "May it fall upon the head of Joab, [and upon all his father's house, and may the house of Joab never be without one who has a discharge or who is leprous or who holds a spindle or who is slain by the sword or who lacks bread]" (2 Sam. 3:29).

III. Matters of Philosophy, Natural Science and Metaphysics

This category remains useless.

28

Leviticus Rabbah Parashah Seventeen

I. Unarticulated Premises: The Givens of Religious Conduct

The category receives nothing here.

II. Unarticulated Premises: The Givens of Religious Conviction

1. That God afflicts Israel is a mark of Israel's election; only Israel is punished so extensively and with such precision:

XVII

I.1   A.   "[The Lord said to Moses and Aaron,] When you come into the land of Canaan, [which I give you for a possession, and I put a leprous disease in a house in the land of your possession, then he who owns the house shall come and tell the priest, 'There seems to me to be some sort of disease in my house']" (Lev. 14:33-34).

    B.   "Truly God is good to Israel, to those who are pure in heart. [But as for me, my feet had almost stumbled, my steps had well nigh slipped, for I was envious of the arrogant, when I saw the prosperity of the wicked]" (Prov. 73:1-3).

    C.   Is it possible [to suppose that God is good] to everybody?

    D.   Scripture says, "...to those who are pure in heart." These are those whose heart is pure in [doing] religious duties.

    E.   "Blessed are the men whose strength is in you, [in whose heart are the highways to Zion]" (Ps. 84:5).

    F.   Is it possible to suppose [that this applies] to everybody?

    G.   Scripture says, "...to those in whose heart are the highways...." These are the ones in whose heart are paved the ways of the Torah.

    H.   "Do good, O Lord, to those who are good, [and to those who are upright in their hearts]" (Ps. 125:4).

    I.   Is it possible to suppose [that this applies] to everybody?

    J.   Scripture says, "...to those who are upright in their hearts."

    K.   "The Lord is good, a stronghold in the day of trouble, [yea, he knows them that trust in him]" (Nah. 1:7).

    L.   Is it possible to suppose [that this applies] to everybody?

	M.	Scripture says, "He knows them that trust in him."
	N.	"The Lord is good to those who wait for him" (Lam. 3:25).
	O.	Is it possible to suppose [that this applies] to everybody?
	P.	Scripture states, "To the soul that seeks him" (Lam. 3:25).
	Q.	"The Lord is near to those that call on him" (Ps. 145:18).
	R.	Is it possible to suppose [that this applies] to everybody?
	S.	Scripture says, "To those that call upon him in truth" (Ps. 145:18).
	T.	"Who is God like you, pardoning iniquity and passing over transgression [for the remnant of his inheritance]" (Mic. 7:18).
	U.	Is it possible to suppose [that this applies] to everybody?
	V.	Scripture says, "For the remnant of his inheritance."
II.1	A.	"The possessions of his house will be carried away [dragged off in the day of God's wrath. This is the wicked man's portion from God, the heritage decreed for him by God]" (Job 20:28-29).
	B.	They will drag and remove [what is in his house].
	C.	When [will this take place]?
	D.	On the day on which the Holy One, blessed be He, pours out his anger on that man.
	E.	How so?
	F.	A person says to his neighbor, "Lend me a qab of wheat," and the other says, "I don't have any."
	G.	"A qab of barley...," "I don't have any."
	H.	"A qab of dates," and he says to him, "I don't have any."
	I.	A woman says to her friend, "Lend me a sieve," and she says, "I don't have any."
	J.	"A sifter," and she says, "I don't have any."
	K.	What does the Holy One, blessed be He, do?
	L.	He brings leprosy signs into his house, and since [the owner] has to bring all of his utensils out into the street, everyone sees and says, "Didn't he say, 'I don't have any?' Now see how much wheat he has! How much barley he has! How many dates he has! A curse on the house of those who live therein!"
II.2	A.	R. Isaac b. Eleazar brings proof for the same proposition from the following word, that appears in a verse of Scripture: "If the plague in the walls of the house be *sheqaarurot*" (Lev. 14:37: deep green).
	B.	"The house sinks (*sheqa*) on account of such cursed people (*arurot*)."
II.3	A.	Therefore Moses admonished the Israelites, saying to them, "When you come into the land of Canaan" (Lev. 14:34).
III.1	A.	[Back to] the body [of discourse:] For ten reasons do plagues of leprosy come: idolatry, promiscuity, murder, profanation of God's name, blasphemy of God's name, robbing from the community, stealing what does not belong to a person, arrogance, gossiping, and grudging ["the evil eye"].
III.2	A.	On account of idolatry:
	B.	[The case derives] from Israel, which gave false testimony against the Holy One, blessed be He, by going and saying to a calf, "This is your God, O Israel" (Ex. 32:4).
	C.	How do we know that they were afflicted with leprosy?
	D.	As it is said, "And Moses saw the people, that it had broken out, [for Aaron had made it break out]" (Ex. 32:25).

E.   For an epidemic of leprosy and discharge had broken out among them.

III.3   A.   Promiscuity:

B.   [The case derives] from the daughters of Zion: "Because the daughters of Zion are haughty" (Isa. 3:16).

C.   How do we know that they were afflicted with leprosy?

D.   As it is said, "The Lord will smite with a scab the heads of the daughters of Zion" (Isa. 3:17).

III.4   A.   Murder:

B.   [The case derives] from Joab: "And the Lord will return his blood upon his own head" (1 Kgs. 2:32).

C.   How do we know that he was smitten with leprosy?

D.   "May it fall upon the head of Joab [and upon all his father's house and may the house of Joab never be without one who has a discharge or who is leprous]" (2 Sam. 3:29).

III.5   A.   Profanation of God's name:

B.   [The case derives] from Gehazi: "Gehazi, the servant of Elisha, the man of God, [said, 'See, my master has spared this Naaman, the Syrian, in not accepting from his hand what he brought. As the Lord lives, I will run after him and get something (*meumah*) from him]'" (2 Kgs. 5:20).

C.   What is the meaning of "something (*meumah*)?" From the blemish (*mumah*) which afflicts him.

D.   And how do we know that he was smitten with leprosy?

E.   "Therefore the leprosy of Naaman will cleave to you and to your descendants forever. [So he went out from his presence a leper, as white as snow]" (2 Kgs. 5:27).

III.6   A.   On account of blasphemy of God's name:

B.   [The case derives] from Goliath: "And the Philistine cursed David [by his God]" (1 Sam. 17:43).

C.   And how do we know that he was smitten with leprosy?

D.   As it is said, "This day the Lord will shut you up [as a leper] through my hands" (1 Sam. 17:46).

E.   And "shutting up" can mean only leprosy, in line with the following verse of Scripture: "And the priest will shut him up for seven days" (Lev. 13:21).

III.7   A.   On account of robbing from the community:

B.   The case derives from Shebna, who made personal use of things that had been consecrated to the Temple.

C.   And how do we know that he was smitten with leprosy?

D.   "Behold, the Lord will hurl you away violently. O you strong young man, he will wrap you around and around" (Isa. 22:17).

E.   This "wrapping around" can refer only to leprosy, as it is said, "And he will wrap around his upper lip" (Lev. 13:45).

III.8   A.   Stealing what one does not own:

B.   [The case derives] from Uzziah, who planned to plunder the high priesthood.

C.   And how do we know that he was smitten with leprosy?

D.   As it is said, "And Uzziah the king was a leper" (2 Chr. 26:21).

III.9   A.   And how do we know that [leprosy comes on account of] arrogance?

B.   "But when he was strong, he grew proud, to his destruction. For he was false to the Lord his God and entered the temple of the Lord [to burn incense on the altar of incense]" (2 Chr. 26:16).

III.10 A.   On account of gossiping:

B.   The case derives from Miriam: "And Miriam and Aaron spoke against Moses" (Num. 12:1).

C.   And how do we know that she was smitten with leprosy?

D.   As it is said, "And when the cloud was removed from the tent, [behold Miriam was leprous]" (Num. 12:10).

III.11 A.   And on account of grudging?

B.   That is in accord with that which R. Isaac b. Eleazar said, "Deep green (*sheqaarurot*)" (Lev. 14:37) – the house sinks because of the curse [as above]."

III.12 A.   Therefore Moses admonished Israel, saying to them, "When you come into the land of Canaan" (Lev. 13:3-4).

III. Matters of Philosophy, Natural Science and Metaphysics

Unsurprisingly, we find nothing relevant here.

29

Leviticus Rabbah Parashah Eighteen

I. Unarticulated Premises: The Givens of Religious Conduct

The parashah has no legal interests.

II. Unarticulated Premises: The Givens of Religious Conviction

1. Just as the flux or leprosy derive from the person's own body, so healing derives from the victim; people are responsible for what happens to them:

XVIII

V.1   A.   R. Joshua of Sikhnin in the name of R. Levi: "Just as a mortal [king] imposes the sentence of exile, so the Holy One, blessed be He, imposes the sentence of exile.

B.   "'Command the children of Israel, that they expel from the camp [every leper, etc.]' (Num. 5:2).

C.   "A mortal [king] imposes imprisonment, and the Holy One, blessed be He, imposes imprisonment: 'And the priest will lock up the one afflicted with a leprosy spot' (Lev. 13:4).

D.   "A mortal [king] decrees banishment, and the Holy One, blessed be He, decrees banishment: 'All by himself he will dwell outside the camp' (Lev. 13:46).

E.   "A mortal [king] imposes the penalty of flogging, and the Holy One, blessed be He, imposes the penalty of flogging: 'Forty stripes will he smite him' (Deut. 25:3).

F.   "A mortal [king] collects a fine, and the Holy One, blessed be He, collects a fine: 'And he will punish him with a fine of a hundred pieces of silver' (Deut. 22:19).

G.   "A mortal [king] gives a royal donation, and the Holy One, blessed be He, gives a royal donation: 'Lo, I bring rain for you, bread from heaven' (Ex. 16:4).

H.   "A mortal [king] passes out rations, and the Holy One, blessed be He, passes out rations: 'Take a census' (Num. 1:2).

I.   "A mortal [king] imposes a head tax, and the Holy One, blessed be He, imposes a head tax: 'An omer for a head for the entire number of your souls' (Ex. 16:16).

J.   "A mortal [king] imposes a flogging on account of the testimony of witnesses, but the Holy One, blessed be He, will impose a penalty on the basis of his own view: 'I have wounded, and I heal, and none besides me can save'" (Deut. 32:39).

K.   R. Berekhiah in the name of R. Levi said, "A mortal [king] wounds with a scalpel and heals with a salve.

L.   "But the Holy One, blessed be He, heals with that with which he wounds: 'For I shall restore your health, and from out of your wounds I shall bring healing to you, says the Lord'" (Jer. 30:17).

III. Matters of Philosophy, Natural Science and Metaphysics

Nothing is relevant here.

30

Leviticus Rabbah Parashah Nineteen

I find nothing that demands inclusion in the three rubrics here.

31

Leviticus Rabbah Parashah Twenty

The chapter yields nothing for our inquiry.

32

Leviticus Rabbah Parashah Twenty-One

I. Unarticulated Premises: The Givens of Religious Conduct

I find nothing relevant to law.

II. Unarticulated Premises: The Givens of Religious Conviction

1. The past history of Israel serves as a metaphor for the human condition of the Israelite, facing a supernatural enemy, saved by God's favor. The Day of Atonement is a day of national salvation from enemies in this world and in the world above. This theory of the history of Israel is spelled out in an elaborate way in the following:

XXI

I.1   A.   "With this shall Aaron come [into the holy place: with a young bull for a sin-offering and a ram for a burnt-offering]" (Lev. 16:3).

      B.   "The Lord is my light and my salvation; whom shall I fear? [The Lord is the stronghold of my life; of whom shall I be afraid?]" (Ps. 27:1).

      C.   R. Eleazar interpreted the cited verse to speak of [Israel at] the Red Sea:

      D.   "'My light': 'It gave light by night' (Ex. 14:20).

      E.   "'And my salvation': 'Stand firm and see the salvation of the Lord' (Ex. 14:13).

      F.   "'Whom shall I fear': 'Do not fear' (Ex. 14:13).

      G.   "'The Lord is the stronghold of my life': 'The Lord is my strength and song' (Ex. 15:2).

      H.   "'Of whom shall I be afraid': 'Trembling and fear fell on them' (Ex. 15:16).

I.   "'When evildoers come near me to eat up my flesh, [my adversaries and foes shall stumble and fall]' (Ps. 27:2):] 'And Pharaoh drew near' (Ex. 14:10).

J.   "'To eat my flesh' (Ps. 27:2): 'Said the enemy, I shall pursue, I shall overtake [my lust shall be satisfied upon them]'" (Ex. 15:9).

I.2   A.   Said R. Samuel b. R. Nahman, "Said the Holy One, blessed be He, 'This wicked man will not leave the world before he declares the sentence against himself from his own mouth.

B.   "'Said the enemy, I will pursue, [I will overtake].' *'We* will overtake' is not written here, but rather, 'I will be pursued, I will be overtaken.'

C.   "'My desire will have its fill of them' is not written here, but rather, 'My desire will have its fill for him.'

D.   "[The meaning is that] they will fill their desire from him.

E.   "'I will put my sword' is not written here, but rather, 'I will draw my sword,' [meaning], 'I will leave my sword white in them [doing them no injury].'

F.   "'My hand will destroy them' is not written here, but rather, 'My hand will cause him to inherit.' [The meaning is,] 'I shall give him over as an inheritance [all of] my wealth and my honor.'"

I.3   A.   (Eleazar continues:) "'My adversaries and foes' (Ps. 27:2): 'But overthrew Pharaoh and his host in the Red Sea' (Ps. 136:15).

B.   "From this point forward [in the cited Psalm] it is Israel that is speaking:

C.   "'If a host encamp against me' (Ps. 27:3): the host of the Egyptians.

D.   "'My heart shall not fear' (Ps. 27:3). 'If war rise up against me': if the Egyptians should come against me.

E.   "'In this I shall trust' (Ps. 27:3): In this which you have promised us in the Torah: 'The Lord will fight for you, and you shall only be still'" (Ex. 14:14).

II.1   A.   R. Samuel b. R. Nahman interpreted [the intersecting verse to speak of] the Philistines:

B.   "'When evildoers drew near me' (Ps. 27:2) refers to Goliath: 'And the Philistine drew near morning and night' (1 Sam. 17:16).

C.   "And it is written, 'And the Philistine came on and drew near to David' (1 Sam. 17:41).

D.   "'To eat my flesh' (Ps. 27:2): 'The Philistine said to David, "Come to me, and I will give your flesh to the birds of the air and to the beasts of the field"'" (1 Sam. 17:44).

II.2   A.   R. Abba b. R. Kahana said, "[Goliath had to tell David to come to him because] the earth held him fast."

B.   R. Tanhuma said, "I shall give scriptural proof for that proposition. 'And I shall come to you' is not what is written here, rather: 'Come to me.' That teaches that the earth held him fast."

C.   R. Yannai in the name of R. Simeon b. R. Yannai: "The Holy One, blessed be He, put two hundred forty locks on his two hundred forty-eight limbs."

D.   At that moment David said, "'Do not, O Lord, grant the desires of the wicked' (Ps. 140:8). Do not grant him his lust.

E.   "'Do not let loose his bit' (Ps. 140:8). Do not unloose it.

F. "'May they be high, *sela'* (*ib.*). Strengthen his bond [so that he cannot get loose].'"

G. R. Yudan said, "[Goliath] wanted David, because he had lovely eyes and was handsome. Thereupon David said, 'Do not, O Lord, grant the desires of the wicked' (Ps. 140:8) – his lust. 'But he will give the desire of the righteous'" (Prov. 10:24).

H. And rabbis say, "He smote him with leprosy, as you find in Scripture: 'He said, This day will the Lord shut you up through my hand' (1 Sam. 17:46). And the words 'shut up' refers only to leprosy, as you find in the verse: 'And the priest will shut up one afflicted by a leprosy sign'" (Lev. 13:4).

II.3 A. [Samuel b. R. Nahman continues:] "'My adversaries and foes, they stumbled and fell' (Ps. 27:2): 'And the stone sank into his forehead, and he fell' (1 Sam. 17:49).

B. "From that point on, it is David who said [the remainder of the Psalm] before the Holy One, blessed be He:

C. "'Though a host encamp against me' (Ps. 27:3): the camp of the Philistines.

D. "'My heart shall not fear' (Ps. 27:3).

E. "'Though war arise against me' (Ps. 27:3): war against the Philistines.

F. "'In this will I trust'" (Ps. 27:3).

G. "In this" (Ps. 27:3):

H. Said R. Levi, "'In the Scripture [farewell blessing] which Moses wrote in the scroll of the Torah for my forefathers: "And this is what he said of Judah: [Hear, O Lord, the voice of Judah and bring him in to his people. With your hands contend for him and be a help against his adversaries]"'" (Deut. 33:7).

III.1 A. R. Joshua b. Levi interpreted [the intersecting verse to speak] of the Amalekites:

B. "'When evildoers come near me' (Ps. 27:2) refers to the Amalekites: 'And the Amalekites made a raid on the Negeb and on Ziklag' (1 Sam. 30:1).

C. "'To eat my flesh' (Ps. 27:2): 'David's two wives also had been taken captive' (1 Sam. 30:5).

D. "'My adversaries and foes': 'And David smote them from twilight until the evening of the next day'" (1 Sam. 30:17).

III.2 A. What is the meaning of "of the next day?"

B. Said R. Joshua b. Levi, "Two nights and one day.

C. "Who provided light for him during the nights?

D. "The Holy One, blessed be He, provided light for him during the nights, through comets and lightning.

E. "It is to this that David speaks: 'For you illumine my lamp'" (Ps. 18:29).

III.3 A. (Joshua b. Levi continues:) "From that point [in the Psalm,] it is David who speaks.

B. "'Though a host encamp against me' – the camp of the Amalekites.

C. "'My heart shall not fear.'

D. "'Though war arise against me': the war of the Amalekites."

E. "In this I shall trust" (Ps. 27:3).

F. Said R. Levi, "In the Scripture [farewell blessing] which Moses wrote in the scroll of the Torah for my forefathers: 'And this is what he said of Judah'" (Deut. 33:7).

IV.1 A. Rabbis interpret [the intersecting] verse to speak of the New Year and Day of Atonement:

B. "'My light' (Ps. 27:1) is on the New Year.

C. "'And my salvation' (Ps. 27:1) is on the Day of Atonement.

D. "'Whom shall I fear' (Ps. 27:1): 'The Lord is my strength and my song' (Ex. 15:2).

E. "'When evildoers come near me' (Ps. 27:2) refers to the princes [of heaven] who represent the nations of the world.

F. "'To eat my flesh' (Ps. 27:2): For the princes representing the nations of the world come and draw an indictment against Israel before the Holy One, blessed be He, saying before him, 'Lord of the world, these [nations] practice idolatry and those [Jews] practice idolatry. These practice fornication and those practice fornication. These shed blood and those shed blood. Why then do these [nations of the world] go down to Gehenna and those do not go down?'

G. "'My adversaries and foes' (Ps. 27:2): You find that the number of days in the solar year are three hundred sixty-five, but the number of names of Satan are three hundred and sixty-four.

H. "For on all the days of the year, Satan is able to draw up an indictment, but on the Day of Atonement, Satan is not able to draw up an indictment.

I. "Said the Israelites before the Holy One, blessed be He, 'Though a host encamp against me' – the host of the nations of the world.

J. "'My heart shall not fear' (Ps. 27:3).

K. "'Though war arise against me' – the war of the nations of the world.

L. "'In this I shall trust' (Ps. 27:3).

M. "In this which you have promised me: 'With this will Aaron come' (Lev. 16:3) [on the Day of Atonement]."

III. Matters of Philosophy, Natural Science and Metaphysics

The parashah bears no interest for this rubric.

33

Leviticus Rabbah Parashah Twenty-Two

I. Unarticulated Premises: The Givens of Religious Conduct

There is nothing that requires our attention.

II. Unarticulated Premises: The Givens of Religious Conviction

1. The demands of the Torah are reasonable and balanced; everything is fair and just, and for each prohibition there is a remission:

XXII

X.1 A. ["Who executes justice for the oppressed, who gives food to the hungry. The Lord permits what is forbidden" (Ps. 146:7).] "Who executes justice for the oppressed" refers to Israel, concerning whom is written, "Thus says the Lord, the children of Israel are oppressed" (Jer. 50:33).

B. "Who gives food to the hungry" (Ps. 146:7) refers to Israel, concerning whom it is written, "And he afflicted you and made you suffer hunger" (Deut. 8:3).

C. "The Lord permits what is forbidden" (Ps. 146:7): "What I forbade to you, I have permitted to you.

D. "I forbade the abdominal fat in the case of domesticated cattle but permitted it in the case of wild beasts.

E. "I forbade you to eat the sciatic nerve in a wild beast, but I permitted it to you in fowl.

F. "I forbade you beasts not killed through proper slaughter in the case of fowl, but I permitted the same in the case of fish."

X.2 A. R. Aha, R. Bisna, and R. Jonathan in the name of R. Meir: "More that I prohibited to you, I permitted to you.

B. "I forbade you to have sexual relations in the presence of menstrual blood, but I permitted you to have sexual relations despite the presence of hymeneal blood.

C. "I forbade you [to have sexual relations with] a married woman but I permitted you [to have sexual relations with] a captive woman [regardless of her marital status].

D. "I forbade you [to have sexual relations with] a brother's wife [or widow], but I permitted you [to marry] the deceased childless brother's widow.

E. "I forbade you to marry a woman along with her sister, but I permitted you to do so after the sister [you married] had died.

F. "I forbade you to wear a garment made of mixed species [wool and linen], but I permitted you to wear a linen cloak with show fringes made of wool.

G. "I forbade you to eat the meat of a pig, but I permitted you to eat the tongue of a fish [which tastes like pork].

H. "I forbade you to eat abdominal fat [of a beast], but I permitted you to eat ordinary fat.

I. "I forbade you to eat blood, but I permitted you to eat liver.

J. "I forbade you to eat meat with milk, but I permitted you to eat the cow's udder."

X.3 A. R. Menahama, R. Aha, R. Yohanan in the name of R. Jonathan: "In place of whatever I forbade to you, I permitted something to you.

B. "In place of the prohibition of certain kinds of fish [you may eat] the Leviathan, a clean fish.

C. "In place of the prohibition of certain kinds of fowl [you may eat] *ziz,* a clean bird.

D. "That is in line with the following verse of Scripture: 'I know all the fowl of the mountains, and the *ziz* of the fields is mine'" (Ps. 50:11).

III. Matters of Philosophy, Natural Science and Metaphysics

This category does not apply.

34

Leviticus Rabbah Parashah
Twenty-Three

I. Unarticulated Premises: The Givens of Religious Conduct

The entry at the second rubric is relevant in a rather general way to the matter of law.

II. Unarticulated Premises: The Givens of Religious Conviction

The Israelites differ from the nations, and on that account will be worthy of being redeemed; God saved the entire world on account of Israel:

XXIII

I.1   A.   "[And the Lord said to Moses, Say to the people of Israel, I am the Lord your God.] You shall not do as they do in the land of Egypt [where you dwelt, and you shall not do as they do in the land of Canaan, to which I am bringing you]" (Lev. 18:1-3).

II.1   A.   R. Eleazar interpreted the same verse to speak of those who came forth from Egypt: "'Like a rose among thorns':

      B.   "Just as it is difficult to pick a rose [among thorns], so it was hard to redeem the Israelites from Egypt.

      C.   "That is in line with the following verse of Scripture: 'Or has God tried to come to take a nation for himself from the midst of another nation'" (Deut. 4:34).

II.2   A.   R. Joshua b. R. Nehemiah in the name of R. Samuel b. Pazzi: "'A nation from the midst of a people' is not written here, nor [do we find], 'a people from the midst of a nation,' but, 'a nation from the midst of a nation.'

      B.   "For [the Egyptians] were uncircumcised, and the Israelites also were uncircumcised. The Egyptians grew [ceremonial] locks, and so did the Israelites. The Egyptians wore garments made of mixed species, and so did the Israelites.

C. "Therefore by the measure of strict justice, the Israelites ought not have been redeemed from Egypt."

D. Said R. Samuel b. R. Nahmani, "If the Holy One, blessed be He, had not bound himself by an oath, the Israelites would never have been redeemed from Egypt.

E. "'Therefore say to the children of Israel, I am the Lord, and I shall take you out of the burdens of Egypt' (Ex. 6:6).

F. "The language, 'therefore,' can refer only to an oath, as it is said, 'Therefore I take an oath concerning the house of Eli'" (1 Sam. 3:14).

II.3 A. Said R. Berekhiah, "'You have redeemed your people with your arm' (Ps. 77:16) – with naked power (tyranny)."

B. Said R. Yudan, "From the phrase, 'To go and take a nation from the midst of another nation' to the phrase 'great terrors' [Deut. 4:34] are seventy-two letters.

C. "Should you claim there are more, you should deduct from the count the last reference to 'nation [= Egypt],' which does not count."

D. R. Abin said, "It was for the sake of his name that he redeemed them, and the name of the Holy One, blessed be He, consists of seventy-two letters."

III.1 A. R. Judah b. R. Simon in the name of R. Azariah interpreted the cited verse to speak of Israel before Mount Sinai:

B. "'Like a rose among thorns': The matter may be compared to a king who had an orchard. He planted in it rows upon rows of figs, grapevines, and pomegranates. After a while the king went down to his vineyard and found it filled with thorns and brambles. He brought woodcutters to cut it down. But he found in the orchard a single red rose. He took it and smelled it and regained his serenity and said, 'This rose is worthy that the entire orchard be saved on its account.'

C. "So, too, the entire world was created only on account of the Torah. For twenty-six generations, the Holy One, blessed be He, looked down upon his world and saw it full of thorns and brambles, for example, the Generation of Enosh, the Generation of the Flood, and the Sodomites.

D. "He planned to render the world useless and to destroy it, as it is said, 'The Lord sat enthroned at the flood' (Ps. 29:10).

E. "But he found in the world a single red rose, Israel, that was destined to stand before Mount Sinai and to say before the Holy One, blessed be He, 'Whatever the Lord has said we shall do and we shall hear' (Ex. 24:7).

F. "Said the Holy One, blessed be He, Israel is worthy that the entire world be saved on its account.'"

Israel's suffering among the nations leads them to look upward to their father in heaven; it is good for Israel to be surrounded by enemies; Israel will be redeemed at the expense of its enemies:

XXIII

V.1 A. R. Hanina son of R. Idi interpreted the verse to speak of the current generations:

B.   "'Like a rose among thorns': Just as, when the north wind blows on the rose, it bends southward, and a thorn pricks it, and when the south wind blows, it bends northward, and a thorn pricks it, and all the while, the heart [of its stem] points upward,

C.   "so even though Israel is enslaved among the nations of the world by surcharges, head taxes, and confiscations, nonetheless their heart points upward toward their father in heaven.

D.   "So did David say, 'My heart is steadfast, O God, my heart is steadfast. I will sing and make melody!' (Ps. 57:8). And what is further written? 'My eyes are always toward the Lord'" (Ps. 25:15).

V.2   A.   R. Abihu interpreted the cited verse to speak of the coming redemption:

B.   "'Like a rose among thorns': Just as when a householder wants to pick a rose, he burns [the thorns] around it and plucks it,

C.   "so: 'The Lord has commanded concerning Jacob that those who are around him should be his enemies' (Lam. 1:17).

D.   "For example, Halamo [which is gentile, is enemy] to Naweh [which is Israelite], Susita to Tiberias, Qastra to Haifa, Jericho to Nauran, Lud to Ono.

E.   "That is in line with the following verse of Scripture: 'This is Jerusalem. I have set her in the midst of the gentiles' (Ezek. 5:5).

F.   "Tomorrow, when redemption comes to Israel, what will the Holy One, blessed be He, do to them? He will bring a flame and burn [the area] around [Israel].

G.   "That is in line with the following verse of Scripture: 'And the peoples will be as burnings of lime, as thorns cut down that are burned in fire'" (Isa. 33:12).

III. Matters of Philosophy, Natural Science and Metaphysics

This rubric serves here no better than it does anywhere else.

35

Leviticus Rabbah Parashah Twenty-Four

I. Unarticulated Premises: The Givens of Religious Conduct

There are no legal points of interest here.

II. Unarticulated Premises: The Givens of Religious Conviction

God's justice is perfect, and it is what exalts him; when God raises up a person, caste, or nation, it is permanent and forever; God's justice is to exalt others:

XXIV

I.1 A. "You shall be holy [for I the Lord your God am Holy]" (Lev. 19:2).

B. "But the Lord of hosts is exalted in justice, [and the holy God shows himself holy in righteousness]" (Isa. 5:16).

C. It has been taught: Said R. Simeon b. Yohai, "When is the name of the Holy One, blessed be He, magnified in his world?

D. "When he applies the attribute of justice to the wicked.

E. "And there are many verses of Scripture [that prove that point]:

F. "'Thus I shall magnify myself and sanctify myself and make myself known [in the eyes of many nations]' (Ezek. 38:23).

G. "'The Lord has made himself known, he has executed judgment' (Ps. 9:7).

H. "'I will make myself known among them when I judge you' (Ezek. 35:11).

I. "'And it shall be known that the hand of the Lord is with his servants, [and his indignation is against his enemies]' (Isa. 66:14).

J. "'This time I shall make them know [my hand and my might]' (Jer. 16:21).

K. "'That you may know the hand of the Lord' (Hos. 4:24).

L. "And this verse: 'But the Lord of hosts is exalted in justice'" (Isa. 5:16).

II.1 A. R. Berekhiah in the name of R. Levi, "It is written, 'But you, O Lord, are on high forever' (Ps. 92:8).

B.   "Your hand is always on top.

C.   "Under ordinary circumstances, when a mortal king sits in judgment, when he hands down an acquittal, everybody praises him, but when he hands down a verdict of guilty, nobody praises him. Why? Because people know that passion affects his judgment.

D.   "But with the Holy One, blessed be He, that is not how things are.

E.   "Rather, whether it is the attribute of goodness or the attribute of punishment: 'But you, O Lord, are on high forever.' Your hand is on top."

II.2   A.   R. Huna in the name of R. Aha produces the following verse: "'A Psalm of David. I will sing of mercy and of justice, to you, O Lord, will I sing' (Ps. 101:1).

B.   "Said David before the Holy One, blessed be He, 'Lord of the world, if you act mercifully with me, I shall sing, if you impose justice on me, I shall sing. One way or the other: 'To you, O Lord, shall I sing.'"

II.3   A.   Said R. Tanhum b. R. Yudan, "It is written, 'In God, whose word I praise, in the Lord, whose word I praise' (Ps. 56:11).

B.   "If it is with the attribute of justice that he comes to deal with me: 'In God, whose word I praise.'

C.   "If it is with the attribute of mercy that he comes to deal with me: 'In the Lord, whose word I praise.'

D.   "One way or the other: 'In the Lord, whose word I praise.'"

II.4   A.   And rabbis say, "'I suffered distress and anguish. Then I called on the name of the Lord' (Ps. 116:3-4). 'I will lift up the cup of salvation and call on the name of the Lord' (Ps. 116:13).

B.   "One way or the other: 'Then I called on the name of the Lord.'"

II.5   A.   Said R. Yudan b. R. Philia, "That is the meaning of what Job said: 'The Lord has given, and the Lord has taken, let the name of the Lord be blessed' (Job 1:21).

B.   "If he gave, he gave in mercy, and if he took, he took in mercy.

C.   "And not only so, but when he gave, he did not consult with any creature, and when he took, he did consult with his court."

D.   Said R. Eleazar, "In any context in which you find the word, 'the Lord...and the Lord...,' it is, as it were, a reference to him and his court.

E.   "The generative source of all of them: 'And the Lord has spoken ill concerning you'" (1 Kgs. 22:23).

II.6   A.   Said R. Yudan, "It is written, 'You, O Lord, are on high forever more' (Ps. 92:9).

B.   "You give high status in your world. You gave the priesthood to Aaron forever: 'It is an everlasting covenant of salt' (Num. 18:19).

C.   "You gave the monarchy to David forever: 'Should you not know that the Lord, God of Israel, gave the monarchy [over Israel to David forever]' (2 Chr. 13:5).

D.   "You gave holiness to Israel forever: 'Speak to all the congregation of the people of Israel, You shall be holy'" (Lev. 19:2).

III. Matters of Philosophy, Natural Science and Metaphysics

I find nothing that pertains.

36

Leviticus Rabbah Parashah Twenty-Five

I. Unarticulated Premises: The Givens of Religious Conduct

While the topic concerns the law, there are no premises of a legal order in this parashah.

II. Unarticulated Premises: The Givens of Religious Conviction

1. The Torah protects Israel and keeps Israel:

XXV

I.1   A.   "When you come into the land and plant [all kinds of trees for food, then you shall count their fruit as forbidden; three years it shall be forbidden to you, it must not be eaten. And in the fourth year all their fruit shall be holy, an offering of praise to the Lord. But in the fifth year you may eat of their fruit, that they may yield more richly for you: I am the Lord your God]" (Lev. 19:23-25).

B.   "She [= wisdom, Torah] is a tree of life to those who lay hold of her; [and those who hold her fast are called happy]" (Prov. 3:18).

C.   R. Huna in the name of R. Aha: "[The meaning is] that the words of Torah should not appear in your sight like the case of a man who had a daughter of marriageable age, whom he wanted to attach to anyone [he could find].

D.   "Rather: 'My son, if you receive my words and treasure up my commandments with you [then you will understand the fear of the Lord and find the knowledge of God]' (Prov. 2:1).

E.   "If you have merit, you will receive my words."

F.   R. Hunia in the name of R. Benjamin b. Levi: "[The matter may be compared] to the case of a king who said to his son, 'Go out and take up trading.'

G.   "He said to him, 'Father, I am afraid, by land of thugs, and by sea of pirates.'

H.   "What did his father do for him? He took a staff and hollowed it out and put an amulet in it and handed it over to his son, saying to him, 'Let this staff be in your hand, and you will not have to be afraid of anybody.'

I.   "So said the Holy One, blessed be He, to Israel, 'My children, keep yourselves busy in the Torah, and you will not have to be afraid of anybody.'"

I.2   A.   [With reference to "She is a tree of life to those that lay hold of her," including those who support the ones who actually study Torah, and now speaking of the following verse: "Cursed be he who does not confirm the words of this law by doing them" (Deut. 27:26)], had the cited verse stated, "Cursed be he who does not study [the words of this Torah]," there would be no enduring [for Israel, since most of the Jews do not study the Torah].

B.   But [it says], "Cursed be he who does not confirm...," [and the Jews do carry out the teachings of the Torah].

C.   If it had said, "She is a tree of life to those that labor in her," there would be no enduring.

D.   But [it says], "She is a tree of life to those that lay hold of her," [by supporting and following the ones who do study the Torah].

I.3   A.   R. Huna said, "If a person stumbles into a transgression so that he becomes liable to death at the hands of heaven, what should he do so that he may live?

B.   "If he was trained to recite a single page of Scripture, let him recite two, if he was trained to repeat one chapter of Mishnah, let him repeat two.

C.   "And if he was not trained either to recite Scripture or to repeat Mishnah, what should he do so as to live?

D.   "Let him go and take up the responsibility of communal leader or charity collector, and he will live.

E.   "For if it had said 'Cursed be he who does not study...,' there would be no enduring. But [it says], 'Cursed be he who does not confirm.'

F.   "If it had said, 'It is a tree of life to those that labor in it,' there would be no enduring, but [it says], 'It is a tree of life to those that lay hold of it.'"

I.4   A.   "For wisdom is a defense as money is a defense" (Qoh. 7:12).

B.   R. Aha in the name of R. Tanhum b. R. Hiyya: "If one had learned Torah and taught it, kept and done [its teachings], but had the power to protest [wrongdoing] and did not protest, or to support [disciples of sages] and did not support them, lo, this one falls into the category of cursed.

C.   "That is in line with the following verse of Scripture: '[Cursed be he] who does not confirm...'" (Deut. 27:26).

D.   R. Jeremiah in the name of R. Hiyya: "If one did not study [Torah] and did not carry out [its teachings], did not keep them and did not teach them to others, and did not have the power to support [disciples of sages] but [nonetheless] he did so, [or] did not have the power to protest [wrongdoing] but nonetheless he did so, lo, this one falls into the category of blessed."

2. The Jew who keeps the Torah is honored even by the enemies of Israel; the Jew who emulates that person without understanding his actions is a nullity:

XXV

V.2 A.   Hadrian (may his bones be ground up) was walking through the paths of Tiberias. He saw an old man standing and digging holes to plant trees. He said to him, "Old man, old man, if you got up early [to do the work, when you were young], you would not have stayed late [to plant in your old age]."

B.   He said to him, "I got up early [and worked in my youth] and I stayed late [working in my old age], and whatever pleases the Master of heaven, let him do."

C.   He said to him, "By your life, old man! How old are you today?"

D.   He said to him, "I am a hundred years old."

E.   He said to him, "Now you are a hundred years old, and you are standing and digging holes to plant trees! Do you honestly think that you're going to eat the fruit of those trees?"

F.   He said to him, "If I have the merit, I shall eat it. But if not, well, just as my forefathers labored for me, so I labor for my children."

G.   He said to him, "By your life! If you have the merit of eating of the fruit of these trees, be sure to let me know about it."

H.   After some time the trees produced figs. The man said, "Lo, the time has come to tell the king."

I.   What did he do? He filled a basket with figs and went up and stood at the gate of the palace.

J.   [The guards] said to him, "What is your business here?"

K.   He said, "To come before the king."

L.   When he had gone in, he said to him, "What are you doing here?"

M.   He said to him, "I am the old man you met. I was the one who was digging holes to plant trees, and you said to me, 'If you have the merit of eating the fruit of those trees, be sure to let me know.' Now I in fact did have the merit, and I ate of their fruit, and these figs here are the fruit of those trees."

N.   Then said Hadrian, "I order you to bring a chair of gold for him to sit on.

O.   "I order you to empty this basket of his and fill it with golden denars."

P.   His servants said to him, "Are you going to pay so much respect to that old Jew?"

Q.   He said to him, "His Creator honors him, and should I not honor him?"

R.   The wife of the neighbor [of that man] was wicked. She said to her husband, "Son of darkness, see how the king loves figs and trades them for golden denars."

S.   What did [the man] do? He filled a sack with figs and went and stood before the palace.

T.   They said to him, "What is your business here?"

U.   He said to them, "I heard that the king loves figs and trades them for golden denars."

V.   They went and told the king, "There is an old man standing at the
      gate of the palace carrying a sackful of figs. When we asked him,
      'What are you doing here,' he told us, 'I heard that the king loves
      figs and trades them for golden denars.'"

W.   [The king] said, "I order you to set him up before the gate of the
      palace. Whoever goes in and out is to throw [a fig] in his face."

X.   Toward evening they freed him and he went home. He said to his
      wife, "For all the honor [that I got], I owe you!"

Y.   She said, "Go and boast to your mother that they were figs and not
      etrogs, that they were soft and not hard!"

III. Matters of Philosophy, Natural Science and Metaphysics

The category is useless.

37

Leviticus Rabbah Parashah Twenty-Six

I. Unarticulated Premises: The Givens of Religious Conduct

Nothing pertains.

II. Unarticulated Premises: The Givens of Religious Conviction

1. Worse than idolatry is the betrayal of the renegade:

XXVI

II.1	A.	R. Yosé of Malehayya and R. Joshua of Sikhnin, in the name of R. Levi: "Children in David's time, before they had tasted the taste of sin [reached sexual maturity], were able to expound the Torah in forty-nine different ways to reach a decision on uncleanness, and in forty-nine different ways to reach a decision on cleanness.
	B.	"And David prayed for them: 'You, O Lord, protect them' (Ps. 12:7).
	C.	"Preserve their learning in their heart.
	D.	"'Protect them forever from this generation'" (Ps. 12:7).
	E.	"From the generation that deserves destruction."
II.2	A.	After all this glory, [that generation of disciples] went out to war and fell.
	B.	It was because there were renegades among them.
	C.	That is in line with what David says, "My soul is in the midst of lions. I lie down among them that are aflame, sons of men whose teeth are spears and arrows, their tongues sharp swords" (Ps. 57:4).
	D.	"My soul is in the midst of lions" refers to Abner and Amasa, who were lions in the Torah.
	E.	"I lie down among them that are aflame" refers to Doeg and Ahitophel, who were burning with gossip.
	F.	"Sons of men whose teeth are spears and arrows" refers to the men of Keilah: "Will the men of Keilah hand me over?" (1 Sam. 32:11).

G.   "Their tongues are sharp swords" refers to the Ziphites: "When the Ziphites came and said to Saul, 'Does David not hide himself with us?'" (1 Sam. 23:19).

H.   At that moment said David, "Now what is the Presence of God doing in the world? 'Be exalted, O God, above the heavens' (Ps. 57:5). Remove your Presence from their midst!"

I.   But the generation of Ahab was made up of idolators. But because there were no renegades among them, they would go out to war and win.

J.   That is in line with what Obadiah said to Elijah: "Has it not been told my lord what I did when Jezebel killed the prophets of the Lord, how I hid a hundred men of the Lord's prophets by fifties in a cave and fed them with bread and water?" (1 Kgs. 18:13).

K.   If bread, why water? But this teaches that it was harder to bring the water than the bread.

L.   Elijah proclaimed on Mount Carmel, saying, "And I alone remain as a prophet to the Lord" (1 Kgs. 18:22).

M.   Now the entire people were well informed [that there were other prophets who had survived], but they did not reveal it to the king.

III. Matters of Philosophy, Natural Science and Metaphysics

This category does not apply.

38

Leviticus Rabbah Parashah Twenty-Seven

I. Unarticulated Premises: The Givens of Religious Conduct

There is some interest in the correspondence of the regulations of the cult to the life of the patriarchs, for example,

XXVII

IX.1 A. "A bull, a sheep, or a goat" (Lev. 22:27):

B. "A bull" on account of the merit of Abraham, as it is said: "And Abraham ran to the herd and took a calf" (Gen. 18:7).

C. "A sheep" on account of the merit of Isaac, as it is written, "And he looked, and behold, a ram caught by its horns" (Gen. 22:13).

D. "A goat" on account of the merit of Jacob, as it is written in his regard, "Now go to the flock and get me two good kid goats" (Gen. 27:9).

That premise is routine; what makes it interesting is the specific points at which it is articulated.

II. Unarticulated Premises: The Givens of Religious Conviction

1. God favors the pursued over the pursuer, the persecuted over the persecutor, and this is proven by the history of Israel:

XXVII

V.1 A. "God seeks what has been driven away" (Qoh. 3:15).

B. R. Huna in the name of R. Joseph said, "It is always the case that 'God seeks what has been driven away' [favoring the victim].

C. "You find when a righteous man pursues a righteous man, 'God seeks what has been driven away.'

D. "When a wicked man pursues a wicked man, 'God seeks what has been driven away.'

E.   "All the more so when a wicked man pursues a righteous man, 'God seeks what has been driven away.'

F.   "[The same principle applies] even when you come around to a case in which a righteous man pursues a wicked man, 'God seeks what has been driven away.'"

V.2 A.   R. Yosé b. R. Yudan in the name of R. Yosé b. R. Nehorai says, "It is always the case that the Holy One, blessed be He, demands an accounting for the blood of those who have been pursued from the hand of the pursuer.

B.   "Abel was pursued by Cain, and God sought [an accounting for] the pursued: 'And the Lord looked [favorably] upon Abel and his meal-offering' (Gen. 4:4).

C.   "Noah was pursued by his generation, and God sought [an accounting for] the pursued: 'You and all your household shall come into the ark' (Gen. 7:1). And it says, 'For this is like the days of Noah to me, as I swore [that the waters of Noah should no more go over the earth]' (Isa. 54:9).

D.   "Abraham was pursued by Nimrod, 'and God seeks what has been driven away': 'You are the Lord, the God who chose Abram and brought him out of Ur' (Neh. 9:7).

E.   "Isaac was pursued by Ishmael, 'and God seeks what has been driven away': 'For through Isaac will seed be called for you' (Gen. 21:12).

F.   "Jacob was pursued by Esau, 'and God seeks what has been driven away': 'For the Lord has chosen Jacob, Israel for his prized possession' (Ps. 135:4).

G.   "Moses was pursued by Pharaoh, 'and God seeks what has been driven away': 'Had not Moses His chosen stood in the breach before Him' (Ps. 106:23).

H.   "David was pursued by Saul, 'and God seeks what has been driven away': 'And he chose David, his servant' (Ps. 78:70).

I.   "Israel was pursued by the nations, 'and God seeks what has been driven away': 'And you has the Lord chosen to be a people to him' (Deut. 14:2).

J.   "And the rule applies also to the matter of offerings. A bull is pursued by a lion, a sheep is pursued by a wolf, a goat is pursued by a leopard.

K.   "Therefore the Holy One, blessed be He, has said, 'Do not make offerings before me from those animals that pursue, but from those that are pursued: 'When a bull, a sheep, or a goat is born'" (Lev. 22:27).

2.   The enmity of the nations assures God's forgiveness of Israel; he will not give them occasion to rejoice over the fall of Israel:

XXVII

VI.1 A.   "O my people, what have I done to you, in what have I wearied you? Testify against me" (Mic. 6:3).

B.   Said R. Aha, "'Testify against me' and receive a reward, but 'Do not bear false witness' (Ex. 20:13) and face a settlement of accounts in the age to come."

VI.2 A. Said R. Samuel b. R. Nahman, "On three occasions the Holy One, blessed be He, came to engage in argument with Israel, and the nations of the world rejoiced, saying, 'Can these ever [dare] engage in an argument with their creator? Now he will wipe them out of the world.'

B. "One was when he said to them, 'Come, and let us reason together, says the Lord' (Isa. 1:18). When the Holy One, blessed be He, saw that the nations of the world were rejoicing, he turned the matter to [Israel's] advantage: 'If your sins are as scarlet, they shall be white as snow' (Isa. 1:18).

C. "Then the nations of the world were astonished, and said, 'This is repentance, and this is rebuke? He has planned only to amuse himself with his children.'

D. "[A second time was] when he said to them, 'Hear, you mountains, the controversy of the Lord' (Mic. 6:2), the nations of the world rejoiced, saying, 'How can these ever [dare] engage in an argument with their creator? Now he will wipe them out of the world.'

E. "When the Holy One, blessed be He, saw that the nations of the world were rejoicing, he turned the matter to [Israel's] advantage: 'O my people, what have I done to you? In what have I wearied you? Testify against me' (Mic. 6:3). 'Remember what Balak king of Moab devised' (Mic. 6:5).

F. "Then the nations of the world were astonished, saying, 'This is repentence, and this is rebuke, one following the other? He has planned only to amuse himself with his children.'

G. "[A third time was] when he said to them, 'The Lord has an indictment against Judah, and will punish Jacob according to his ways' (Hos. 12:2), the nations of the world rejoiced, saying, 'How can these ever [dare] engage in an argument with their creator? Now he will wipe them out of the world.'

H. "When the Holy One, blessed be He, saw that the nations of the world were rejoicing, he turned the matter to [Israel's] advantage. That is in line with the following verse of Scripture: 'In the womb he [Jacob = Israel] took his brother [Esau = other nations] by the heel [and in his manhood he strove with God. He strove with the angel and prevailed, he wept and sought his favor]'" (Hos. 12:3-4).

VI.3 A. Said R. Yudan b. R. Simeon, "The matter may be compared to a widow who was complaining to a judge about her son. When she saw that the judge was in session and handing out sentences of punishment by fire, pitch, and lashes, she said, 'If I report the bad conduct of my son to that judge, he will kill him now.' She waited until he was finished. When he had finished, he said to her, 'Madam, this son of yours, how has he behaved badly toward you?'

B. "She said to him, 'My lord, when he was in my womb, he kicked me.'

C. "He said to her, 'Now has he done anything wrong to you?'

D. "She said to him, 'No.'

E. "He said to her, 'Go your way, there is nothing wrong in the matter [that you report].

F. "So, when the Holy One, blessed be He, saw that the nations of the world were rejoicing, he turned the matter to [Israel's] advantage:

G.   "'In the womb he took his brother by the heel' (Mic. 12:3).

H.   "Then the nations of the world were astonished, saying, 'This is repentence and this is rebuke, one following the other? He has planned only to amuse himself with his children.'"

III. Matters of Philosophy, Natural Science and Metaphysics

Nothing belongs here.

39

Leviticus Rabbah Parashah Twenty-Eight

I. Unarticulated Premises: The Givens of Religious Conduct

We find a reference to a Mishnah law but no extensive analysis of its contents, nor interest in generalizing through a premise or presupposition pertinent elsewhere.

II. Unarticulated Premises: The Givens of Religious Conviction

1. In the end of time God will give to Israel the dominions of those who have persecuted them:

XXVIII

IV.1 A. "His harvest the hungry eat, and he takes it even without a buckler; and the thirsty pant after their wealth" (Job 5:5).

B. "His harvest" refers to the four kingdoms [of Gen. 14:1].

C. "The hungry eat" refers to our father, Abraham.

D. "And he takes it even without a buckler" – without a sword, without a shield, but with prayer and supplications.

E. This is in line with the following verse of Scripture: "He led forth his trained servants [empty-handed, understanding the Hebrew word RK as empty], those born of his house, three hundred and eighteen" (Gen. 14:14).

F. Said R. Simeon b. Laqish, "It was Eliezer alone [whom Abraham took with him]. And how do we know? [The numerical value of the letters that make up the Hebrew name] Eliezer adds up to three hundred and eighteen.

G. "And the thirsty pant after their wealth" – who trampled on the wealth of the four kingdoms? It was Abraham and all those who were allied with him.

IV.2 A. Another interpretation: "His harvest" refers to Pharaoh.

B. "The hungry eat" refers to Moses.

C.   "And he takes it even without a buckler" – without a sword, without a shield, but with prayer and supplications.

D.   "And the Lord said to Moses, 'Why do you cry out to me?'" (Ex. 14:15).

E.   "And the thirsty pant after their wealth" – who trampled the wealth of Pharaoh? It was Moses and all those who were allied with him.

IV.3 A.   Another interpretation: "His harvest" refers to Sihon and Og.

B.   "The hungry eat" refers to Moses.

C.   "And he takes it even without a buckler" – without a sword, without a shield, but with a [mere] word.

D.   "And the Lord said to Moses, 'Be not afraid of him, because I have given him into your hand'" (Num. 21:34).

E.   "And the thirsty pant after their wealth" – who trampled on the wealth of Sihon and Og? It was Moses and all those who were allied with him.

IV.4 A.   Another interpretation: "His harvest" refers to the Canaanites.

B.   "The hungry eat" refers to Joshua.

C.   "And he takes it even without a buckler" – without a sword, without a shield, but with hailstones.

D.   That is in line with the following verse of Scripture: "And as they fled before Israel, while they were going down the ascent of Beth-horon, the Lord threw down great stones from heaven upon them [as far as Azekah, and they died; there were more who died because of the hailstones than the men of Israel killed with the sword]" (Josh. 10:11).

E.   "And the thirsty pant after their wealth" – who trampled upon the wealth of the Canaanites? It was Joshua and all those who were allied with him.

IV.5 A.   Another interpretation: "His harvest" refers to Sisera.

B.   "The hungry eat" refers to Deborah and Barak.

C.   "And he takes it even without a buckler" – without a sword, without a shield, but [solely] by means of good deeds.

D.   That is in line with the following verse of Scripture: "Was shield or spear to be seen among forty thousand in Israel?" (Jud. 5:8).

E.   "And the thirsty pant after their wealth" – who trampled on the wealth of Sisera? It was Deborah and Barak and all those who were allied with them.

IV.6 A.   Another interpretation: "His harvest" refers to Sennacherib.

B.   "The hungry eat" refers to Hezekiah.

C.   "And he takes it even without a buckler" – without a sword, without a shield, but [solely] through prayer.

D.   "And Hezekiah the king and Isaiah ben Amoz, the prophet, prayed concerning this matter" (2 Chr. 32:20).

E.   "And the thirsty pant after their wealth" – who trampled on the wealth of Sennacherib? It was Hezekiah and all those who were allied with him.

IV.7 A.   Another interpretation: "His harvest" refers to Haman.

B.   "The hungry eat" refers to Mordecai.

C.   "And he takes it even without a buckler" – without a sword, without a shield, but solely with sack and ashes, as it is said, "Many lay in sackcloth and ashes" (Est. 4:3).

D.   "And the thirsty pant after their wealth" – who trampled upon the wealth of Haman? It was Mordecai and Esther and all those who were allied with them.

IV.8   A.   Said the Holy One, blessed be He, to Israel, "My children, I have fed you the harvest of the kingdoms. Take care that others not come and eat your harvest."

B.   Therefore Moses admonished the Israelites, saying to them, "When you come into the land which I give you and reap its harvest, you shall bring the sheaf of the first fruits of your harvest to the priest" (Lev. 23:10).

III. Matters of Philosophy, Natural Science and Metaphysics

The category is irrelevant.

40

Leviticus Rabbah Parashah Twenty-Nine

I. Unarticulated Premises: The Givens of Religious Conduct

1. Scripture supports changes in the law when these are called for:

XXIX

XII.1 A. R. Yohanan and R. Simeon b. Laqish were in session, raising a question about traditions. Kahana came by. They said, "Lo, here comes the authority for the tradition. Let us arise and raise our question for him."

B. They arose and asked him as follows: "We have learned [at M.R.H. 4:1], 'In the case of the festival day of the New Year that coincided with the Sabbath, in the sanctuary they would sound the shofar horn, but not in the countryside. When the house of the sanctuary was destroyed, Rabban Yohanan ben Zakkai made the ordinance that they should sound the shofar horn wherever a court was located.'

C. "Now if it is a matter of Torah law [that the shofar is sounded], then it should override [the considerations of Sabbath rest even] in the provinces. And if it is not [a matter of Torah law], then even in the sanctuary, [sounding the shofar horn] should not override [the considerations of Sabbath rest]."

D. He said to them, "One verse of Scripture states, 'You will have a day for sounding the horn' (Num. 29:1). Another verse of Scripture says, 'A Sabbath of remembrance of the sounding of the horn, a holy convocation' (Lev. 23:24).

E. "Now how [may the two verses be harmonized]? On an occasion on which [the holiday] coincides with an ordinary day [not a Sabbath], 'You will have a day for sounding the horn' (Num. 29:1). On an occasion on which [the holiday] coincides with the Sabbath, 'A Sabbath of remembrance of the sounding of the horn, a holy convocation,' (Lev. 23:24), meaning that they make mention [of the sounding of the horn] but they do not sound [the horn]."

II. Unarticulated Premises: The Givens of Religious Conviction

1. The nations rise and fall. Israel's history is eternal; even though God punishes Israel, Israel will endure in the world to come. Its history follows a different paradigm from that of the nations:

XXIX

II.1 A. R. Nahman commenced (discourse by citing the following verse): "'Then fear not, O Jacob my servant, says the Lord, nor be dismayed, O Israel, for lo, I will save you from afar, and your offspring from the land of their captivity. Jacob shall return and have quiet and ease, and none shall make him afraid' (Jer. 30:10).

B. "The verse speaks of Jacob: 'And he dreamed that there was a ladder set up on the earth, and the top of it reached to heaven, and behold the angels of God were ascending and descending on it'" (Gen. 28:12).

C. Said R. Samuel b. R. Nahman, "Now do you think that they were ministering angels? Were they not only the princes of [representing] the nations of the world. [God] showed [Jacob] the prince of Babylonia going up seventy steps, the one of Media going up fifty-two steps, the one of Greece one hundred eighty steps. And as to the one representing Edom [Rome], he kept going up and [Jacob] did not know how many [steps he was going up, thus how long he would rule].

D. "[Jacob] said before him, 'Lord of the ages! Will you say that he, too, is subject to decline?'

E. "Said to him the Holy One, blessed be He, 'Jacob! Even if you see that he reaches heaven, I shall bring him down.'

F. "That is in line with the following verse of Scripture: 'Though you make your nest as high as the eagle, and though you set it among the stars, I will bring you down from there'" (Obad. 1:4).

G. R. Berekhiah, R. Helbo in the name of R. Simeon b. Menassia in the name of R. Meir: "He showed him the prince of Babylonia going up and coming down, and the one of Media going up and coming down, and the one of Greece going up and coming down, and also the one of Edom going up and coming down.

H. "He said before him, 'Lord of the ages! Is it the case that just as these are subject to decline, so I, too, am subject to decline?'

I. "He said to him, 'Fear not. For the [sort of] ascent that you will make, there is no descent.' Nonetheless, he feared and did not ascend."

J. R. Berekhiah, R. Helbo, and R. Simeon b. Menassia: "Meir expounded [the following verse:] 'Nonetheless they still sinned and did not believe in his wondrous works' (Ps. 78:32). [This verse] speaks of Jacob, who did not believe and so did not ascend.

K. "Said to him the Holy One, blessed be He, 'Jacob! If you had believed and ascended, you would never again have gone down. Now that you did not believe and did not ascend, lo, your sons will be held fast among the nations and wander aimlessly among the kingdoms, from one to the next, from Babylonia to Media, from Media to Greece, and from Greece to Edom.'

L.   "He said before him, 'Lord of the ages, is it forever?'

M.   "Said to him the Holy One, blessed be He, 'Then fear not, O Jacob my servant...nor be dismayed, O Israel, for lo, I will save you from afar' (Jer. 30:10): from Gallia and Aspamea and nearby lands.

N.   "'And your offspring from the land of their captivity': 'Jacob shall return from Babylonia.

O.   "'And have quiet' from Media.

P.   "'And ease' from Greece.

Q.   'And none shall make him afraid' on account of Edom."

II.2 A.   "I will make a full end of all the nations" (Jer. 30:11). As to the nations of the world, because they make a full end [when they harvest even the corner of] their field, "I will make a full end of all the nations among whom I scattered you."

B.   But as to Israel, because they do not make a full end [when they harvest, for they leave the corner of] their field, therefore: "But of you I will not make a full end" (Jer. 30:11).

C.   "I will chasten you in just measure, and I will by no means leave you unpunished" (Jer. 30:11). I shall chasten you through suffering in this world, so as to leave you unpunished in the world to come.

D.   When? On the New Year.

E.   "In the seventh month, on the first day of the month" (Lev. 23:24).

2.   Israel endures through the merit of the patriarchs, beginning with Abraham:

XXIX

X.1 A.   R. Judah b. R. Simon in the name of R. Joshua b. Levi: "It is written, 'And Abraham raised his eyes, and he saw, and behold, a ram' (Gen. 22:13).

B.   "[That verse] teaches that the Holy One, blessed be He, showed Abraham a ram tearing itself out of one thicket and getting caught in another, over and over again. He said to him, 'So will your children be trapped among the nations and entangled among the kingdoms, but in the end they will be redeemed through the horn of a ram [sounded on the New Year].'

C.   "That is in line with the following verse of Scripture: 'And in that day a great trumpet will be blown'" (Isa. 27:13).

X.2 A.   R. Abba, son of R. Papi, and R. Joshua of Sikhnin in the name of R. Levi: "It is written, 'And Abraham raised his eyes, and he saw, and behold, a ram trapped in a bush by its horns' (Gen. 22:13).

B.   "[That verse] teaches that the Holy One, blessed be He, showed Abraham a ram tearing itself out of one thicket and getting caught in another, over and over again. He said to him, 'So will your children be trapped by transgressions and entangled by troubles, but in the end they will be redeemed through the horn of a ram.'

C.   "That is in line with the following verse of Scripture: 'Then the Lord will appear over them, and his arrow go forth like lightning; the Lord God will sound the trumpet, and march forth in the whirlwinds of the south. The Lord of hosts will protect them' (Zech. 9:14-15).

D. "May the Lord of hosts protect you, may the Lord of hosts protect us."

III. Matters of Philosophy, Natural Science and Metaphysics

This category does not serve.

41

Leviticus Rabbah Parashah Thirty

I. Unarticulated Premises: The Givens of Religious Conduct

The performed rites correspond to the figures of the patriarchs and matriarchs; the concrete deeds of the law stand for figures in Israel's sanctified life:

XXX

1. A. Another interpretation: "The fruit of goodly (HDR) trees" (Lev. 23:40):
   B. This refers to Abraham, whom the Holy One, blessed be He, honored (HDR) with a goodly old age,
   C. as it is said, "And Abraham was an old man, coming along in years" (Gen. 24:1).
   D. And it is written, "And you will honor (HDR) the face of an old man" (Lev. 19:32).
   E. "Branches (KPWT) of palm trees" (Lev. 23:40):
   F. This refers to Isaac, who was tied (KPWT) and bound upon the altar.
   G. "And boughs of leafy trees" (Lev. 23:40):
   H. This refers to Jacob. Just as a myrtle is rich in leaves, so Jacob was rich in children.
   I. "Willows of the brook" (Lev. 23:40):
   J. This refers to Joseph. Just as the willow wilts before the other three species do, so Joseph died before his brothers did.

2. A. Another interpretation: "The fruit of goodly trees" (Lev. 23:40):
   B. This refers to Sarah, whom the Holy One, blessed be He, honored with a goodly old age, as it is said, "And Abraham and Sarah were old" (Gen. 18:11).
   C. "Branches of palm trees" (Lev. 23:40): this refers to Rebecca. Just as a palm tree contains both edible fruit and thorns, so Rebecca produced a righteous and a wicked son [Jacob and Esau].
   D. "Boughs of leafy trees" (Lev. 23:40): this refers to Leah. Just as a myrtle is rich in leaves, so Leah was rich in children.

> E. "And willows of the brook" (Lev. 23:40): this refers to Rachel. Just as the willow wilts before the other three species do, so Rachel died before her sister.

They also pertain to the sages and to Israel.

The powerful result of the exegesis is to link the species of the Festival to the patriarchs and matriarchs of Israel. It is continuous with the foregoing, linking the species to God, and with what is to follow, as the species will be compared to Israel's leadership, on the one side, as well, finally, to ordinary people, on the other:

XXX

XI.1   A.   Another interpretation: "The fruit of goodly trees" (Lev. 23:40): this refers to the great Sanhedrin of Israel, which the Holy One, blessed be He, honored (HDR) with old age, as it is said, "You will rise up before old age" (Lev. 19:32).

       B.   "Branches (KPWT) of palm trees" (Lev. 23:40): this refers to disciples of sages, who compel (KWPYN) themselves to study Torah from one another.

       C.   "Boughs of leafy trees": this refers to the three rows of disciples who sit before them.

       D.   "And willows of the brook" (Lev. 23:40): this refers to the court scribes, who stand before them, one on the right side, the other on the left, and write down the opinions of those who vote to acquit and those who vote to convict.

XII.1   A.   Another interpretation: "The fruit of goodly trees" refers to Israel.

       B.   Just as a citron has both taste and fragrance, so in Israel are people who have [the merit of both] Torah and good deeds.

       C.   "Branches of palm trees" (Lev. 23:40): refers to Israel. Just as a palm has a taste but no fragrance, so in Israel are people who have [the merit of] Torah but not of good deeds.

       D.   "Boughs of leafy trees": refers to Israel. Just as a myrtle has a fragrance but no taste, so in Israel are people who have the merit of good deeds but not of Torah.

       E.   "Willows of the brook": refers to Israel. Just as a willow has neither taste nor fragrance, so in Israel are those who have the [merit] neither of Torah nor of good deeds.

       F.   What does the Holy One, blessed be He, do for them? Utterly to destroy them is not possible.

       G.   Rather, said the Holy One, blessed be He, "Let them all be joined together in a single bond, and they will effect atonement for one another.

       H.   "And if you have done so, at that moment I shall be exalted."

       I.   That is in line with the following verse of Scripture: "He who builds his upper chambers in heaven" (Amos 9:6).

       J.   And when is he exalted? When they are joined together in a single bond, as it is said, "When he has founded his bond upon the earth" (Amos 9:6).

       K.   Therefore Moses admonishes Israel: "And you shall take..." (Lev. 23:40).

II. Unarticulated Premises: The Givens of Religious Conviction

1. Israel serves the nations of the world because it does not sufficiently study the Torah:

XXX

I.1   A.   "[On the fifteenth day of the seventh month, when you have gathered in the produce of the land, you shall keep the feast of the Lord seven days....] And you shall take on the first day [the fruit of goodly trees, branches of palm trees and boughs of leafy trees and willows of the brook, and you shall rejoice before the Lord your God for seven days]" (Lev. 23:39-40).

B.   R. Abba bar Kahana commenced [discourse by citing the following verse]: "Take my instruction instead of silver, [and knowledge rather than choice gold]" (Prov. 8:10).

C.   Said R. Abba bar Kahana, "Take the instruction of the Torah instead of silver.

D.   "'Why do you weigh out money? Because there is no bread' (Isa. 55:2).

E.   "'Why do you weigh out money to the sons of Esau [Rome]? [It is because] "there is no bread," because you did not sate yourselves with the bread of the Torah.

F.   "'And [why] do you labor? Because there is no satisfaction' (Isa. 55:2).

G.   "'Why do you labor while the nations of the world enjoy plenty? 'Because there is no satisfaction,' that is, because you have not sated yourselves with the wine of the Torah.

H.   "For it is written, 'Come, eat of my bread, and drink of the wine I have mixed'" (Prov. 9:5).

2. Study of the Torah outweighs in value the possession of wealth in the form of real estate:

XXX

I.4   A.   R. Yohanan was going up from Tiberias to Sepphoris. R. Hiyya bar Abba was supporting him. They came to a field. He said, "This field once belonged to me, but I sold it in order to acquire merit in the Torah."

B.   They came to a vineyard, and he said, "This vineyard once belonged to me, but I sold it in order to acquire merit in the Torah."

C.   They came to an olive grove, and he said, "This olive grove once belonged to me, but I sold it in order to acquire merit in the Torah."

D.   R. Hiyya began to cry.

E.   Said R. Yohanan, "Why are you crying?"

F.   He said to him, "It is because you left nothing over to support you in your old age."

G.   He said to him, "Hiyya, my disciple, is what I did such a light thing in your view? I sold something which was given in a spell of six days [of creation] and in exchange I acquired something which was given in a spell of forty days [of revelation].

H. "The entire world and everything in it was created in only six days, as it is written, 'For in six days the Lord made heaven and earth' (Ex. 20:11).

I. "But the Torah was given over a period of forty days, as it was said, 'And he was there with the Lord for forty days and forty nights' (Ex. 34:28).

J. "And it is written, 'And I remained on the mountain for forty days and forty nights'" (Deut. 9:9).

I.5 A. When R. Yohanan died, his generation recited concerning him [the following verse of Scripture]: "If a man should give all the wealth of his house for the love" (Song 8:7), with which R. Yohanan loved the Torah, "he would be utterly destitute" (Song 8:7).

B. When R. Hoshaiah of Tiria died, they saw his bier flying in the air. His generation recited concerning him [the following verse of Scripture]: "If a man should give all the wealth of his house for the love," with which the Holy One, blessed be He, loved Abba Hoshaiah of Tiria, "he would be utterly destitute" (Song 8:7).

C. When R. Eleazar b. R. Simeon died, his generation recited concerning him [the following verse of Scripture]: "Who is this who comes up out of the wilderness like pillars of smoke, perfumed with myrrh and frankincense, with all the powders of the merchant?" (Song 3:6).

D. What is the meaning of the clause, "With all the powders of the merchant"?

E. [Like a merchant who carries all sorts of desired powders,] he was a master of Scripture, a repeater of Mishnah traditions, a writer of liturgical supplications, and a poet.

III. Matters of Philosophy, Natural Science and Metaphysics

There is nothing pertinent.

42

Leviticus Rabbah Parashah Thirty-One

I find nothing of interest in this parashah.

43

Leviticus Rabbah Parashah Thirty-Two

I. Unarticulated Premises: The Givens of Religious Conduct
There is nothing that belongs here.

II. Unarticulated Premises: The Givens of Religious Conviction
1. Israel will be redeemed because it remains separate and different from the gentiles, particularly in regard to sexual relations:

XXXII

V.1 A. "A garden locked is my sister, my bride, a garden locked, a fountain sealed" (Song 4:12).

B. [Regarding the sister as Israel, and the locked garden as evidence that Israelite women did not commit sexual relations with Egyptians], said R. Phineas, "'A garden locked' refers to the virgins. 'A garden locked' refers to women who had had sexual relations. 'A fountain sealed' refers to the males."

C. It was taught in the name of R. Nathan, "'A garden locked, a garden locked' – these refer to two modes of sexual relations, frontwards, backwards."

V.2 A. Another interpretation: "A garden locked" (Song 4:12):

B. R. Phineas in the name of R. Hiyya bar Abba: "Because the Israelites locked themselves up [and avoided] licentious sexual behavior with the Egyptians, they were redeemed from Egypt.

C. "On that account was 'Your being sent forth' [lit.: Your shoots are an orchard of pomegranates, with all choicest fruits] (Song 4:13).

D. "That interpretation is in line with the following: 'And it came to pass, when Pharaoh sent forth...' (Ex. 13:17). [The 'shoots' of Song 4:13 calls to mind the 'sending forth' of Pharaoh, and the Israelites were sent forth by virtue of the fact that they had protected the integrity of their 'shoots,' their offspring.]"

V.3 A. R. Huna in the name of R. Hiyya bar Abba: "Sarah went down to Egypt and fenced herself off from sexual licentiousness and all the other [Israelite] women were kept fenced off on account of the merit that she had attained.

B.   "Joseph went down to Egypt and fenced himself off from sexual licentiousness, and all the other [Israelite] men kept fenced off on account of the merit that he had attained."

C.   Said R. Hiyya bar Abba, "It was truly worthy that through the fence that kept people from licentious behavior, Israel should be redeemed."

V.4   A.   R. Huna in the name of Bar Qappara: "It was on four counts that the Israelites were redeemed from Egypt:

B.   "Because they did not change their names [from Jewish to Egyptian ones], because they did not change their language, because they did not gossip, because they did not go beyond the bounds of sexual decency.

C.   "Because they did not change their names: Reuben and Simeon – whoever went down Reuben and Simeon came up bearing the same names.

D.   "They did not call Reuben, Rufus, Judah, Julian, Joseph, Justus, or Benjamin, Alexander.

E.   "Because they did not change their language: Elsewhere it is written, 'And a refugee came and told Abram the Hebrew' (Gen. 14:13). Here it is written, 'The God of the Hebrews has met with us' (Ex. 3:18).

F.   "And it is written, 'For my mouth it is that speaks with you' (Gen. 45:12). That was in the holy language.

G.   "Because they did not gossip: For it is written, 'Speak into the ears of the people [and let them ask...jewels or silver from their neighbors]' (Ex. 11:2). Now you find that this matter [of taking away the wealth of Egypt] had been set in trust with them for twelve months [prior to the actual exodus], but not a single one of them turned out to have revealed the secret, and not a single one of them squealed on his fellow [Jews].

H.   "Because they did not go beyond the bounds of sexual decency: You may find evidence that that was the case, for there was only a single [Israelite] woman who actually did so, and Scripture explicitly identified her: 'And the name of his mother was Shulamit, daughter of Dibri, of the tribe of Dan' (Lev. 24:11). [So she was the only one who bore a child to an Egyptian man.]"

III. Matters of Philosophy, Natural Science and Metaphysics

Nothing pertains.

44

Leviticus Rabbah Parashah
Thirty-Three

The parashah is barren of interest for our project.

45

Leviticus Rabbah Parashah Thirty-Four

I. Unarticulated Premises: The Givens of Religious Conduct
I find nothing relevant.

II. Unarticulated Premises: The Givens of Religious Conviction
1. The value of the Torah outweighs that of real estate:

XXXIV

XVI.1 A. "And your ancient ruins shall be rebuilt" (Isa. 58:12).

B. R. Tarfon gave to R. Aqiba six silver *centenarii,* saying to him, "Go, buy us a piece of land, so we can get a living from it and labor in the study of Torah together."

C. He took the money and handed it out to scribes, Mishnah teachers, and those who study Torah.

D. After some time R. Tarfon met him and said to him, "Did you buy the land that I mentioned to you?"

E. He said to him, "Yes."

F. He said to him, "Is it any good?"

G. He said to him, "Yes."

H. He said to him, "And do you not want to show it to me?"

I. He took him and showed him the scribes, Mishnah teachers, and people who were studying Torah, and the Torah that they had acquired. He said to him, "Is there anyone who works for nothing? Where is the deed covering the field?"

J. He said to him, "It is with King David, concerning whom it is written, 'He has scattered, he has given to the poor, his righteousness endures forever'" (Ps. 112:9).

III. Matters of Philosophy, Natural Science and Metaphysics
The chapter contains nothing pertinent.

46

Leviticus Rabbah Parashah Thirty-Five

This parashah contains nothing pertinent to our inquiry.

47

Leviticus Rabbah Parashah Thirty-Six

I. Unarticulated Premises: The Givens of Religious Conduct

No legal materials occur here.

II. Unarticulated Premises: The Givens of Religious Conviction

The perfect God created the perfect Israel, every detail of the life and history of which accords with God's plan:

XXXVI

II.1   A.   "You did bring a vine out of Egypt; [you did drive out the nations and plant it. You did clear the ground for it; it took deep root and filled the land. The mountains were covered with its shade, the mighty cedars with its branches]" (Ps. 80:8-10).

       B.   Just as, in the case of a vine, people do not plant it among unbroken clods but break up the ground beneath it and afterward plant it, so in the case of Israel: "You did drive out the nations and plant it" (Ps. 80:8).

       C.   Just as in the case of a vineyard, people do not plant the shoots in a haphazard way but in rows, so the Israelites encamped in the wilderness in rows and according to their standards: "Every man with his own standard, according to the ensigns" (Num. 2:2).

       D.   Just as in the case of a vine, it thrives in accord with the space that you are able to create round about it, so with Israel, you cleared away thirty-one kings, and afterward: "You did clear the ground for it; it took deep root and filled the land" (Ps. 80:9).

       E.   Just as the vine is the lowliest of all trees, so Israelites are low in this world, but in the world to come they are going to inherit from one end of the world to the other.

       F.   Just as in the case of a vine, a single shoot sprouts from it and ultimately eclipses all trees, so in the case of Israel, a single righteous man shoots out from it and rules from one end of the world to the other.

G. That is in line with the following verse of Scripture: "And Joseph was the ruler over the earth" (Gen. 42:6). "And the Lord was with Joshua" (Josh. 6:27). "And the name of David went forth through all the lands" (2 Chr. 14:17). "And Solomon ruled over all kingdoms" (1 Kgs. 5:1). "For Mordecai was great in the house of the king and his reputation traveled among all provinces" (Est. 9:4).

H. Just as in the case of a vine, the leaves cover the grape clusters, so are the Israelites: the common folk cover the disciples of sages.

I. Just as in the case of the vine, there are large grape clusters and small ones. So in the case of Israel, there are people who are completely righteous and others who are only middling.

J. Just as in the case of the vine, there are great grape clusters and small grape clusters, and the larger one is lower than the smaller one, so in the case of Israel, whoever is greater than his fellow in knowledge of the Torah appears to be lower than his fellow.

K. Just as in the case of the vine, there are grapes and raisins, so in the case of Israel, there is [knowledge of] Scripture, Mishnah, Talmud, and lore.

L. Just as in the case of the vine, there will be wine and vinegar, this one bearing its blessing and that one bearing its blessing, so in the case of Israel, people are obligated to say a blessing over bad things that happen just as they are obligated to say a blessing over the good.

M. For the good: "Blessed...who is good and does good." For the bad: "Blessed is...the true judge."

N. Just as the [fruit of the] vine requires three blessings [to be said after consuming the fruit of the vine (M. Ber. 6:8)], so Israel are blessed with three blessings: "May the Lord bless you and keep you. May the Lord lift up the light of his face to you and be gracious to you. May the Lord lift up his face to you and give you peace" (Num. 6:24-26).

O. Just as in the case of the vine, anyone who drinks wine has his face glisten and his teeth set on edge, so in the case of Israel, whoever joins issue with them in the end gets his just desserts from them as at the outset.

P. Just as in the case of the vine, at the outset it is trodden underfoot but in the end it ascends to the table of kings, so in the case of Israel, they appear to be oppressed in this world, but in the world to come they are going to inherit from one end of the world to the other.

Q. [That is in line with the following verse of Scripture:] "And kings will be your nursemaids" (Isa. 49:23). "The Lord your God will place you above" (Deut. 28:1).

R. Just as [the fruit of the] vine ascends to the table of kings at the beginning and at the end of the meal, so will Israel be in this world and in the world to come.

S. Just as the vine climbs over one prop after another, so does Israel become more numerous than each king[dom].

T. Just as in the case of the vine, they train it to grow over high cedars, so in the case of Israel: "The mountains were covered with its shade, the mighty cedars with its branches" (Ps. 80:10).

U.   Just as in the case of the vine, the one who guards it climbs above it
       and watches it, so in the case of Israel, their guardian stands above
       them and guards them, as it is written, "Lo, the guardian of Israel
       does not slumber or sleep" (Ps. 121:4).

V.   Just as a vineyard rests upon a reed, so Israel rests upon the merit
       accruing for study of the Torah, which is written with a reed.

W.   Just as a vineyard rests upon dry wood while it remains fresh, so
       Israel rests upon the merit of the patriarchs, even though they are
       asleep [dead]: "And I shall remember my covenant with Jacob"
       (Lev. 26:42).

2. The merit of the patriarchs protects Israel, and also protects the
    patriarchs themselves, Jacob's serving Abraham, for example:

XXXVI

IV.2   A.   R. Berekhiah and R. Levi in the name of Samuel bar Nahman:
              "Abraham was saved from the furnace of fire only because of the
              merit of Jacob.

       B.   "The matter may be compared. To what is it like? It is like the case
              of someone who was judged before the ruler, and the judgment
              came forth from the ruler that he was to be put to death through
              burning.

       C.   "The ruler perceived through his astrological science that [the
              condemned man] was going to beget a daughter, who was going to
              be married to a king. He said, 'This one is worthy to be saved
              through the merit of the daughter that he is going to beget, who is
              going to be married to a king.'

       D.   "So in the case of Abraham, judgment against him came forth from
              Nimrod that he was to be put to death through burning. But the
              Holy One, blessed be He, foresaw that Jacob was going to come
              forth from him. So he said, 'That one is worthy of being saved on
              account of the merit of Jacob.'

       E.   "That is in line with the following verse of Scripture: 'Thus said the
              Lord to the House of Jacob, who redeemed Abraham'" (Isa. 29:22).

       F.   And rabbis say, "Abraham himself was created only on account of
              the merit of Jacob.

       G.   "That is in line with the following verse of Scripture: 'For I have
              known him, that he may charge his children and his household
              after him to keep the way of the Lord by doing righteousness and
              justice' (Gen. 18:19).

       H.   "Now righteousness and justice are only with Jacob, for it is written,
              'You have made justice and righteousness in Jacob'" (Ps. 99:4).

V.1   A.   Why (at Lev. 26:42) are the patriarchs listed in reverse order [Jacob,
              Isaac, Abraham]?

       B.   It is as if to say, if the deeds of Jacob are insufficient, there are the
              deeds of Isaac, and if the deeds of Isaac are insufficient, there are
              the deeds of Abraham.

       C.   Each one of them is sufficient for [his merit] to sustain [the world].

VI.1   A.   [Returning to] the body [of the matter:] How long does the merit of
              the patriarchs endure?

B. R. Tanhuma made this statement, Rab in the name of R. Hiyya the Elder, R. Menehama said it, R. Berekhiah and R. Helbo in the name of R. Abba bar Zabeda: "Down to Jehoahaz. 'But the lord was gracious to them and had compassion on them [and he turned toward them, because of his covenant with Abraham, Isaac, and Jacob, and would not destroy them; nor has he cast them from his presence until now]' (2 Kgs. 13:23).

C. "Until now [the time of Jehoahaz, 2 Kgs. 13:22] the merit of the patriarchs has endured."

D. R. Joshua b. Levi said, "Until the time of Elijah: 'And it came to pass at the time of the evening-offering, that Elijah the prophet came near and said, "O Lord, [the God of Abraham, Isaac, and Israel, this day let it be known that you are God"' (1 Kgs. 18:36). Thus, to this day the merit endured, but not afterward.]"

E. Samuel said, "Down to the time of Hosea: 'Now will I uncover her shame in the sight of her lovers, and no man will [ever again] deliver her out of my hand' (Hos. 2:12).

F. "'Man' refers then to Abraham, as it is said in Scripture: 'And now, return the wife of the man' (Gen. 20:7).

G. "'Man' refers only to Isaac, as it is said, 'Who is this man?' (Gen. 24:65).

H. "'Man' refers only to Jacob, as it is said, 'Jacob, a quiet man, dwelling in tents'" (Gen. 28:27).

I. R. Yudan said, "Down to the time of Hezekiah: 'That the government may be increased [and of peace there be no end...the zeal of the Lord of hosts [thus: not the merit of the patriarchs] does this'" (Isa. 9:6).

J. R. Yudan bar Hanan in the name of R. Berekiah said, "If you see that the merit of the patriarchs is slipping away, and the merit of the matriarchs is trembling, then go and cleave to the performance of deeds of loving kindness.

K. "That is in line with the following verse of Scripture: 'For the mountains will melt (YMWSW), and the hills will tremble, [but my love will not depart from you]' (Isa. 54:10).

L. "'Mountains' refers to the patriarchs, and 'hills' to the matriarchs.

M. "Henceforward: 'But my love will not (YMWS) depart from you'" (Isa. 54:10).

N. Said R. Aha, "The merit of the patriarchs endures forever. Forever do people call it to mind, saying, 'For the Lord your God is a merciful God. He will not fail you nor destroy you nor forget the covenant he made with your fathers'" (Deut. 4:31).

III. Matters of Philosophy, Natural Science and Metaphysics

Nothing pertains; the discussion of which was created first, heaven or earth, cannot be classed as "metaphysics."

48

Leviticus Rabbah Parashah
Thirty-Seven

I. Unarticulated Premises: The Givens of Religious Conduct

The laws emerge from the conduct of sages:

XXXVII

III.1   A.   The story is told of Rabban Gamaliel, who was going on the road from Acre to Akhzib, and Tabi, his servant, was walking in front of him, and R. Ilai was walking behind him.

       B.   He found a loaf of cheap bread on the road. [He said to Tabi, his slave, "Take the loaf." (Y. A.Z. 1:9)]

       C.   He saw a gentile coming toward him. He said to him, "Mabgai, Mabgai, take this loaf of bread."

       D.   R. Ilai ran after [Mabgai] and said to him, "What is your name?"

       E.   He said to him, "Mabgai."

       F.   "And where do you come from?"

       G.   "From one of the [nearby] station keeper's villages."

       H.   "Now did Rabban Gamaliel ever in your whole life meet you?"

       I.   He said to him, "No."

       J.   And from what he said we learn three things:

       K.   We learn that the leaven of a gentile is permitted immediately after Passover (see M. Pes. 2:2).

       L.   [On the basis of this event we learn that] Rabban Gamaliel divined by the Holy Spirit that his name was Mabgai.

       M.   And that they do not pass by food [but pick it up].

       N.   (Y. A.Z. 1:9 adds:) And that they follow the status of the majority of those who travel the roads [in a given place, in this instance, gentile] [T. Pes. 2:15].

       O.   R. Jacob bar Zabedai in the name of R. Abbahu: "That rule [about not walking past food, but stopping and picking it up] was valid in the past, but now they do pass by foodstuffs because of the possibility of witchcraft."

       P.   When they reached Akhzib, they ate and drank there.

Q. When he was leaving Akhezib, someone came along and besought from him [absolution of] his vow. Rabban Gamaliel said to Ilai [who was with him], "Do you reckon that we have drunk so much as a quarter-log of Italian wine?" He said to him, "Yes." He said to the one who asked the question, "Travel with us until the effect of our wine has worn off." He walked with them to the Ladder of Tyre.

R. Once they got to the Ladder of Tyre, Rabban Gamaliel got off [his ass] and wrapped himself in his cloak and sat down and declared his vow to be absolved.

S. From these statements of his we learn three things: [that a quarter-log of wine causes drunkenness] (Y. A.Z. 1:9),

T. [that traveling wears down the effects of wine] (Y. A.Z. 1:9),

U. that [sages] do not grant absolution from vows or give decisions when they are drunk

V. and that they do not absolve vows either while riding on an ass or while walking or while standing,

W. but only sitting down and wrapped in a cloak (T. Pes. 2:16).

II. Unarticulated Premises: The Givens of Religious Conviction

I find here nothing of theological weight.

III. Matters of Philosophy, Natural Science and Metaphysics

The parashah presents nothing relevant.

Part Three

PESIQTA DERAB KAHANA

49

Pesiqta deRab Kahana Pisqa One

I. The Character of Pesiqta deRab Kahana

A compilation of twenty-eight propositional discourses, Pesiqta deRab Kahana innovates because it appeals for its themes and lections to the liturgical calendar, rather than to a Pentateuchal book. Pesiqta deRab Kahana marks a stunning innovation in Midrash compilation because it abandons the pretense that fixed associative connections derive solely from Scripture.

The text that governs the organization of Pesiqta deRab Kahana comprises a liturgical occasion of the synagogue, which is identical to a holy day, has told our authorship what topic it wishes to take up – and therefore also what verses of Scripture (if any) prove suitable to that topic and its exposition.

Adar-Nisan-Sivan

Passover-Pentecost: *Pisqaot* 2-12
[possible exception: *Pisqa* 6]

Tammuz-Ab-Elul

The Ninth of Ab: *Pisqaot* 13-22

Tishré

Tishré 1-22: *Pisqaot* 23-28

Only *Pisqa* 1 (possibly also *Pisqa* 6) falls out of synchronic relationship with a long sequence of special occasions in the synagogal lections.

The twenty-eight *parashiyyot* of Pesiqta deRab Kahana in order follow the synagogal lections from early spring through fall, in the Western calendar, from late February or early March through late September or early October, approximately half of the solar year, 27 weeks, and somewhat more than half of the lunar year. On the very surface, the basic building block is the theme of a given lectionary

Sabbath – that is, a Sabbath distinguished by a particular lection – and not the theme dictated by a given passage of Scripture, let alone the exposition of the language or proposition of such a scriptural verse. The topical program of the document may be defined very simply: expositions of themes dictated by special Sabbaths or festivals and their lections.

Pisqa	Base verse	Topic or Occasion
1.	*On the day Moses completed* (Num. 7:1)	Torah lection for the Sabbath of Hanukkah
2.	*When you take the census* (Ex. 30:12)	Torah lection for the Sabbath of Sheqalim, first of the four Sabbaths prior to the advent of Nisan, in which Passover falls
3.	*Remember Amalek* (Deut. 25:17-19)	Torah lection for the Sabbath of Zakhor, second of the four Sabbaths prior to the advent of Nisan, in which Passover falls
4.	*Red heifer* (Num. 19:1ff.)	Torah lection for the Sabbath of Parah, third of the four Sabbaths prior to the advent of Nisan, in which Passover falls
5.	*This month* (Ex. 12:1-2)	Torah lection for the Sabbath of Hahodesh, fourth of the four Sabbaths prior to the advent of Nisan, in which Passover falls
6.	*My offerings* (Num. 28:1-4)	Torah lection for the New Moon which falls on a weekday
7.	*It came to pass at midnight* (Ex. 12:29-32)	Torah lection for the first day of Passover
8.	*The first sheaf* (Lev. 23:11)	Torah lection for the second day of Passover on which the first sheaves of barley were harvested and waved as an offering
9.	*When a bull or sheep or goat is born* (Lev. 22:26)	Lection for Passover
10.	*You shall set aside a tithe* (Deut. 14:22)	Torah lection for Sabbath during Passover in the Land of Israel or for the eighth day of Passover outside of the Land of Israel

11.	*When Pharaoh let the people go* (Ex. 13:17-18)	Torah lection for the Seventh Day of Passover
12.	*In the third month* (Ex. 19:1ff.)	Torah lection for Pentecost
13.	*The words of Jeremiah* (Jer. 1:1-3)	Prophetic lection for the first of three Sabbaths prior to the Ninth of Ab
14.	*Hear* (Jer. 2:4-6)	Prophetic lection for the second of three Sabbaths prior to the Ninth of Ab
15.	*How lonely sits the city* (Lam. 1:1-2)	Prophetic lection for the third of three Sabbaths prior to the Ninth of Ab
16.	*Comfort* (Isa. 40:1-2)	Prophetic lection for the first of three Sabbaths following the Ninth of Ab
17.	*But Zion said* (Isa. 49:14-16)	Prophetic lection for the second of three Sabbaths following the Ninth of Ab
18.	*O afflicted one, storm tossed* (Isa. 54:11-14)	Prophetic lection for the third of three Sabbaths following the Ninth of Ab
19.	*I even I am he who comforts you* (Isa. 51:12-15)	Prophetic lection for the fourth of three Sabbaths following the Ninth of Ab
20.	*Sing aloud, O barren woman* (Isa. 54:1ff.)	Prophetic lection for the fifth of three Sabbaths following the Ninth of Ab
21.	*Arise, Shine* (Isa. 60:1-3)	Prophetic lection for the sixth of three Sabbaths following the Ninth of Ab
22.	*I will greatly rejoice in the Lord* (Isa. 61:10-11)	Prophetic lection for the seventh of three Sabbaths following the Ninth of Ab
23.	*The New Year*	No base verse indicated. The theme is God's justice and judgment.
24.	*Return O Israel to the Lord your God* (Hos. 14:1-3)	Prophetic lection for the Sabbath of Repentance between New Year and Day of Atonement
25.	*Selihot*	No base verse indicated. The theme is God's forgiveness.
26.	*After the death of the two sons of Aaron* (Lev. 16:1ff.)	Torah lection for the Day of Atonement
27.	*And you shall take on the first day* (Lev. 23:39-43)	Torah lection for the first day of the Festival of Tabernacles
28.	*On the eighth day* (Num. 29:35-39)	Torah lection for the Eighth Day of Solemn Assembly

This catalogue draws our attention to three eccentric *pisqaot*, distinguished by their failure to build discourse upon the base verse. These are No. 4, which may fairly claim that its topic, the red cow, occurs in exact verbal formulation in the verses at hand; No. 23, the New Year, and No. 25, *Selihot*. The last named may or may not take an integral place in the structure of the whole. But the middle item, the New Year, on the very surface is essential to a structure that clearly wishes to follow the line of holy days onward through the Sabbath of Repentance, the Day of Atonement, the Festival of Tabernacles, and the Eighth Day of Solemn Assembly.

It follows that, unlike Genesis Rabbah and Leviticus Rabbah, the document focuses upon the life of the synagogue. Its framers set forth propositions in the manner of the authorship of Leviticus Rabbah. But these are framed by appeal not only to the rules governing the holy society, as in Leviticus Rabbah, but also to the principal events of Israel's history, celebrated in the worship of the synagogue. What we do not find in this Midrash compilation is exposition of Pentateuchal or prophetic passages, verse by verse; the basis chosen by our authorship for organizing and setting forth its propositions is the character and theme of holy days and their special synagogue Torah lections. That is, all of the selected base verses upon which the *parashiyyot* are built, Pentateuchal or prophetic, are identified with synagogal lections for specified holy days, special Sabbaths or festivals.

The contrast to the earlier compilations – this one is generally assigned to ca. 500 – is striking. The framers of Sifra and Sifré to Numbers and Sifré to Deuteronomy follow the verses of Scripture and attach to them whatever messages they wish to deliver. The authorship of Genesis Rabbah follows suit, though less narrowly guided by verses and more clearly interested in their broader themes. The framers of Leviticus Rabbah attached rather broad, discursive and syllogistic statements to verses of the book of Leviticus, but these verses do not follow in close sequence, one, then the next, as in Sifra and its friends. That program of exposition of verses of Scripture read in or out of sequence, of organization of discourse in line with biblical books, parallel to the Tosefta's and Talmuds' authorships' exposition of passages of the Mishnah, read in close sequence or otherwise, we see, defines what our authorship has not done. Pesiqta deRab Kahana has been so assembled as to exhibit a viewpoint, a purpose of its particular authorship, one quite distinctive, in its own context (if not in a single one of its propositions!) to its framers or collectors and arrangers.

Rhetoric

Following the model of Leviticus Rabbah, Pesiqta deRab Kahana consists of twenty-eight syllogisms, each presented in a cogent and systematic way by the twenty-eight *pisqaot*, respectively. Each *pisqa* contains an implicit proposition, and that proposition may be stated in a simple way. It emerges from the intersection of an external verse with the base verse that recurs through the *pisqa*, and then is restated by the systematic dissection of the components of the base verse, each of which is shown to say the same thing as all the others.

A *pisqa* in Pesiqta deRab Kahana systematically presents a single syllogism, which is expressed through, first the contrast of an external verse with the base verse – hence, the base verse/intersecting verse form, in which the implicit syllogism is stated through the intervention of a contrastive verse into the basic proposition established by the base verse, and then through the systematic exegesis of the components of the base verse on their own, hence through the exegetical form. There is a third form, a syllogistic list, familiar of course from the Mishnah and prior Midrash compilations as well. The first two forms occur in the same sequence, because the former of the two serves to declare the implicit syllogism, and the latter, to locate that implicit syllogism in the base verse itself. The third will then be tacked on at the end. Otherwise it would disrupt the exposition of the implicit syllogism. All of these forms are familiar and require no further explanation.

Logic of Coherent Discourse

The document as a whole appeals to the fixed associations defined by synagogal lections, in sequence. The individual compositions of course are syllogistic. The pattern is the same as for Leviticus Rabbah, but different, of course, from Genesis Rabbah.

Topical Program

These synagogal discourses read in their entirety form a coherent statement of three propositions.

1. God loves Israel, that love is unconditional, and Israel's response to God must be obedience to the religious duties that God has assigned, which will produce merit. Israel's obedience to God is what will save Israel. That means doing the religious duties as required by the Torah, which is the mark of God's love for – and regeneration of – Israel. The tabernacle symbolizes the union of Israel and God. When Israel does what God asks above, Israel will prosper down

below. If Israel remembers Amalek down below, God will remember Amalek up above and will wipe him out. A mark of Israel's loyalty to God is remembering Amalek. God does not require the animals that are sacrificed, since man could never match God's appetite, if that were the issue, but the savor pleases God [as a mark of Israel's loyalty and obedience]. The first sheaf returns to God God's fair share of the gifts that God bestows on Israel, and those who give it benefit, while those who hold it back suffer. The first sheaf returns to God God's fair share of the gifts that God bestows on Israel, and those who give it benefit, while those who hold it back suffer. Observing religious duties, typified by the rites of the Festival, brings a great reward of that merit that ultimately leads to redemption. God's ways are just, righteous and merciful, as shown by God's concern that the offspring remain with the mother for seven days. God's love for Israel is so intense that he wants to hold them back for an extra day after the Festival in order to spend more time with them, because, unlike the nations of the world, Israel knows how to please God. This is a mark of God's love for Israel.

2.   God is reasonable and when Israel has been punished, it is in accord with God's rules. God forgives penitent Israel and is abundant in mercy. The good and the wicked die in exactly the same circumstance or condition. Laughter is vain because it is mixed with grief. A wise person will not expect too much joy. But when people suffer, there ordinarily is a good reason for it. That is only one sign that God is reasonable and God never did anything lawless and wrong to Israel or made unreasonable demands, and there was, therefore, no reason for Israel to lose confidence in God or to abandon him. God punished Israel to be sure. But this was done with reason. Nothing happened to Israel of which God did not give fair warning in advance, and Israel's failure to heed the prophets brought about her fall. And God will forgive a faithful Israel. Even though the Israelites sinned by making the golden calf, God forgave them and raised them up. On the New Year, God executes justice, but the justice is tempered with mercy. The rites of the New Year bring about divine judgment and also forgiveness because of the merit of the fathers. Israel must repent and return to the Lord, who is merciful and will forgive them for their sins. The penitential season of the New Year and Day of Atonement is the right

time for confession and penitence, and God is sure to accept penitence. By exercising his power of mercy, the already merciful God grows still stronger in mercy.

3.   God will save Israel personally at a time and circumstance of his own choosing. Israel may know what the future redemption will be like, because of the redemption from Egypt. The paradox of the red cow, that what imparts uncleanness, namely touching the ashes of the red cow, produces cleanness is part of God's ineffable wisdom, which man cannot fathom. Only God can know the precise moment of Israel's redemption. That is something man cannot find out on his own. But God will certainly fulfill the predictions of the prophets about Israel's coming redemption. The Exodus from Egypt is the paradigm of the coming redemption. Israel has lost Eden – but can come home, and, with God's help, will. God's unique power is shown through Israel's unique suffering. In God's own time, he will redeem Israel.

To develop this point, the authorship proceeds to further facts, worked out in its propositional discourses. The lunar calendar, particular to Israel, marks Israel as favored by God, for the new moon signals the coming of Israel's redemption, and the particular new moon that will mark the actual event is that of Nisan. When God chooses to redeem Israel, Israel's enemies will have no power to stop him, because God will force Israel's enemies to serve Israel, because of Israel's purity and loyalty to God. Israel's enemies are punished, and what they propose to do to Israel, God does to them. Both directly and through the prophets, God is the source of true comfort, which he will bring to Israel. Israel thinks that God has forsaken them.

But it is Israel who forsook God, God's love has never failed, and will never fail. Even though he has been angry, his mercy still is near and God has the power and will to save Israel. God has designated the godly for himself and has already promised to redeem them. He will assuredly do so. God personally is the one who will comfort Israel. While Israel says there is no comfort, in fact, God will comfort Israel. Zion/Israel is like a barren woman, but Zion will bring forth children, and Israel will be comforted. Both God and Israel will bring light to Zion, which will give light to the world. The rebuilding of Zion will be a source of joy for the entire world, not for Israel alone. God will rejoice in Israel, Israel in God, like bride and groom.

II. Unarticulated Premises: The Givens of Religious Conduct

There are no points of law to examine here.

III. Unarticulated Premises: The Givens of Religious Conviction

1. God's principal habitation on earth was with humanity, but gradually, as people sinned, God went up from one firmament to the next, withdrawing from humanity; but with the coming of Israel's patriarchs and prophets, God gradually returned to earth, finally meeting humanity at Sinai:

I

I.6   A.   The principal locale of God's presence had been among the lower creatures, but when the first man sinned, it went up to the first firmament.

B.   The generation of Enosh came along and sinned, and it went up from the first to the second.

C.   The generation of the flood [came along and sinned], and it went up from the second to the third.

D.   The generation of the dispersion [came along] and sinned, and it went up from the third to the fourth.

E.   The Egyptians in the time of Abraham our father [came along] and sinned, and it went up from the fourth to the fifth.

F.   The Sodomites [came along], and sinned, ...from the fifth to the sixth.

G.   The Egyptians in the time of Moses...from the sixth to the seventh.

H.   And, corresponding to them, seven righteous men came along and brought it back down to earth:

I.   Abraham our father came along and acquired merit, and brought it down from the seventh to the sixth.

J.   Isaac came along and acquired merit and brought it down from the sixth to the fifth.

K.   Jacob came along and acquired merit and brought it down from the fifth to the fourth.

L.   Levi came along and acquired merit and brought it down from the fourth to the third.

M.   Kahath came along and acquired merit and brought it down from the third to the second.

N.   Amram came along and acquired merit and brought it down from the second to the first.

O.   Moses came along and acquired merit and brought it down to earth.

P.   Therefore it is said, "On the day that Moses completed the setting up of the Tabernacle, he anointed and consecrated it" (Num. 7:1).

IV. Matters of Philosophy, Natural Science and Metaphysics

Nothing remotely qualifies.

50

Pesiqta deRab Kahana Pisqa Two

I. Unarticulated Premises: The Givens of Religious Conduct

There are no legal components to this *pisqa*.

II. Unarticulated Premises: The Givens of Religious Conviction

1. While David and Israel have sinned, both are forgiven by God and restored to their throne and fortunes, respectively:

II

I.1   A.   "O Lord, how many are my foes! Many are rising against me; many are saying of me, there is no help for him in God. Sela" (Ps. 3:2-3):

B.   R. Samuel bar Immi and Rabbis:

C.   R. Samuel bar Immi interpreted the verse to speak of Doeg and Ahitophel:

D.   "'...many are saying of me,' refers to Doeg and Ahitophel. Why does he refer to them as 'many'?

E.   "For they formed a majority in Torah study.

F.   "'...many are saying of me' – They say to David, 'A man who has seized a ewe lamb, killed the shepherd, and made Israelites fall by the sword – will he have salvation? "There is no help for him in God."'

G.   "Said David, 'And you, O Lord, have concurred with them, writing in your Torah, saying, "The adulterer and the adulteress will surely die" (Lev. 20:10).

H.   "'"But you, O Lord, are a shield about me" (Ps. 3:4): For you have formed a protection for me through the merit attained by my ancestors.

I.   "'"My glory" (Ps. 3:4): For you restored me to the throne.

J.   "'"And the lifter of my head" (Ps. 3:4): While I was liable to you to have my head removed, you raised my head through the prophet, Nathan, when he said to me, "Also the Lord has removed your sin and you will not die" (2 Sam. 12:13).'"

K.   And rabbis interpreted the verse to refer to the nations of the world:

L.   "'Many' – these are the nations of the world.

M.   "Why does he call them many? For it is written, 'Ah the uproar of
     many peoples' (Isa. 17:12).

N.   "'...many are saying of me': this refers to Israel.

O.   "'A nation that heard from the mouth of its God at Mount Sinai,
     "You shall have no other gods before me" (Ex. 20:3), and yet after
     forty days said to the calf, "This is your god, O Israel" (Ex. 32:4) –
     will such a nation have salvation?

P.   "'"...there is no help for him in God. Sela."' [so said the nations of
     the world].

Q.   "The Israelites said, 'And you, O Lord, have concurred with them,
     writing in your Torah, "And you shall say, one who sacrifices to
     other gods will be utterly exterminated" (Ex. 22:19).'

R.   "'"But you, O Lord, are a shield about me" (Ps. 3:4): For you have
     afforded protection for us on account of the merit accrued by our
     ancestors.

S.   "'"My glory" (Ps. 3:4): For you have brought your Presence to come
     to rest among us.

T.   "'"And the lifter of my head" (Ps. 3:4): While I was liable to you to
     have my head removed, you raised my head through Moses:
     "When you lift up the head [RSV: take the census] of the people of
     Israel, then each shall give a ransom for himself to the Lord when
     you number them, that there be no plague among them when you
     number them" (Ex. 30:12).'"

Along these same lines, God forgave Israel for the sin of the golden calf,
and the support of the tabernacle commemorates God's forgiveness of
sin; the Temple marks the reconciliation of God and Israel:

II

III.1   A.   R. Jonathan opened discourse [by citing the following verse]: "'A
             man shall be brought low, all men shall be humbled; and how can
             they raise themselves' (Isa. 2:9).

        B.   "'A man shall be brought low' refers to Israel, concerning whom it
             is written, 'You, my sheep, the sheep of my pasture, are man' (Ezek.
             34:31).

        C.   "'...all men shall be humbled' refers to Moses, concerning whom it
             is written, 'And the man, Moses, was very humble' (Num. 12:3).

        D.   "Said Moses before the Holy One, blessed be He, 'Lord of the ages, I
             know that the Israelites have bowed down to the calf, and I was
             humiliated. "And how can they raise themselves?"'

        E.   "He said to him, 'I shall raise them up.'

        F.   "'When you lift up the head [RSV: take the census] of the people of
             Israel, then each shall give a ransom for himself to the Lord when
             you number them, that there be no plague among them when you
             number them' (Ex. 30:12)."

III. Matters of Philosophy, Natural Science and Metaphysics

Nothing pertains.

51

Pesiqta deRab Kahana Pisqa Three

I. Unarticulated Premises: The Givens of Religious Conduct
This category does not pertain.

II. Unarticulated Premises: The Givens of Religious Conviction

1. The redemption of Israel is the counterpart to the fall of her enemies, Amalek-Esau-Rome: one will fall by the hand of one who did fear God, with the consequent interest in the contrast of Joseph and Esau = Amalek. The salvation of Israel also marks the downfall of Israel's enemies.

III

XIII.1 A. "Remember [what the Amalekites did to you on your way out of Egypt, how they met you on the road] when you were faint and weary [and cut off your rear, which was lagging behind exhausted; they showed no fear of God. When the Lord your God gives you peace from your enemies on every side, in the land which he is giving you to occupy as your patrimony, you shall not fail to blot out the memory of the Amalekites from under heaven]" (Deut. 25:17-19):

B. "...faint": from thirst.

C. "...and weary": from the journey.

XIII.2 A. "...they showed no fear of God": R. Phineas in the name of R. Samuel bar Nahman, "There is a tradition concerning the narrative that the seed of Esau will fall only by the hand of the sons of Rachel.

B. "'Surely the youngest of the flock shall drag them' (Jer. 49:20).

C. "Why does he refer to them as the youngest of the flock? Because they were the youngest of all the tribes.

D. "[Now we shall see the connection to the downfall of Esau = Amalek = Rome:] This one is called a youth, and that one is called young.

E. "This one is called a youth: 'And he was a youth' (Gen. 37:2).

F.   "And that one is called young: 'Lo, I have made you the youngest among the nations' (Obad. 1:2).

G.   "This one [Esau] grew up between two righteous men and did not act like them, and that one [Joseph] grew up between two wicked men and did not act like them.

H.   "Let this one come and fall by the hand of the other.

I.   "This one showed concern for the honor owing to his master, and that one treated with disdain the honor owning to his master.

J.   "Let this one come and fall by the hand of the other.

K.   "In connection with this one it is written, 'And he did not fear God' (Deut. 25:18), and in connection with that one it is written, 'And I fear God' (Gen. 42:18).

L.   "Let this one come and fall by the hand of that one."

III. Matters of Philosophy, Natural Science and Metaphysics

I see nothing relevant.

52

Pesiqta deRab Kahana Pisqa Four

I. Unarticulated Premises: The Givens of Religious Conduct

There are laws that have no rational basis in this-worldly facts but express a miracle that God alone can do:

IV

I.1   A.   "Who can bring forth something clean out of something unclean? Is it not the one?" (Job 14:4) [that is, the one God]:

       B.   For examples [of bringing the clean out of the unclean]: Abraham from Terah, Hezekiah from Ahaz, Mordecai from Shimei, Israel from the nations, the world to come from this world.

       C.   Who has done so? Who has commanded so? Who has decreed so? Is it not the one, is it not the Unique One of the world?

I.2   A.   There we have learned: **If a white spot the size of a bean [is on a person's flesh], he is unclean. But if it flowered throughout the person's body, he is clean** [M. Neg. 8:2].

       B.   Who has done so? Who has commanded so? Who has decreed so? Is it not the one, is it not the Unique One of the world?

I.3   A.   There we have learned: **In the case of a woman whose fetus has died in her womb, if the midwife stuck in her hand and touched it, the midwife is unclean with an uncleanness that lasts for seven days [by reason of touching the corpse], while the woman remains in a state of cleanness until the offspring comes forth** [M. Hul. 4:3]. While the corpse is in the "house," [that is, the womb, the woman's body], it is clean, but when it comes forth therefrom, lo, it is unclean.

       B.   Who has done so? Who has commanded so? Who has decreed so? Is it not the one, is it not the Unique One of the world?

I.4   A.   And we have learned there: **All those who are engaged in the work of preparing the ashes of the red cow from beginning to end impart uncleanness to clothing** [M. Par. 4:4], while the cow itself effects purification.

       B.   [Supply:] Who has done so? Who has commanded so? Who has decreed so? Is it not the one, is it not the Unique One of the world?

I.5   A.   Said the Holy One, blessed be He, "An ordinance have I ordained, a
             decree have I made, and you have no right to transgress my
             decrees: 'Now the Lord said to Moses and to Aaron, "This is the
             statute of the Torah which the Lord has commanded: [Tell the
             people of Israel to bring you a red heifer without defect, in which
             there is no blemish, and upon which a yoke has never come.... And
             a man who is clean shall gather up the ashes of the heifer and
             deposit them outside the camp in a clean place; and they shall be
             kept for the congregation of the people of Israel for the water for
             impurity, for the removal of sin. And he who gathers the ashes of
             the heifer shall wash his clothes and be unclean until evening.... He
             who touches the dead body of any person shall be unclean seven
             days; he shall cleanse himself with the water on the third day and
             on the seventh day and so be clean; but if he does not cleanse
             himself on the third day and on the seventh day he will not become
             clean. Whoever touches a dead person...and does not cleanse
             himself defiles the tabernacle of the Lord, and that person shall be
             cut off from Israel, because the water for impurity was not thrown
             upon him, he shall be unclean; his uncleanness is still on him]"'
             (Num. 19:1-13, pass.)."

II. Unarticulated Premises: The Givens of Religious Conviction

1.   There are laws in the Torah that bear no rational sense at all, but God
       makes decrees that humanity must accept without cavil:

IV

VII.5 A.   A gentile asked Rabban Yohanan ben Zakkai, saying to him, "These
             rites that you carry out look like witchcraft. You bring a cow and
             slaughter it, burn it, crush the remains, take the dust, and if one of
             you contracts corpse uncleanness, you sprinkle on him two or three
             times and say to him, 'You are clean.'"
       B.   He said to him, "Has a wandering spirit never entered you?"
       C.   He said to him, "No."
       D.   He said to him, "And have you ever seen someone into whom a
             wandering spirit entered?"
       E.   He said to him, "Yes."
       F.   He said to him, "And what do you do?"
       G.   He said to him, "People bring roots and smoke them under him and
             sprinkle water on the spirit and it flees."
       H.   He said to him, "And should your ears not hear what your mouth
             speaks? So this spirit is the spirit of uncleanness, as it is written, 'I
             will cause prophets as well as the spirit of uncleanness to flee from
             the land' (Zech. 13:2)."
       I.   After the man had gone his way, his disciples said to him, "My lord,
             this one you have pushed off with a mere reed. To us what will you
             reply?"
       J.   He said to them, "By your lives! It is not the corpse that imparts
             uncleanness nor the water that effects cleanness. But it is a decree
             of the Holy One, blessed be He.

K. "Said the Holy One, blessed be He, 'A statute have I enacted, a decree have I made, and you are not at liberty to transgress my decree: "This is the statute of the Torah" (Num. 19:1).'"

III. Matters of Philosophy, Natural Science and Metaphysics

The category is irrelevant to this document.

53

Pesiqta deRab Kahana Pisqa Five

I. Unarticulated Premises: The Givens of Religious Conduct

I find nothing that demands inclusion.

II. Unarticulated Premises: The Givens of Religious Conviction

1. The patriarchs determined the future history of Israel, knowing what would happen and choosing the fate of the people:

V

II.1 A. "Great things have you done, O Lord my God; your wonderful purposes are all for our good; none can compare with you; I would proclaim them and speak of them, but they are more than I can tell" (Prov. 40:5):

B. R. Hinenah bar Papa says two [teachings in respect to the cited verse]: "All those wonders and plans which you made so that our father, Abraham, would accept the subjugation of Israel to the nations were 'for our good,' for our sake, so that we might endure in the world."

C. Simeon bar Abba in the name of R. Yohanan: "Four things did the Holy One, blessed be He, show to our father, Abraham: the Torah, the sacrifices, Gehenna, and the rule of the kingdoms.

D. "The Torah: '...and a flaming torch passed between these pieces' (Gen. 15:17).

E. "Sacrifices: 'And he said to him, Take for me a heifer divided into three parts' (Gen. 15:9).

F. "Gehenna: 'behold a smoking fire pot.'

G. "The rule of the kingdoms: 'Lo, dread, a great darkness' (Gen. 15:12)."

H. "The Holy One, blessed be He, said to our father, Abraham, 'So long as your descendants are occupied with the former two, they will be saved from the latter two. If they abandon the former two of them, they will be judged by the other two.

I. "'So long as they are occupied with study of the Torah and performance of the sacrifices, they will be saved from Gehenna and from the rule of the kingdoms.

J. "'But [God says to Abraham] in the future the house of the sanctuary is destined to be destroyed and the sacrifices nullified. What is your preference? Do you want your children to go down into Gehenna or to be subjugated to the four kingdoms?'"

K. R. Hinenah bar Papa said, "Abraham himself chose the subjugation to the four kingdoms.

L. "What is the scriptural basis for that view? 'How should one chase a thousand and two put ten thousand to flight, except their rock had given them over' (Deut. 32:30). That statement concerning the rock refers only to Abraham, as it is said, 'Look at the rock from which you were hewn' (Isa. 51:1).

M. "'But the Lord delivered them up' (Deut. 32:30) teaches that God then approved what he had chosen."

II.2   A. R. Berekhiah in the name of R. Levi: "Now Abraham sat and puzzled all that day, saying, 'Which should I choose, Gehenna or subjugation to the kingdoms? The one is worse than the other.'

B. "Said the Holy One, blessed be He, to him, 'Abraham, how long are you going to sit in puzzlement? Choose without delay.' That is in line with this verse: 'On that day the Lord made a covenant with Abraham saying' (Gen. 15:18)."

C. What is the meaning of, 'saying'?

D. R. Hinenah bar Papa said, "Abraham chose for himself the subjugation to the four kingdoms."

E. We have reached the dispute of R. Yudan and R. Idi and R. Hama bar Haninah said in the name of a single sage in the name of Rabbi: "The Holy One, blessed be He, [not Abraham] chose the subjugation to the four kingdoms for him, in line with the following verse of Scripture: 'You have caused men to ride over our heads' (Ps. 66:12). That is to say, 'you have made ride over our heads various nations, and it is as though we went through fire and through water' (Ps. 66:21)."

2. God goes from synagogue to schoolhouse to bless Israel, on account of the merit of Abraham:

V

VIII.2   A. ["My beloved is like a gazelle":] Said R. Isaac, "Just as a gazelle skips and jumps from tree to tree, hut to hut, fence to fence, so the Holy One, blessed be He, skipped from Egypt to the Sea, from the sea to Sinai.

B. "In Egypt they saw him: 'And I shall pass through the land of Egypt on that night' (Ex. 12:12).

C. "At the sea they saw him: 'And Israel saw the great hand' (Ex. 14:32).

D. "At Sinai they saw him: 'And the Lord spoke from Sinai, he came and shone from Seir to him' (Deut. 32:2)."

VIII.5   A. ["My beloved is like a gazelle":] Said R. Isaac, "Just as a gazelle skips and jumps from tree to tree, hut to hut, fence to fence, so the

Holy One, blessed be He, skips from one synagogue to another, one study house to another.

B.   "On what account? So as to bless Israel.

C.   "On account of whose merit? On account of the merit of Abraham, who remained seated at the oak of Mamre [where he was praying and studying].

D.   "That is in line with this verse of Scripture: 'And the Lord appeared to him at the oak of Mamre, when he was sitting down at the door of the tent' (Gen. 18:1)."

3.   Israel is small now but will be great in time to come; Rome is great now but will diminish:

V

XIV.1 A.   "This month is for you [the first of months, you shall make it the first month of the year]" (Ex. 12:2):

B.   You count by it, but the nations of the world will not count by it. [They use the solar calendar, you the lunar one.]

XIV.2 A.   R. Levi in the name of R. Yosé b. R. Ilai: "It is merely natural that someone who presently is great should count by what is great, and someone who presently is small should count by what is small.

B.   "Accordingly, Esau [Rome] counts by the sun, because it is great, while Jacob [Israel] counts by the moon, for it is small."

C.   Said R. Nahman, "That really is a good omen. Esau counts by the sun, because it is great. But just as the sun rules by day but does not rule by night, so the wicked Esau rules in this world but not in the world to come.

D.   "Jacob counts by the moon, which is small, and just as the moon rules by night and also by day [making its appearance both by night and by day], so, too, will Jacob rule in this world and in the world to come."

E.   R. Nahman said, "So long as the light of the great luminary glows splendidly in the world, the light of the lesser luminary is not going to be noted. Once the light of the great light sets, then the light of the lesser one shines forth.

F.   "So too, as long as the light of the wicked Esau lasts, the light of Jacob will not be seen. Once the light of the wicked Esau sets, then the light of Jacob will shine forth.

G.   "That is in line with this verse: 'Arise, shine [for behold, darkness shall cover the earth, and gross darkness the peoples, but upon you the Lord will arise, and his glory shall be seen upon you]' (Isa. 60:1)."

III. Matters of Philosophy, Natural Science and Metaphysics

Nothing could be further from the present category than the materials collected in this document.

54

Pesiqta deRab Kahana Pisqa Six

For the purpose of this study I find nothing in this *pisqa*.

55

Pesiqta deRab Kahana Pisqa Seven

I. Unarticulated Premises: The Givens of Religious Conduct

1. First, property is afflicted, then the person; and that rule is shown in both scriptural narrative and law:

VII

X.1　A. R. Huna and R. Joshua bar Abin, son-in-law of R. Levi, in the name of R. Levi: "The Merciful God does not touch lives first of all [but exacts vengeance on property]. From whom do you learn that fact? From Job: 'A messenger came to Job and said, The oxen were plowing and the asses feeding beside them' (Job 1:14)."

X.2　A. [The same proposition derives from the case] also of Mahlon and Chilion. First their horses, camels, and asses died, and then he died,

　　B. as it is said: "And Elimelech, Naomi's husband, died" (Ruth 1:3), then the two sons: "Mahlon and Chilian died, both of them" (Ruth 1:5). [Delete: And then she died.]

X.3　A. So, too, is the rule applying to skin ailments which affect man.

　　B. **First of all, it begins on his house, and, if the man repents, the affected stone has only to be removed: "They shall dismantle the stones" (Lev. 14:40). If the man does not repent, then the whole house has to be dismantled: "And he will dismantle the house" (Lev. 14:45). And then it affects his clothing. If he repents, the clothing has to be ripped: "And he shall tear the affected patch out of the garment or the hide or from the warp or from the woof" (Lev. 13:56). If he does not repent, then the clothing has to be burned: "And he will burn the clothing" (Lev. 13:52). Then it affects his body. If he repents, it goes away, and he departs, and if not, it comes back on him: "And he shall sit solitary, his dwelling will be outside of the camp" (Lev. 13:46) [T. Neg. 6:4].**

X.4　A. So, too, is the rule as to the events in Egypt:

　　B. First the measure of justice affected their property: "He smote their vines and their fig trees" (Ps. 105:33).

　　C. Then: "He gave over their cattle to the hail and their flocks to fiery bolts of lightning" (Ps. 78:48).

　　D. Then at the end: "He smote all the firstborn of Egypt" (Ps. 78:51).

II. Unarticulated Premises: The Givens of Religious Conviction

1. God favors Israel over the nations, as shown by the striking contrast between the justice done to Israel and the decrees of punishment issued against the nations.

VII

IV.4 A. What is the meaning of "the justice of your decrees"?

       B. [Thanks are due for] the decree of judgment that you carried out against the wicked Pharaoh, and the justice that you did with our elder, Sarah.

       C That is in line with this verse: "And the Lord afflicted Pharaoh with great plagues" (Gen. 12:17).

IV.5 A. Another interpretation of "the justice of your decrees":

       B. [David said,] "[Thanks are due for] the decree of judgment that you carried out against the nations of the world [Ammon and Moab], and the justice that you did with our ancestor and our ancestress [reference here is to Boaz and Ruth].

       C. "For if he [Boaz] had [Braude and Kapstein, p. 143:] slipped into her as she lay at his feet, whence would I have had my origin?

       D. "Instead you set a blessing into his heart, so he said, 'Blessed are you of the Lord, my daughter' (Ruth 3:10)."

IV.6 A. Another interpretation of "the justice of your decrees":

       B. [Thanks are due for] the decree of judgment that you carried out against the Egyptians in Egypt.

       C. And for the righteousness that you carried out with our forefathers in Egypt.

       D. For they had to their credit only two religious duties on account of which they should be redeemed, the blood of the Passover-offering and the blood of circumcision.

       E. That is in line with this verse: "And I passed over you and I saw you wallowing in your bloods, and I said to you, In your bloods, live" (Ezek. 16:6).

       F. "In your bloods": the blood of the Passover-offering and the blood of circumcision.

III. Matters of Philosophy, Natural Science and Metaphysics

Obviously, this category is useless.

56

Pesiqta deRab Kahana Pisqa Eight

The parashah is shared with Leviticus Rabbah XXVIII.

57

Pesiqta deRab Kahana Pisqa Nine

The *pisqa* goes over ground covered in Leviticus Rabbah.

58

Pesiqta deRab Kahana Pisqa Ten

I see nothing of special interest here.

59

Pesiqta deRab Kahana Pisqa Eleven

I find nothing that requires inclusion in this repertoire.

60

Pesiqta deRab Kahana Pisqa Twelve

I. Unarticulated Premises: The Givens of Religious Conduct

I find nothing of halakhic interest here.

II. Unarticulated Premises: The Givens of Religious Conviction

1. The numerous religious duties that have been assigned to Israel are marks of God's engagement with the life of Israel. The mark of the election of Israel is the commandments:

XII

I.1   A.   R. Judah bar Simon commenced discourse by citing the following verse: "'Many daughters show how capable they are, but you excel them all. [Charm is a delusion and beauty fleeting; it is the God-fearing woman who is honored. Extol her for the fruit of her toil and let her labors bring her honor in the city gate]' (Prov. 31:29-31):

     B.   "The first man was assigned six religious duties, and they are: not worshiping idols, not blaspheming, setting up courts of justice, not murdering, not practicing fornication, not stealing.

     C.   "And all of them derive from a single verse of Scripture: 'And the Lord God commanded the man, saying, "You may freely eat of every tree of the garden, [but of the tree of the knowledge of good and evil you shall not eat, for in the day that you eat of it you shall die]"' (Gen. 2:16).

     D.   "'And the Lord God commanded the man, saying': this refers to idolatry, as it is said, 'For Ephraim was happy to walk after the command' (Hos. 5:11).

     E.   "'The Lord': this refers to blasphemy, as it is said, 'Whoever curses the name of the Lord will surely die' (Lev. 24:16).

     F.   "'God': this refers to setting up courts of justice, as it is said, 'God [in context, the judges] you shall not curse' (Ex. 22:27).

     G.   "'the man': this refers to murder, as it is said, 'He who sheds the blood of man by man his blood shall be shed' (Gen. 9:6).

H.   "'saying': this refers to fornication, as it is said, 'Saying, will a man divorce his wife...' (Jer. 3:1).

I.   "'You may freely eat of every tree of the garden': this refers to the prohibition of stealing, as you say, 'but of the tree of the knowledge of good and evil you shall not eat.'

J.   "Noah was commanded, in addition, not to cut a limb from a living beast, as it is said, 'But as to meat with its soul – its blood you shall not eat' (Gen. 9:4).

K.   "Abraham was commanded, in addition, concerning circumcision, as it is said, 'And as to you, my covenant you shall keep' (Gen. 17:9).

L.   "Isaac was circumcised on the eighth day, as it is said, 'And Abraham circumcised Isaac, his son, on the eighth day' (Gen. 21:4).

M.   "Jacob was commanded not to eat the sciatic nerve, as it is said, 'On that account the children of Israel will not eat the sciatic nerve' (Gen. 32:33).

N.   "Judah was commanded concerning marrying the childless brother's widow, as it is said, 'And Judah said to Onen, Go to the wife of your childless brother and exercise the duties of a levir with her' (Gen. 38:8).

O.   "But as to you, at Sinai you received six hundred thirteen religious duties, two hundred forty-eight religious duties of commission [acts to be done], three hundred sixty-five religious duties of omission [acts not to be done],

P.   "the former matching the two hundred forty-eight limbs that a human being has.

Q.   "Each limb says to a person, 'By your leave, with me do this religious duty.'

R.   "Three hundred sixty-five religious duties of omission [acts not to be done] matching the days of the solar calendar.

S.   "Each day says to a person, 'By your leave, on me do not carry out that transgression.'"

I.4   A.   "Extol her for the fruit of her toil and let her labors bring her honor in the city gate":

B.   Said R. Yosé bar Jeremiah, "On what account does Scripture compare prophets to women? Just as a woman is not ashamed to demand from her husband what her household needs, so the prophets are not ashamed to demand before the Holy One, blessed be He, the needs of Israel.

C.   "Said the Holy One, blessed be He, to Israel, 'My children, read this passage every year, and I shall credit it to you as if you were standing before me at Mount Sinai and receiving the Torah.'

D.   "When is that the case?

E.   "'In the third month after Israel had left Egypt, [they came to the wilderness of Sinai. They set out from Rephidim and entered the wilderness of Sinai, where they encamped, pitching their tent opposite the Mountain. Moses went up the mountain of God, and the Lord called to him from the mountain and said, "Speak thus to the house of Jacob and tell this to the sons of Israel: You have seen with your own eyes what I did to Egypt and how I have carried you on eagles' wings and brought you here to me. If only you will now listen to me and keep my covenant, then out of all peoples you shall become my special possession; for the whole earth is mine. You shall be my kingdom of priests, my holy nation"'] (Ex. 19:1-6)."

III. Matters of Philosophy, Natural Science and Metaphysics

This category remains useless.

61

Pesiqta deRab Kahana Pisqa Thirteen

The notion that documents rest on identifiable and useful premises is called into question by this *pisqa*, as by others of its type.

62

Pesiqta deRab Kahana Pisqa Fourteen

I. Unarticulated Premises: The Givens of Religious Conduct

This category does not pertain.

II. Unarticulated Premises: The Givens of Religious Conviction

1. There is no fault to be found with God; the fathers found no fault with their punishment; there is no reason to complain against God on any grounds whatsoever:

XIV

V.1 A.   It is written, "Thus said the Lord, What wrong did your fathers find in me that they went far from me and went after worthlessness and became worthless?" (Jer. 2:5)

B.   Said R. Isaac, "This refers to one who leaves the scroll of the Torah and departs. Concerning him, Scripture says, 'What wrong did your fathers find in me that they went far from me.'

C.   "Said the Holy One, blessed be He, to the Israelites, 'My children, your fathers found no wrong with me, but you have found wrong with me.

D.   "'The first Man found no wrong with me, but you have found wrong with me.'

E.   "To what may the first Man be compared?

F.   "To a sick man, to whom the physician came. The physician said to him, 'Eat this, don't eat that.'

G.   "When the man violated the instructions of the physician, he brought about his own death.

H.   "[As he lay dying,] his relatives came to him and said to him, 'Is it possible that the physician is imposing on you the divine attribute of justice?'

I.   "He said to them, 'God forbid. I am the one who brought about my own death. This is what he instructed me, saying to me, 'Eat this, don't eat that,' but when I violated his instructions, I brought about my own death.

222

J. "So, too, all the generations came to the first Man, saying to him, 'Is it possible that the Holy One, blessed be He, is imposing the attribute of justice on you?'

K. "He said to them, 'God forbid. I am the one who has brought about my own death. Thus did he command me, saying to me, "Of all the trees of the garden you may eat, but of the tree of the knowledge of good and evil you may not eat" (Gen. 2:17). When I violated his instructions, I brought about my own death, for it is written, "On the day on which you eat it, you will surely die" (Gen. 2:17).'

L. "[God's speech now continues:] 'Pharaoh found no wrong with me, but you have found wrong with me.'

M. "To what may Pharaoh be likened?

N. "To the case of a king who went overseas and went and deposited all his possessions with a member of his household. After some time the king returned from overseas and said to the man, 'Return what I deposited with you.'

O. "He said to him, 'I did not such thing with you, and you left me nothing.'

P. "What did he do to him? He took him and put him in prison.

Q. "He said to him, 'I am your slave. Whatever you left with me I shall make up to you.'

R. "So, at the outset, said the Holy One, blessed be He, to Moses, 'Now go and I shall send you to Pharaoh' (Ex. 3:10).

S. "That wicked man said to him, 'Who is the Lord that I should listen to his voice? I do not know the Lord' (Ex. 2:5).

T. "But when he brought the ten plagues on him, 'The Lord is righteous and I and my people are wicked' (Ex. 9:27).

U. "[God's speech now continues:] 'Moses found no wrong with me, but you have found wrong with me.'

V. "To what may Moses be compared?

W. "To a king who handed his son over to a teacher, saying to him, 'Do not call my son a moron.'"

X. What is the meaning of the word moron?

Y. Said R. Reuben, "In the Greek language they call an idiot a moron."

Z. [Resuming the discourse:] "One time the teacher belittled the boy and called him a moron. Said the king to him, 'With all my authority I instructed you, saying to you, Do not call my son a fool,' and yet you have called my son a fool. It is not the calling of a smart fellow to go along with fools. [You're fired!]'

AA. "Thus it is written, 'And the Lord spoke to Moses and to Aaron and commanded them concerning the children of Israel' (Ex. 6:13).

BB. "What did he command them? He said to them, 'Do not call my sons morons.' But when they rebelled at the waters of rebellion, Moses said to them, 'Listen, I ask, you morons' (Num. 20:10).

CC. "Said the Holy One, blessed be He, to them, 'With all my authority I instructed you, saying to you, Do not call my sons fools,' and yet you have called my sons fools. It is not the calling of a smart fellow to go along with fools. [You're fired!]'

DD. "Therefore, what is written is not 'You [singular] therefore shall not bring,' but 'you [plural] therefore shall not bring' (Num. 20:12).

> [For God said,] 'Neither you nor your brother nor your sister will enter the Land of Israel.'

EE. "[God's speech now continues:] Said the Holy One, blessed be He, to Israel, 'Your fathers in the wilderness found no wrong with me, but you have found wrong with me.'

FF. "'I said to them, "One who makes an offering to other gods will be utterly destroyed" (Ex. 22:19), but they did not do so, but rather, "They prostrated themselves to it and worshiped it" (Ex. 32:8).

GG. "'After all the wicked things that they did, what is written, "And the Lord regretted the evil that he had considered doing to his people" (Ex. 32:14).'"

V.2 A. Said R. Judah bar Simon, "Said the Holy One, blessed be He, to Israel, 'Your fathers in the wilderness found no wrong with me, but you have found wrong with me.'

B. "'I said to them, "For six days you will gather [the manna] and on the seventh day it is a Sabbath, on which there will be no collecting of manna" (Ex. 16:26).

C. "'But they did not listen, but rather: "And it happened that on the seventh day some of the people went out to gather manna and did not find it" (Ex. 16:27).

D. "'Had they found it, they would have gathered it [and violated his wishes, so he did not give manna on the seventh day, therefore avoiding the occasion of making them sin].'"

III. Matters of Philosophy, Natural Science and Metaphysics

This category serves no purpose.

63

Pesiqta deRab Kahana Pisqa Fifteen

I. Unarticulated Premises: The Givens of Religious Conduct

There is nothing of legal consequence here.

II. Unarticulated Premises: The Givens of Religious Conviction

1. God mourned for Israel the way a mortal king mourns:

XV

III.1 A. Bar Qappara opened discourse by citing the following verse: "In that day the Lord God of hosts called to weeping and mourning, to baldness and girding with sackcloth; [and behold, joy and gladness, slaying oxen and killing sheep, eating meat and drinking wine. 'Let us eat and drink for tomorrow we die.' The Lord of hosts has revealed himself in my ears: 'Surely this iniquity will not be forgiven you until you die,' says the Lord of hosts]" (Isa. 15:12-14).

B. "Said the Holy One, blessed be He, to the ministering angels, 'When a mortal king mourns, what does he do?'

C. "They said to him, 'He puts sack over his door.'

D. "He said to them, 'I, too, shall do that. "I will clothe the heavens with blackness [and make sackcloth for their covering]" (Isa. 50:3).'

E. "He further asked them, 'When a mortal king mourns, what does he do?'

F. "They said to him, 'He extinguishes the torches.'

G. "He said to them, 'I, too, shall do that. "The sun and moon will become black [and the stars stop shining]" (Joel 4:15).'

H. "He further asked them, 'When a mortal king mourns, what does he do?'

I. "They said to him, 'He goes barefooted.'

J. "He said to them, 'I, too, shall do that. "The Lord in the whirlwind and in the storm will be his way and the clouds [the dust of his feet]" (Nah. 1:3).'

K. "He further asked them, 'When a mortal king mourns, what does he do?'

L.   "They said to him, 'He sits in silence.'

M.   "He said to them, 'I, too, shall do that. "He will sit alone and keep silence because he has laid it upon himself" (Lam. 3:28).'

N.   "He further asked them, 'When a mortal king mourns, what does he do?'

O.   "They said to him, 'He overturns the beds.'

P.   "He said to them, 'I, too, shall do that. "I beheld to the seats of thrones [having been overturned, now] were placed right side up" (Dan. 7:9).'

Q.   "He further asked them, 'When a mortal king mourns, what does he do?'

R.   "They said to him, 'He tears his [royal] purple garment.'

S.   "He said to them, 'I, too, shall do that. "The Lord has done that which he devised, he tore his word" (Lam. 2:17).'"

T.   What is the meaning of the phrase, "he tore his word"?

U.   R. Jacob of Kefar Hanan said, "He tears his purple garments."

V.   [Resuming the earlier account,] "He further asked them, 'When a mortal king mourns, what does he do?'

W.   "They said to him, 'He sits and laments.'

X.   "He said to them, 'I, too, shall do that. "How lonely sits the city [that was full of people! How like a widow has she become, she that was great among the nations! She that was a princess among the cities has become a vassal. She weeps bitterly in the night, tears on her cheeks, among all her lovers she has none to comfort her; all her friends have dealt treacherously with her, they have become her enemies]" (Lam. 1:1-2).'"

2.   Sin is atoned for by the Temple sacrifices:

XV

VII.4 A.   "...Righteousness lodged in her":

B.   Said R. Yudan in the name of R. Simon, "No one ever spent the night in Jerusalem while still bearing sin.

C.   "How so? The daily whole-offering of the morning would effect atonement for the sins that had been committed overnight, and the daily whole-offering of dusk would effect atonement for the transgressions that had been committed by day.

D.   "In consequence, no one ever spent the night in Jerusalem while still bearing sin.

E.   "And what verse of Scripture makes that point? 'Righteousness lodged in her' (Isa. 1:21)."

III. Matters of Philosophy, Natural Science and Metaphysics

Not surprisingly, we find nothing pertinent.

64

Pesiqta deRab Kahana Pisqa Sixteen

I. Unarticulated Premises: The Givens of Religious Conduct

This category does not pertain.

II. Unarticulated Premises: The Givens of Religious Conviction

1. Ultimately, God and all the angels will comfort Jerusalem:

XVI

VIII.1 A. "How will you comfort me through vanity, and as for your answers, there remains only faithlessness" (Job 21:34):

B. Said R. Abba bar Kahana [on the meaning of the word translated as faithlessness], "Your words [of comfort and consolation, that Job's friends had provided him] require clarification."

C. Rabbis say, "Your words contain contradictions." [We shall now have a long series of examples of how God's messages to the prophets contradict themselves.]

VIII.2 A. The Holy One said to the prophets, "Go and comfort Jerusalem."

B. Hosea went to give comfort. He said to her [the city], "The Holy One, blessed be He, has sent me to you to bring you comfort."

C. She said to him, "What do you have in hand."

D. He said to her, "I will be as the dew to Israel" (Hos. 14:6).

E. She said to him, "Yesterday, you said to me, 'Ephraim is smitten, their root is dried up, they shall bear no fruit' (Hos. 9:16), and now you say this to me? Which shall we believe, the first statement or the second?"

VIII.3 A. Joel went to give comfort. He said to the city, "The Holy One, blessed be He, has sent me to you to bring you comfort."

B. She said to him, "What do you have in hand."

C. He said to her, "It shall come to pass in that day that the mountains shall drop down sweet wine and the hills shall flow with milk" (Joel 4:18).

D. She said to him, "Yesterday, you said to me, 'Awake you drunkards and weep, wail, you who drink wine, because of the sweet wine, for it is cut off from your mouth' (Joel 1:5), and now you say this to me? Which shall we believe, the first statement or the second?"

VIII.4 A. Amos went to give comfort. He said to the city, "The Holy One, blessed be He, has sent me to you to bring you comfort."

B. She said to him, "What do you have in hand."

C. He said to her, "On that day I will raise up the fallen tabernacle of David" (Amos 9:11).

D. She said to him, "Yesterday, you said to me, 'The virgin of Israel is fallen, she shall no more rise' (Amos 5:2), and now you say this to me? Which shall we believe, the first statement or the second?"

VIII.5 A. Micah went to give comfort. He said to the city, "The Holy One, blessed be He, has sent me to you to bring you comfort."

B. She said to him, "What do you have in hand."

C. He said to her, "Who is like God to you who pardons iniquity and passes by transgression" (Mic. 7:18).

D. She said to him, "Yesterday, you said to me, 'For the transgression of Jacob is all this and for the sins of the house of Israel' (Mic. 1:56), and now you say this to me? Which shall we believe, the first statement or the second?"

VIII.6 A. Nahum went to give comfort. He said to the city, "The Holy One, blessed be He, has sent me to you to bring you comfort."

B. She said to him, "What do you have in hand."

C. He said to her, "The wicked one shall no more pass through you, he is utterly cut off" (Nah. 2:1).

D. She said to him, "Yesterday, you said to me, 'Out of you came he forth who devises evil against the Lord, who counsels wickedness' (Nah. 1:11), and now you say this to me? Which shall we believe, the first statement or the second?"

VIII.7 A. Habakkuk went to give comfort. He said to the city, "The Holy One, blessed be He, has sent me to you to bring you comfort."

B. She said to him, "What do you have in hand."

C. He said to her, "You have come forth for the deliverance of your people, for the deliverance of your anointed" (Hab. 3:13).

D. She said to him, "Yesterday, you said to me, 'How long, O Lord, shall I cry and you will not hear, I cry to you of violence' (Hab. 1:22), and now you say this to me? Which shall we believe, the first statement or the second?"

VIII.8 A. Zephaniah went to give comfort. He said to the city, "The Holy One, blessed be He, has sent me to you to bring you comfort."

B. She said to him, "What do you have in hand."

C. He said to her, "It shall come to pass at that time that I will search Jerusalem with the lamps" (Zeph. 1:12).

D. She said to him, "Yesterday, you said to me, 'A day of darkness and gloominess, a day of clouds and thick darkness' (Zeph. 1:15), and now you say this to me? Which shall we believe, the first statement or the second?"

VIII.9 A. Haggai went to give comfort. He said to the city, "The Holy One, blessed be He, has sent me to you to bring you comfort."

B. She said to him, "What do you have in hand."

C. He said to her, "Shall the seed ever again remain in the barn? Shall the vine, the fig tree, the pomegranate, and the olive tree ever again bear no fruit? Indeed not, from this day I will bless you" (Hag. 2:19).

D. She said to him, "Yesterday, you said to me, 'You sow much and bring in little' (Hag. 1:6), and now you say this to me? Which shall we believe, the first statement or the second?"

VIII.10 A. Zechariah went to give comfort. He said to the city, "The Holy One, blessed be He, has sent me to you to bring you comfort."

B. She said to him, "What do you have in hand."

C. He said to her, "I am very angry with the nations that are at ease" (Zech. 1:15).

D. She said to him, "Yesterday, you said to me, 'The Lord was very angry with your fathers' (Zech. 1:2), and now you say this to me? Which shall we believe, the first statement or the second?"

VIII.11 A. Malachi went to give comfort. He said to the city, "The Holy One, blessed be He, has sent me to you to bring you comfort."

B. She said to him, "What do you have in hand."

C. He said to her, "All the nations shall call you happy, for you shall be a happy land" (Mal. 3:12).

D. She said to him, "Yesterday, you said to me, 'I have no pleasure in you says the Lord of hosts' (Mal. 1:10), and now you say this to me? Which shall we believe, the first statement or the second?"

VIII.12 A. The prophets went to the Holy One, blessed be He, saying to him, "Lord of the ages, Jerusalem has not accepted the comfort [that we brought her]."

B. Said to them the Holy One, blessed be He, "You and I together shall go and comfort her."

C. Thus we say: "Comfort, comfort my people" but read the letters for "my people as with me."

D. Let the creatures of the upper world comfort her, let the creatures of the lower world comfort her.

E. Let the living comfort her, let the dead comfort her.

F. Comfort her in this world, comfort her in the world to come.

G. Comfort her on account of the Ten Tribes, comfort her on account of the tribe of Judah and Benjamin.

H. [Thus we must understand the statement, "Comfort, comfort my people, says your God. Speak tenderly to the heart of Jerusalem and cry to her that her warfare is ended, that her iniquity is pardoned, that she has received from the Lord's hand double for all her sins" (Isa. 40:1-2) in this way:] "Comfort, comfort my people but read the letters for my people as with me."

This will come about at the end of time, and the comfort that the prophets foresaw has yet to take place; it is not over but in the future:

XVI

X.1 A. "[Comfort, comfort my people,] *will* your God say. [Speak tenderly to the heart of Jerusalem and cry to her that her warfare is ended, that her iniquity is pardoned, that she has received from the Lord's hand double for all her sins]" (Isa. 40:1-2):

B. R. Hanina bar Pappa and R. Simeon:

C. [Focusing on the future tense of the phrase, "Comfort, comfort my people, *will* your God say,"] R. Hanina bar Pappa said, "The Israelites said to Isaiah, 'Our lord, Isaiah, is it possible that you have come to comfort only that generation in the days of which the house of the sanctuary was destroyed?'

D. "He said to them, 'It is to all generations that I have come to bring comfort. What is said is not, "Your God *has* said," but rather, "Your God will say."'"

E. Said R. Simon, "The Israelites said to Isaiah, 'Our lord, Isaiah, is it possible that all these things that you say you have made up on your own?'

F. "He said to them, 'It is to all generations that I have come to bring comfort. What is said is not, "Your God *has* said," but rather, "Your God will say."'"

G. Said R. Hinenah son of R. Abba, "In eight passages [Isa. 1:11, 18, 33:10, 40:1, 25, 41:21 (2x), 66:9 (Mandelbaum, p. 278n.)], it is written, 'Your God will say,' matching the eight prophets who prophesied after the house of the sanctuary [was first destroyed] and these are they: Joel, Amos, Zephanaiah, Haggai, Zechariah, Malachi, Ezekiel, and Jeremiah."

The comfort that is coming will more than compensate for the anguish of the past:

XVI

XI.1 A. "[Comfort, comfort my people, says your God.] Speak tenderly to the heart of Jerusalem and declare to her [that her warfare is ended, that her iniquity is pardoned, that she has received from the Lord's hand double for all her sins]" (Isa. 40:1-2).

B. When they sinned with the head, they were smitten at the head, but they were comforted through the head.

C. When they sinned with the head: "Let us make a head and let us return to Egypt" (Num. 14:4).

D. ...they were smitten at the head: "The whole head is sick" (Isa. 1:5).

E. ...but they were comforted through the head: "Their king has passed before them and the Lord is at the head of them" (Mic. 2:13).

XI.2 A. When they sinned with the eye, they were smitten at the eye, but they were comforted through the eye.

B. When they sinned with the eye: "[The daughters of Zion...walk]...with wanton eyes" (Isa. 3:16).

C. ...they were smitten at the eye: "My eye, my eye runs down with water" (Lam. 1:16).

D. ...but they were comforted through the eye: "For every eye shall see the Lord returning to Zion" (Isa. 52:8).

XI.3 A. When they sinned with the ear, they were smitten at the ear, but they were comforted through the ear.

B. When they sinned with the ear: "They stopped up their ears so as not to hear" (Zech. 7:11).

C. ...they were smitten at the ear: "Their ears shall be deaf" (Mic. 7:16).

D. ...but they were comforted through the ear: "Your ears shall hear a word saying, [This is the way]" (Isa. 30:21).

XI.4	A.	When they sinned with the nose [spelled *af*, which can also mean, *yet* or *also*] [Braude and Kapstein, p. 299, add: with obscene gestures], they were smitten at the nose, but they were comforted through the nose.
	B.	When they sinned with the nose: "And lo, they put the branch to their noses" (Ezek. 8:17).
	C.	...they were smitten at the word *af* [also]: "I also will do this to you" (Lev. 26:16).
	D.	...but they were comforted through the word *af* [now meaning *yet*]: "And yet for all that, when they are in the land of their enemies, I will not reject them" (Lev. 26:44).
XI.5	A.	When they sinned with the mouth, they were smitten at the mouth, but they were comforted through the mouth.
	B.	When they sinned with the mouth: "Every mouth speaks wantonness" (Isa. 9:16).
	C.	...they were smitten at the mouth: "[The Aramaeans and the Philistines] devour Israel with open mouth" (Isa. 9:11).
	D.	...but they were comforted through the mouth: "Then was our mouth filled with laughter" (Ps. 126:2).
XI.6	A.	When they sinned with the tongue, they were smitten at the tongue, but they were comforted through the tongue.
	B.	When they sinned with the tongue: "They bend their tongue, [their bow of falsehood]" (Jer. 9:2).
	C.	...they were smitten at the tongue: "The tongue of the sucking [child cleaves to the roof of his mouth for thirst]" (Lam. 4:4).
	D.	...but they were comforted through the tongue: "And our tongue with singing" (Ps. 126:2).
XI.7	A.	When they sinned with the heart, they were smitten at the heart, but they were comforted through the heart.
	B.	When they sinned with the heart: "Yes, they made their hearts as a stubborn stone" (Zech. 7:12).
	C.	...they were smitten at the heart: "And the whole heart faints" (Isa. 1:5).
	D.	...but they were comforted through the heart: "Speak to the heart of Jerusalem" (Isa. 40:2).
XI.8	A.	When they sinned with the hand, they were smitten at the hand, but they were comforted through the hand.
	B.	When they sinned with the hand: "Your hands are full of blood" (Isa. 1:15).
	C.	...they were smitten at the hand: "The hands of women full of compassion have boiled their own children" (Lam. 4:10).
	D.	...but they were comforted through the hand: "The Lord will set his hand again the second time [to recover the remnant of his people]" (Isa. 11:11).
XI.9	A.	When they sinned with the foot, they were smitten at the foot, but they were comforted through the foot.
	B.	When they sinned with the foot: "The daughters of Zion...walk... making a tinkling with their feet" (Isa. 3:16).
	C.	...they were smitten at the foot: "Your feet will stumble upon the dark mountains" (Jer. 13:16).

D.   ...but they were comforted through the foot: "How beautiful upon the mountains are the feet of the messenger of good tidings" (Isa. 52:7).

XI.10 A.   When they sinned with *this*, they were smitten at *this*, but they were comforted through *this*.

B.   When they sinned with *this*: "[The people said...Go, make us a god], for as for *this* man Moses..., [we do not know what has become of him]" (Ex. 32:1).

C.   ...they were smitten at *this*: "For *this* our heart is faint" (Lam. 5:17).

D.   ...but they were comforted through *this*: "It shall be said in that day, Lo, *this* is our God" (Isa. 25:9).

XI.11 A.   When they sinned with *he*, they were smitten at *he*, but they were comforted through *he*.

B.   When they sinned with *he*: "They have denied the Lord and said, It is not *he*" (Jer. 5:12).

C.   ...they were smitten at *he:* "Therefore he has turned to be their enemy, and *he himself* fought against them" (Isa. 63:10).

D.   ...but they were comforted through *he:* "I even I am *he* who comforts you" (Isa. 51:12).

XI.12 A.   When they sinned with fire, they were smitten at fire, but they were comforted through fire.

B.   When they sinned with fire: "The children gather wood and the fathers kindle fire" (Jer. 7:18).

C.   ...they were smitten at fire: "For from on high he has sent fire into my bones" (Lam. 1:13).

D.   ...but they were comforted through fire: "For I, says the Lord, will be for her a wall of fire round about" (Zech. 2:9).

XI.13 A.   When they sinned in double measure, they were smitten in double measure, but they were comforted in double measure.

B.   When they sinned in double measure: "Jerusalem has sinned a sin" (Lam. 1:8).

C.   ...they were smitten in double measure: "that she has received from the Lord's hand double for all her sins" (Isa. 40:2).

D.   ...but they were comforted in double measure: "Comfort, comfort my people, says your God. [Speak tenderly to the heart of Jerusalem and cry to her that her warfare is ended, that her iniquity is pardoned, that she has received from the Lord's hand double for all her sins]" (Isa. 40:1-2).

III. Matters of Philosophy, Natural Science and Metaphysics

The category does not apply.

65

Pesiqta deRab Kahana Pisqa Seventeen

This *pisqa* goes over the same conceptions as the foregoing.

66

Pesiqta deRab Kahana Pisqa Eighteen

I. Unarticulated Premises: The Givens of Religious Conduct
There is nothing of legal interest, therefore no premise emerges.

II. Unarticulated Premises: The Givens of Religious Conviction
1. Though God has removed his presence from Jerusalem for a time, it is not forever; God will assuredly return to Zion:

XVIII

I.1   A.   "O sons of a man, how long shall my honor suffer shame? [How long will you love vain words and seek after lies? But know that the Lord has set apart the faithful for himself; the Lord hears when I call to him]" (Ps. 4:2-3):

      B.   The reference to "sons of a man" alludes to Doeg and Ahitophel.

      C.   Why does Scripture refer to them as sons of a man?

      D.   For they are the sons of Abraham, Isaac and Jacob.

      E.   The word "man" refers only to our father, Abraham, as it is said: "And now, return the wife of the man, because he is a prophet" (Gen. 20:7).

      F.   The word "man" refers only to our father, Isaac, as it is said: "Who is this man, who is going" (Gen. 24:65).

      G.   The word "man" refers only to our father, Jacob, as it is said: "A simple man" (Gen. 25:27).

I.2   A.   "...how long shall my honor suffer shame? [How long will you love vain words and seek after lies?]" (Ps. 4:3):

      B.   Said David, "How long will you bring shame on my honor and call me merely, 'Son of Jesse': 'Why has the son of Jesse not come' (1 Sam. 20:27). 'I saw the son of Jesse' (1 Sam. 16:18). 'Will the son of Jesse give everyone of you [fields]' (1 Sam. 22:7). Do I not have a name?"

I.3   A.   "...how long will you love vain words and seek after lies?" (Ps. 4:3):

      B.   ...pursuing after words of vanity: "[The Lord] has abandoned him, forgotten him, the kingdom will never again return to him."

I.4   A.   "...and seek after lies?" (Ps. 4:3):

234

	B.	"What are you thinking? Is it that because my kingdom has been taken away from me for a while, that it is forever?"
I.5	A.	"But know that the Lord has set apart the godly for himself; [the Lord hears when I call to him]":
	B.	"He has already sent word to me through the prophet Nathan and said to me, 'The Lord will indeed remove your sin and you will not die' (2 Sam. 13:14)."
I.6	A.	Another interpretation of the verse "O sons of a man, how long will you love vain words and seek after lies? [But know that the Lord has set apart the faithful for himself; the Lord hears when I call to him]" (Ps. 4:2-3):
	B.	"O sons of a man" refers to the nations of the world.
	C.	And why does Scripture refer to them as sons of a man?
	D.	For they come from the sons of Noah's sons, and the word for "man" refers only to Noah, as it is said, "And Noah was a righteous man" (Gen. 6:9).
I.7	A.	"...how long shall my honor suffer shame" refers to the house of the sanctuary.
	B.	The Holy One, blessed be He, says, "How long will you bring shame to the honor of my house, spitting at it, dirtying it, doing your transgressions in it?"
I.8	A.	"...How long will you love vain words":
	B.	...pursuing after words of vanity: "[The Lord] has abandoned it, forgotten it, the Presence of God will never again return to it."
I.9	A.	"...and seek after lies?" (Ps. 4:3):
	B.	"What are you thinking? Is it that because I removed my presence from it for a while, that it is forever?"
I.10	A.	"But know that the Lord has set apart the faithful for himself; the Lord hears when I call to him":
	B.	"I have already sent word to him through the prophet Isaiah and I have said to [Jerusalem]: 'O afflicted one, storm-tossed [and not comforted, behold, I will set your stones in antimony, and lay your foundations with sapphires. I will make your pinnacles of agate, your gates of carbuncles, and all your wall of precious stones. All your sons shall be taught by the Lord, and great shall be the prosperity of your sons. In righteousness you shall be established; you shall be far from oppression, for you shall not fear; and from terror, for it shall not come near you]' (Isa. 54:11-14)."

III. Matters of Philosophy, Natural Science and Metaphysics

The category remains inert.

67

Pesiqta deRab Kahana Pisqa Nineteen

I. Unarticulated Premises: The Givens of Religious Conduct

There is no point of relevance.

II. Unarticulated Premises: The Givens of Religious Conviction

1. Israel's sin brings about its fate, but the gentiles who deliver the divine punishment themselves have sinned and will be punished too:

XIX

I.1   A.   "[You know what reproaches I bear, all my anguish is seen by you.] Reproach has broken my heart, my shame and my dishonor are past hope; I looked for consolation and received none, for comfort and did not find any" (Ps. 69:19-21):

    B.   "The reproach that has broken us are the Ammonites and Moabites."

    C.   You find that when sin had made it possible for the gentiles to enter Jerusalem, the Ammonites and Moabites came in with them.

    D.   They came into the house of the holy of holies and took the cherubim and put them onto a bier and paraded them around the streets of Jerusalem, saying, "Did not the Israelites say, 'We do not worship idols'? See what they were doing."

    E.   That is in line with this verse of Scripture: "Moab and Seir say, [Behold the house of Judah is like all the other nations]" (Ezek. 25:8).

    F.   What did they say? "Woe, woe, all of them are as one."

    G.   From that time the Holy One, blessed be He, said, "I have heard the shame of Moab and the blaspheming of the children of Ammon, who have shamed my people, the children of Israel, and aggrandized their border.... Therefore as I live, says the Lord of hosts, the God of Israel, surely Moab shall be as Sodom and the children of Amon as Gomorrah" (Zeph. 2:8-9).

III. Matters of Philosophy, Natural Science and Metaphysics

Nothing pertains.

68

Pesiqta deRab Kahana Pisqa Twenty

I. Unarticulated Premises: The Givens of Religious Conduct

No rules of conduct occur here.

II. Unarticulated Premises: The Givens of Religious Conviction

1. Zion is now barren but ultimately will bear:

XX

I.1　A.　"...who makes the woman in a childless house a happy mother of children" (Ps. 113:9):

　　　B.　There are seven childless women [in Scripture]: Sarah, Rebecca, Rachel, Leah, the wife of Manoah, Hannah, and Zion.

I.2　A.　Another interpretation of the verse "...who makes the woman in a childless house a happy mother of children" (Ps. 113:9):

　　　B.　This refers to our mother, Sarah: "And Sarah was barren" (Gen. 11:30).

　　　C.　"As a joyful mother of children" (Ps. 113:9): "Sarah has given children suck" (Gen. 21:7).

I.3　A.　Another interpretation of the verse "...who makes the woman in a childless house a happy mother of children" (Ps. 113:9):

　　　B.　This refers to our Rebecca: "And Isaac entreated to the Lord on account of his wife, because she was barren" (Gen. 25:21).

　　　C.　"As a joyful mother of children" (Ps. 113:9): "And the Lord was entreated by him and his wife Rebecca conceived" (Gen. 25:21).

I.4　A.　Another interpretation of the verse "...who makes the woman in a childless house a happy mother of children" (Ps. 113:9):

　　　B.　This refers to Leah: "And the Lord saw that Leah was hated and he opened her womb" (Gen. 29:31). On the basis of that statement we learn that Leah had been barren.

　　　C.　"As a joyful mother of children" (Ps. 113:9): "For I have born him six sons" (Gen. 30:20).

I.5　A.　Another interpretation of the verse "...who makes the woman in a childless house a happy mother of children" (Ps. 113:9):

　　　B.　This refers to Rachel: "And Rachel was barren" (Gen. 29:31).

C. "As a joyful mother of children" (Ps. 113:9): "The children of Rachel: Joseph and Benjamin" (Gen. 35:24).

I.6 A. Another interpretation of the verse "...who makes the woman in a childless house a happy mother of children" (Ps. 113:9):

B. This refers to the wife of Manoah: "And the angel of the Lord looked at the woman and said to her, Lo, you are barren and have not born children" (Judg. 13:3).

C. "As a joyful mother of children" (Ps. 113:9): "And you will conceive and bear a son" (Judg. 13:3).

I.7 A. Another interpretation of the verse "...who makes the woman in a childless house a happy mother of children" (Ps. 113:9):

B. This refers to Hannah: "And Peninah had children but Hannah had no children" (1 Sam. 1:2).

C. "As a joyful mother of children" (Ps. 113:9): "And she conceived and bore three sons and two daughters" (1 Sam. 2:21).

I.8 A. Another interpretation of the verse "...who makes the woman in a childless house a happy mother of children" (Ps. 113:9):

B. This refers to Zion: "Sing aloud, O barren woman [who never bore a child, break into cries of joy, you who have never been in labor; for the deserted wife has more sons than she who lives in wedlock, says the Lord. Enlarge the limits of your home, spread wide the curtains of your tent; let out its ropes to the full and drive the pegs home; for you shall break out of your confines right and left, your descendants shall dispossess wide regions and repeople cities now desolate. Fear not; you shall not be put to shame, you shall suffer no insult, have no cause to blush. It is time to forget the shame of your younger days and remember no more the reproach of your widowhood; for your husband is your maker, whose name is the Lord of hosts; your redeemer is the Holy One of Israel who is called God of all the earth. The Lord has acknowledged you a wife again, once deserted and heartbroken, your God has called you a bride still young though once rejected. On the impulse of a moment I forsook you, but with tender affection I will bring you home again. In sudden anger I hid my face from you for a moment; but now have I pitied you with a love which never fails, says the Lord who ransoms you]" (Isa. 54:1-8).

2. The Temple today is more a center of the righteous than it was when it was standing:

XX

V.1 A. "...for the deserted wife has more sons than she who lives in wedlock, says the Lord":

B. Said R. Abba bar Kahana, "It is written, 'And your mouth is comely' [Braude and Kapstein, p. 333: 'When the Dwelling is become thy desolation.' Note: 'Thy mouth can also mean thy wilderness, thy desolation'; and 'comely' is construed as though spelled as 'residence, temple'] (Song 4:3).

C. "Even though the habitation is turned into a wilderness, still, [unclean persons who entered into the Temple area] are liable for [contaminating] the space within its bounds though the building is destroyed, even as they are liable for violating its bounds when the Temple is built [and standing]."

D.   Said R. Levi, "When it was standing, it made a place for me for the wicked, such as Ahaz, Manasseh, and Amon. When it was destroyed, it made a place for me for righteous, such as Daniel and his allies, Mordecai and his allies, Ezra and his allies."

E.   R. Aha in the name of R. Yohanan: "It made a place for me for many more righteous ones when it was destroyed than it did when it was standing."

III. Matters of Philosophy, Natural Science and Metaphysics

Nothing in this *pisqa* warrants consideration.

69

Pesiqta deRab Kahana Pisqa Twenty-One

I. Unarticulated Premises: The Givens of Religious Conduct

This rubric does not serve.

II. Unarticulated Premises: The Givens of Religious Conviction

1.   God has foreseen all that has happened and has a plan for the future as well:

XXI

V.1   A.   R. Hiyya taught on Tannaite authority, "At the beginning of the creation of the world the Holy One, blessed be He, foresaw that the Temple would be built, destroyed, and rebuilt.

   B.   "'In the beginning God created the heaven and the earth' (Gen. 1:1) [refers to the Temple] when it was built, in line with the following verse: 'That I may plant the heavens and lay the foundations of the earth and say to Zion, You are my people' (Isa. 51:16).

   C.   "'And the earth was unformed' – lo, this refers to the destruction, in line with this verse: 'I saw the earth, and lo, it was unformed' (Jer. 4:23).

   D.   "'And God said, Let there be light' – lo, it was built and well constructed in the age to come."

III. Matters of Philosophy, Natural Science and Metaphysics

There is nothing philosophical in this *pisqa*.

70

Pesiqta deRab Kahana Pisqa Twenty-Two

This *pisqa* offers nothing for our study.

71

Pesiqta deRab Kahana Pisqa Twenty-Three

The *pisqa* yields nothing of broad and general consequence.

72

Pesiqta deRab Kahana Pisqa Twenty-Four

I. Unarticulated Premises: The Givens of Religious Conduct

This category does not pertain.

II. Unarticulated Premises: The Givens of Religious Conviction

1. God is the source of forgiveness, and he accords forgiveness in response to repentance, which attains atonement:

XXIV

VII.1 A. "Good and upright is the Lord, because he teaches sinners in the way" (Ps. 25:78):

     B. They asked wisdom, "As to the sinner, what is his punishment?"

     C. She said to them, "'Evil pursues sinners' (Prov. 13:21)."

     D. They asked prophecy, "As to the sinner, what is his punishment?"

     E. She said to them, "'The soul that sins shall die' (Ezek. 18:4)."

     F. They asked the Torah, "As to the sinner, what is his punishment?"

     G. She said to them, "Let him bring a guilt-offering and it will attain atonement for him."

     H. They asked the Holy One, blessed be He, "As to the sinner, what is his punishment?"

     I. He said to them, "Let him repent, and it will attain atonement for him,"

     J. That is in line with the verse of Scripture: "Good and upright is the Lord, because he teaches sinners in the way" (Ps. 25:78).

2. God has accepted the repentance of the most reprobate of sinners and will certainly accept the repentance of Israel:

XXIV

XI.1   A.   What is written prior to [the base verse, Hos. 14:2]? It is the following: "Samaria shall bear her guilt [for she has rebelled against her God]" (Hos. 14:1).

        B.   And thereafter: "Return O Israel [to the Lord your God, for you have stumbled because of your iniquity. Take with you words and return to the Lord and say to him, Take away all iniquity; accept that which is good, and we will render the fruit of our lips. Assyria shall not save us, we will not ride upon horses; and we will say no more, Our God, to the work of our hands. In you the orphan finds mercy]" (Hos. 14:1-3).

        C.   R. Eleazar in the name of R. Samuel bar Nahman: "The matter may be compared to the case of a town that rebelled against the king, who sent against it a general of the army to destroy it. The general was skilled and cool.

        D.   "He said to them, 'Take time for yourselves, so that the king not do to you what he did to such-and-such a town and its environs, and to such-and-such a district and its area.'

        E.   "So said Hosea to Israel, 'My children, repent, so that the Holy One, blessed be He, will not do to you what he did to Samaria and its environs.'

        F.   "Said Israel before the Holy One, blessed be He, 'Lord of the ages, if we repent, will you accept us?'

        G.   "He said to them, 'The repentance of Cain I accepted, will I not accept yours?'"

        H.   "'For a harsh decree was issued against him.'"

XI.4   A.   "I accepted the repentance of Ahab, and shall I not accept your repentance?"

        B.   For a harsh decree was issued against him, in line with this verse: "You shall speak to him saying, Have you killed and also taken possession? And you shall speak to him saying, Thus says the Lord: In the place where dogs licked the blood of Naboth shall dogs lick your blood, even yours" (1 Kgs. 21:29).

        C.   "And it came to pass when Ahab heard these words that he tore his clothes and put sackcloth on his flesh and fasted and lay in sackcloth" (1 Kgs. 21:27).

        D.   How did he fast? If he was accustomed to eat at three hours, he would eat at six, and if he was accustomed to eat at six, he ate at nine.

        E.   What is the meaning of "And he walked softly" (1 Kgs. 21:29)?

        F.   R. Joshua b. Levi said, "He went barefooted."

        G.   What is written there? "The word of the Lord came to Elijah the Tishbite saying, Do you see that Ahab humbles himself before me? Because he humbles himself before me, I will not bring the evil in his days" (1 Kgs. 21:28-29).

        H.   Said the Holy One, blessed be He, to Elijah, "You have seen that Ahab repented: 'Do you see that Ahab humbles himself before me? [Because he humbles himself before me, I will not bring the evil in his days.]'

        I.   "And shall I not accept your repentance?"

XI.5 A. "I accepted the repentance of the men of Anathoth, and shall I not accept your repentance?"

B. For a harsh decree was issued against them: "Thus says the Lord concerning the men of Anathoth who seek your life, saying, You shall not prophesy in the name of the Lord that you die not by our hand, therefore thus says the Lord, Behold I will punish them...there shall be no remnant of them" (Jer. 11:21, 23).

C. But when they repented, they had the merit of producing descendants: "The men of Anathoth a hundred and twenty-eight" (Ezra 2:23).

D. "And shall I not accept your repentance?"

XI.6 A. "I accepted the repentance of the men of Nineveh, and shall I not accept your repentance?"

B. For a harsh decree was issued against them, in line with this verse of Scripture: "Jonah began to enter into the city a day's journey [and he proclaimed and said, Yet forty days and Nineveh shall be overthrown]" (Jonah 3:4).

C. "And the tidings reached the king of Nineveh and he arose from his throne and laid his robe from him and covered himself with sackcloth and proclaimed through Nineveh by the decree of the king and his nobles, saying, ['Let neither man nor beast...taste anything; let them not feed nor drink water; but let them be covered with sackcloth both man and beast and let them cry mightily to God']" (Jonah 3:7-8).

D. Said R. Simeon b. Laqish, "The men of Nineveh carried out an essentially deceitful repentance."

E. What did they do?

F. R. Huniah in the name of R. Simeon b. Halputa: "They set up calves inside with their mothers outside, and these lowed from inside and the mothers from outside, so these groaned on this side and those on that side. They said, if you do not have mercy on us, we shall not have mercy on them.'"

G. Said R. Aha, "This is what they do also in Arabia: 'How are the beasts groaning! the herds of cattle are confused [because they have no pasture]' (Joel 1:18)."

H. "...but let them be covered with sackcloth both man and beast and let them cry mightily to God" (Jonah 3:7-8):

I. What is the meaning of "mightily"?

J. Said R. Simeon b. Halputa, "The impudent one conquers even the wicked one, all the more so the One who is the goodness of the world."

K. "Let them turn every one [from his evil way, from the violence that is in their hands]" (Jonah 3:8):

L. Said R. Yohanan, "What they had in hand they returned, but what they had put away in boxes, arks, and cupboards they did not return."

M. "And rend your hearts and not your garments" (Joel 2:13):

N. Said R. Joshua b. Levi, "If you rend your hearts in repentance, you will not have to render your garments on account of the death of your sons and daughters.

O. "Why not?

P. "'Because he is merciful and long-suffering' (Joel 2:13).'"

Q. R. Aha and R. Tanhum in the name of R. Hiyya in the name of R. Yohanan, "What is written is not long-suffering [in the singular] but longer-suffering [in the dual], indicating that he is patient with the righteous but also patient with the wicked.

R. "He is patient with the righteous and collects from them the modicum on account of the bad deeds which they did in this world so as to give them their full and complete reward in the world to come.

S. "And he accords prosperity to the wicked in this world so as to give them the modicum of the reward for the good deeds that they have done in this world in order to exact from them full and complete penalty in the world to come."

T. R. Samuel bar Nahman in the name of R. Yohanan: "What is written is not long-suffering [in the singular] but longer-suffering [in the dual], indicating that he is patient before he comes to collect [exacting punishment], and what he comes to collect, he extends the time [same word as patience] for collecting payment."

U. Said R. Hanina, "Whoever has said that the All-Merciful is [loose in] forgiving will get loose bowels. But he is indeed patient but then collects what is coming to him."

V. Said R. Levi, "What is the meaning of long-suffering? He is very far from anger.

W. "The matter may be compared to the case of a king who had two tough legions. Said the king, 'If the legions stay with me in the town, then when the townsfolk make me angry, they will take off on their own against them and wipe them out. Lo, I shall send them some distance away. If the people make me angry, while I am still sending for them, the people will come and make their peace with me, and I shall accept their appeasement.'

X. "That is in line with this verse of Scripture: 'They come from a country far away, from the end of heaven the weapons of his indignation' (Isa. 13:5)."

Y. Said R. Isaac, "And not only so, but he locks the gate against [his own legions], in line with this verse of Scripture: 'The Lord has unlocked his armory and has brought forth the weapons of his indignation' (Jer. 50:25).

Z. "While he is opening up, while he is still occupied, his mercy will be aroused."

AA. It was taught on Tannaite authority in the name of R. Meir, "'For lo, the Lord goes forth from his place' (Isa. 26:21). He goes forth from the attribute of justice to the attribute of mercy for Israel."

XI.7 A. "I accepted the repentance of Manasseh, and shall I not accept your repentance?"

B. For a harsh decree was issued against him.

C. This is in line with this verse of Scripture: "The Lord spoke to Manasseh and to his people but they did not listen. Therefore the Lord brought upon them the captains of the host of the king of Assyria, who took Manasseh with hooks" (2 Chr. 33:10, 11).

D. What is the meaning of "hooks"?

E. R. Abba bar Kahana said, "Manacles."

F.   "And they imprisoned him in fetters" (2 Chr. 33:11):

G.   What are fetters?

H.   R. Levi bar Haita, "They made him a kind of copper pot and made holes in it and put him into it and began to heat it from beneath. And when the pain of it began to affect him, there was not a single idol in the world on which he did not call: 'idol of so-and-so, come and save me.'

I.   "But when nothing helped, he said, 'I remember that father would recite for me this verse: "In your distress when all these things come upon you in the end of days return to the Lord your God and listen to his voice, for the Lord your God is a merciful God, he will not fail you nor destroy you" (Deut. 4:30, 31).

J.   "'Lo, I shall call on him. If he answers me, well and good, and if not, then they're all alike.'

K.   "Now the ministering angels were closing the windows of the firmament, so that the prayer of Manasseh would not come before the Holy One, blessed be He, 'Lord of the ages, a man who set up an idol in the temple – should such a man be able to repent?'

L.   "Said to them the Holy One, blessed be He, 'If I do not accept him in repentance, lo, I shall lock the door before all those who come to repent.'

M.   "What did the Holy One, blessed be He, do for him?

N.   "He dug a little opening under the throne of glory that was his, and through it he listened to his supplication. That is in line with this verse of Scripture: 'And he prayed to the Lord and he was entreated of him' (2 Chr. 33:13).

O.   "What is written in the verse for the word for 'entreat' is 'dug for him.'"

P.   "And he listened to his supplications" (2 Chr. 33:13):

Q.   Said R. Eleazar b. R. Simeon, "In Arabia they shift the *ayin* for a *het* [so yielding the word exchange just now cited]."

R.   "And he brought him back to Jerusalem to his kingdom" (2 Chr. 33:13):

S.   How did he "bring him back"?

T.   R. Samuel bar Nahman in the name of R. Aha: "He brought him back with a wind, as you say [in the Prayer], Who brings back the wind.'"

U.   "Manasseh knew that the Lord is God" (2 Chr. 33:13): At that time said Manasseh, "There is justice and a Judge."

V.   "I accepted the repentance of Jeconiaiah, and shall I not accept your repentance?"

XI.8 A.   "I accepted the repentance of Jeconaiah, and shall I not accept your repentance?"

B.   For a harsh decree was issued against him.

C.   That is in line with the following verse of Scripture: "Is this man Coniah a despised, broken pot, a vessel no one cares for? Why are he and his children hurled and cast into a land which they do not know?" (Jer. 22:28).

D.   R. Abba bar Kahana said, "[A broken pot] is like a bone of marrow, which, when you break it open, turns out to be worthless."

E.   R. Helbo said, "It is like a date wrapper, which, when you shake it out, turns out to contain nothing."

F.   "...a vessel no one cares for":

G.   R. Hama b. R. Hanina said, "It may be compared to a piss pot."

H.   R. Samuel bar Nachman: "[It is] like a vessel of those who take blood."

I.   Said R. Meir, "The Holy One, blessed be He, took an oath that he would not bring from Jeconaiah son of Jehoiakim, another king of Judah, in line with this verse: 'As I live says the Lord, if Coniah the son of Jehoiakim were the signet on a hand, yet by my right hand I would pluck you hence' (Jer. 22:24)."

J.   R. Hinena bar Isaac said, "'From there [that is, from Jeconaiah] I shall pull up the kingdom from the house of David.'"

K.   "Another explanation: What is written is not 'I shall remove you' but rather 'I shall restore you'; the meaning is, 'From there I shall restore in you in repentance.' The source of his retribution turned into the source of his restoration."

L.   Said R. Zeira, "I heard something from R. Ishmael b. R. Isaac, who expounded the present passage, but I don't remember what it was."

M.   Said to him R. Aha Arika, "Perhaps this is what it was: 'Thus says the Lord, Write this man as childless, a man who will not prosper in his days [for none of his offspring shall succeed in sitting on the throne of David and ruling again in Judah]' (Jer. 22:30)."

N.   He said to him, "Yes, in his days he will not succeed, but in the days of his son he will succeed."

O.   R. Aha bar Abun bar Benjamin in the name of R. Abba son of R. Pappi: "Great is the power of repentance for it annulled both an oath and a decree.

P.   "How do we know that it annulled an oath? 'As I live says the Lord, if Coniah the son of Jehoiakim were the signet on a hand, yet by my right hand I would pluck you hence' (Jer. 22:24). Yet it is written, 'In that day says the Lord of hosts I will take you O Zerubbabel, son of Shealtiel, [and make you as a signet]' (Hag. 2:23).

Q.   "And how do we know that it annulled a decree? It is written, 'Thus says the Lord, Write this man as childless, [a man who will not prosper in his days for none of his offspring shall succeed in sitting on the throne of David and ruling again in Judah]' (Jer. 22:30). Yet it is written, 'The sons of Jeconaiah, Assir Shealtiel, his son' (1 Chr. 3:17)."

R.   Said R. Tanhum bar Jeremiah, "The meaning of the name 'Assir' is that he was imprisoned in a prison [with the same letters serving the name 'Assir' and the word for 'prison']."

S.   "'Shealtiel': For from him a sapling of the kingdom of the house of David was planted.

T.   Said R. Tanhuma, "'Assir' [the prisoner] refers to the Holy One, blessed be He, who imprisoned himself through an oath. 'Shealtiel' [which uses the letters for the word for 'ask'] is because God brought the question of the validity of the lath to the heavenly court, which released him from his vow."

III. Matters of Philosophy, Natural Science and Metaphysics

This category cannot apply.

73

Pesiqta deRab Kahana Pisqa Twenty-Five

This brief *pisqa* yields nothing of interest.

74

Pesiqta deRab Kahana Pisqa Twenty-Six

Nothing surprising and noteworthy emerges here.

75

Pesiqta deRab Kahana Pisqa Twenty-Seven

The *pisqa* goes over ground covered in Leviticus Rabbah.

76

Pesiqta deRab Kahana Pisqa
Twenty-Eight

I. Unarticulated Premises: The Givens of Religious Conduct

The legal passages simply recapitulate well-known rules; there is no analytical program that would yield premises of note.

II. Unarticulated Premises: The Givens of Religious Conviction

1. When God blesses the nations, they do not appreciate it and do not respond properly, but Israel appreciates it and knows how to respond:

XXVIII

I.1 A. "On the eighth day you shall have a solemn assembly. [You shall do no laborious work, but you shall offer a burnt-offering, an offering by fire, a pleasing odor to the Lord.... These you shall offer to the Lord at your appointed feasts in addition to your votive-offerings and your freewill-offerings, for your burnt-offerings and for your cereal-offerings and for your drink-offerings and for your peace-offerings]" (Num. 29:35-9):

  B. "But you have increased the nation, O Lord, you have increased the nation; [you are glorified; you have enlarged all the borders of the land]" (Isa. 17:25):

  C. You gave security to the wicked Pharaoh. Did he then call you "Lord"? Was it not with blasphemies and curses that he said, "Who is the Lord, that I should listen to his voice" (Ex. 5:2)!

  D. You gave security to the wicked Sennacherib. Did he then call you "Lord"? Was it not with blasphemies and curses that he said, "Who is there among all the gods of the lands..." (2 Kgs. 18:35).

  E. You gave security to the wicked Nebuchadnezzar. Did he then call you "Lord"? Was it not with blasphemies and curses that he said, And who is God to save you from my power (Dan. 3:15).

  F. "...you have increased the nation; you are glorified":

G. You gave security to David and so he blessed you: "David blessed the Lord before all the congregation" (1 Chr. 29:10).

H. You gave security to his son, Solomon, and so he blessed you: "Blessed is the Lord who has given rest to his people Israel" (1 Kgs. 8:56).

I. You gave security to Daniel and so he blessed you: "Daniel answered and said, Blessed be the name of God" (Dan. 2:20).

I.2 A. "[But you have increased the nation, O Lord, you have increased the nation; you are glorified;] you have enlarged all the borders of the land" (Isa. 17:25):

B. Said R. Levi, "You have examined those who are near you and you have examined those who are distant from you. Draw near those who are near you, and send distant those who are distant from you.

C. "Draw near those who are near you: 'The Lord is near those who call upon him' (Ps. 145:18).

D. "...and send distant those who are distant from you: 'The Lord is distant from those who do wickedly' (Prov. 15:29)."

I.3 A. Another interpretation of the verse "But you have increased the nation, [O Lord, you have increased the nation; you are glorified; you have enlarged all the borders of the land]" (Isa. 17:25):

B. In the case of the nations of the world, if you give them a male child, he draws forward his foreskin and grows a lock [that is cut off in the honor of the idol.] When he grows up, he brings him to the temple of his idol and outrages you.

C. But in the case of Israel, if you give one of them a male child, he counts eight days and circumcises him. If he was a firstborn, he redeems him after thirty days. When he grows up, he brings him to synagogues and study hours and blesses you every day: Blessed be the Lord who is to be blessed.

I.4 A. Another interpretation of the verse "But you have increased the nation, [O Lord, you have increased the nation; you are glorified; you have enlarged all the borders of the land]" (Isa. 17:25):

B. The nations of the world, if you increase the number of festivals for them, they eat and drink and carouse and go to theaters and circuses and outrage you with their words and deeds.

C. But in the case of Israel, if you give them festival days, they eat, drink, rejoice, go to synagogues and schoolhouses, increase their praying and increase their prayers for additional offerings and other offerings.

D. Therefore it was necessary for Scripture to say, "On the eighth day you shall have a solemn assembly. [You shall do no laborious work, but you shall offer a burnt-offering, an offering by fire, a pleasing odor to the Lord....] These you shall offer to the Lord at your appointed feasts in addition to your votive-offerings and your freewill-offerings, for your burnt-offerings and for your cereal-offerings and for your drink-offerings and for your peace-offerings]" (Num. 29:35-39).

III. Matters of Philosophy, Natural Science and Metaphysics

Nothing fits into this category.

Index

257

South Florida Studies in the History of Judaism